Informal Economic Activity in Belfast

MADELEINE LEONARD
Department of Sociology and Social Policy
Queen's University
Belfast

Avebury
Aldershot · Brookfield USA · Hong Kong · Singapore · Sydney

Published by
Avebury
Ashgate Publishing Limited
Gower House
Croft Road
Aldershot
Hants GU11 3HR
England

Ashgate Publishing Company
Old Post Road
Brookfield
Vermont 05036
USA

British Library Cataloguing in Publication Data

Leonard, Madeleine
Informal Economic Activity in Belfast
I. Title
339.34167

ISBN 1 85628 478 6

Printed and Bound in Great Britain by
Athenaeum Press Ltd, Newcastle upon Tyne.

Contents

Tables

Acknowledgements

I would like to thank the people of Newbury estate for assisting me in carrying out this research, particularly the people who work in Newbury Community House. I would also like to acknowledge the help of Pam McIntyre for her assistance in preparing the manuscript for publication. I owe a great deal of gratitude to Liam O'Dowd who supervised my PhD thesis on which this book is based. I am also grateful to Richard Jenkins for his constructive advice and criticisms. Thanks also to my three children Cathy, Christopher and Colin for not always putting their needs first. But most of all, I would like to thank my husband Martin for remaining my main source of support and encouragement.

For Martin.

Introduction

This book is concerned with examining the ways in which particular social structures and localities shape, foster and constrain informal economic activities. The book is based on data collected in a working class housing estate in West Belfast, referred to by the pseudonym Newbury. Numerous studies have consistently confirmed an above average unemployment rate for the area. Hence for most of the occupants of Newbury, the 'normality' of full time formal employment has not been established. Unemployment is the norm and has been the norm for several decades. This does not mean that the residents of Newbury do not want to work or do not work. Rather they have accepted that the formal economy has been closed off to many of them and as a result, they have reformulated their attitudes to work, employment and unemployment. The dole (unemployment benefit) is viewed as a necessary but inadequate means of 'getting by' that has to be supplemented by engaging in 'work on the side' either for cash or kind.

Chapter One examines the theoretical context in which the research is situated. Particular attention is given to Pahl's (1984) research in the Isle of Sheppey and to his observation that the unemployed are the group least likely to engage in informal work. Following Gallie (1985), the research suggests that more attention needs to be focused on areas of long term unemployment as people living in such areas may have had less exposure to dominant norms about work, employment and unemployment.

Chapter Two presents the research methods used to investigate informal economic activity in Newbury. Specific attention is given to the difficulties of carrying out research of this nature, particularly in Northern Ireland.

Chapter Three introduces the estate where the research is based. A key feature of the chapter will be an outline of the emergence of the negative image of the estate and how this image influenced formal and informal economic opportunities.

Chapters Four to Eight focus on the various informal economic strategies utilised by members of the estate. Chapter Four looks at the internal workings of the household. When money is scarce, households may attempt to ease their financial situation by providing goods and services internally for their members, rather than purchasing such commodities from outside sources. The self sufficiency of Newbury households will be the main theme of this chapter.

Of course, poverty and unemployment are not individual or household experiences for the residents of Newbury. Rather, poverty and unemployment are collective community experiences and hence often involve collective community responses. One way the rigours of unemployment and poverty can be managed is by building up reciprocal favours among those in similar situations. These favours can then be called upon as the need arises. The extent to which the inhabitants of the community participate in forming these mutual obligations will be the focus of Chapter Five.

Chapter Six concentrates on community economic enterprises. This chapter will focus on individuals who provide a range of goods and services from the home or within the community for their relatives, friends, neighbours and occasionally outside formal organisations. These people are mainly paid in cash for their services, although their return rarely seems to compensate for the amount of time and effort they expend. Again their activities provide an additional supplement to the family budget and provide the wider community with a range of goods and services not otherwise available.

Chapter Seven deals with 'doing the double'. This term refers to the practice of claiming welfare benefits while undertaking undeclared paid employment. The chapter will outline the residents' motivations for engaging in this economic practice. Contrary to the popular image of the lucrative benefits attached to this activity, the chapter will demonstrate that earnings from 'doing the double' are a supplement to and not a replacement for inadequate welfare benefits. Indeed, most of the jobs discussed in this chapter are not at all economically viable without the benefit cushion. The chapter will also throw light on a much neglected issue, the employers of people 'doing the double'.

Others engage in more dubious practices such as stealing from formal enterprises or private households. These people may be motivated by financial necessity or simple greed. While their activities are sometimes condemned by their co-residents, nonetheless as Chapter Eight will illustrate, their trading in stolen goods provides their neighbours with another means of obtaining scarce resources.

Finally, Chapter Nine provides a summary and conclusion of the main ideas presented in the book. The research outlines the importance of local kinship and friendship networks within Newbury for providing access to informal economic activity. These networks provide the lynchpin for the economic exchanges which take place within the estate. They are also important for linking individuals with the labour market outside the area. The book illustrates how stability of residence, duration of unemployment, social homogeneity, extensive kinship and friendship networks and low levels of access to external resources are all conducive to the development of informal economic practices.

1 The separation of work from employment in a Belfast working class community

> People sometimes talk as if all that a man wants is regular work. It is nothing of the sort. What they really want is a regular income. Regular work is of no great value to anyone except as a kind of discipline for the young (Wm. Beveridge Speech of 10th Aug. 1910 in Harris 1977,p.98).

In his autobiography, J.S. Mill (1924,p.30) tells us how, during his model upbringing as an early nineteenth century child, he was granted a certain amount of leisure each day. But, he adds, there were to be no complete holidays - 'lest the habit of work should be broken and a taste for idleness acquired'. This 'habit of work' has now been broken for a vast number of the British population. Estimates on the actual extent of unemployment vary. Official government statistics tend to underestimate the extent of unemployment because for many groups of unwaged people there is no financial incentive to register as unemployed and this generally results in their exclusion from the statistics. Yet, even the official unemployment rate looks set to continue on an upward trend. One forecast predicts that by early in the next century, only 10 per cent of the present labour force will be needed to supply a technologically advanced society with all its material needs (Shankland 1984,p.1). When similar forecasts were first made in the late 1970's, they were regarded as ridiculous because the unemployment total then was about one and a half million. Now these predictions look more plausible since the jobless numbers have doubled, accelerated by conservative fiscal measures and consolidated by the installation of technology to replace humans. But even the present government which began by discouraging the expansion of jobs in the private sector with high interest rates and continues to reduce them in the public sector with expenditure cuts is now spending millions on creating temporary work for the jobless while waiting in anticipation for the permanent real jobs to emerge to reverse the unemployment trend. However, it seems likely that western civilization has irretrievably passed the stage where it will ever again need a workforce on the pre-1980 scale. The post war employment boom which lasted up until the late 1960's looks set to take its place in the history books as the abnormal phase in the history of industrial Britain.

Moreover, this overwhelming concentration on the 'golden years' of full employment, and the commitment by political parties from various ideological persuasions to strive towards achieving its return, operates with an extremely limited definition of work which excludes, both now and in the past, various forms of activities and groups of people from its vision.

The nature of work has undoubtedly changed in the post war period. Advances in technology have made existing jobs in both the manufacturing and service sectors obsolete and opened up possibilities for limited work in wholly new areas. Production has become more internationalized and capitalists are now even less accountable to national governments. As a result, existing industries in many developed countries face a much more risky and unpredictable future and many have already suffered extensive job losses to developing countries. The United Kingdom, in particular is facing what many now view as an unacceptable level of unemployment.

Commentators from various disciplines have outlined the individual's basic need for work and painted gloomy forecasts of the social, psychological and political consequences for a society 'without work'. Yet, what exactly do we mean by 'work'. Because this area has only recently emerged as a central focus for concern in academic research, there is a tendency to assume that 'work' as a problematic concept is only a relatively recent phenomenon. What most commentators fail to acknowledge is that work in the conventional sense of the word has never been a sufficient category because it has always been limited to certain forms of activity and to certain groups.

The Oxford English Dictionary defines work first and foremost as any 'physical or mental effort directed towards doing or making something'. Such a wide, general, all encompassing definition is clearly of little use to us as most activities involve us, in either doing something or making something. Such a definition indicates to us that before we can consider how a lack of work affects the individual or society and before we can offer prognostications to the government or society in general, we need to clearly define what we mean by work and assess how this meaning has evolved. We need to pose several questions about the purpose of work, particularly its importance as a human act. In other words, we need to redefine the nature of work as a totality and not simply focus on its conventional economic aspects.

Work in pre-industrial societies

The most obvious contrasts to the working habits of the modern industrial world are provided by the pre-industrial societies with which anthropologists are most familiar. In such societies the distinction between work and leisure is impossible to draw. Rather life in such a world is one in which work and non work are inextricably linked. While idleness did incur social disapproval, nonetheless, the motives leading men to engage in productive work were only partly economic. The Trobriand Islanders driven by a desire for prestige grew twice as many vegetables as they could possibly hope to eat while sheer pleasure in craftsmanship induced the Maori fisherman to get up in the middle of the night to polish his club (Thomas 1964,p.52). Moreover, in these societies, work was not regulated by the clock but by the requirements of the task and there were no clearly defined periods separating work from non work. Each shaded into the other almost imperceptibly.

In a number of respects pre-industrial Britain displayed a similar attitude towards work and non work. The links and associations between work, employment and unemployment were very different from what they were to become with the developing industrial economy of the nineteenth and twentieth centuries. Irregularity was a central characteristic of employment. The work pattern alternated between bouts of intense labour and of idleness determined by seasonal and climatic fluctuations. As Kumar points out, however (1984,p.195-198), the effects of this lack or loss of regular employment was significantly lessened by two crucial features of the eighteenth century labourer's position. Firstly, the eighteenth century labourer was a pluralist in so far as occupation was concerned. Thus, when one occupation went slack on him, he could often resort to another. Secondly, work was organized largely around the home and this in itself reduced the degree of dependence on employment for wages. The household economy could, and indeed had to, draw on the labour of all its members. Few families could have subsisted for very long on the earnings of the head of household alone. Households were based on an economic partnership between men, women, children and other household members. A household strategy developed which made the best use of resources for getting by under given social and economic conditions (Pahl 1988,p.10). The work of all members of the household had to be co-ordinated to achieve the overall viability of the household. It was assumed that family sustenance would depend on the productive contributions of all its members, each of whom helped to sustain the whole. Marriage itself was an economic partnership and children were often put to work at an early age (Malcolmson 1988,p.59). A wife was always a working woman engaged in a wide variety of domestic industries such as spinning, knitting, lace making, silk winding, glove making, the repairing of fishing nets; and in many of these trades children, particularly females, were expected to actively participate.

The household also tried, where possible, to achieve some degree of self sufficiency. The more the household could produce for their direct consumption, the less they would have to rely on market purchases. This in turn meant they would be less dependent for their livelihood on the wages provided by employers. Providing for one's own needs by one's own efforts without the mediation of wage employment, made for greater self reliance and independence, and these were the goals most people adhered to (Malcolmson 1988,p.59). This is not to say that the family economy was perfect, rather it was nearly always stretched to the limit, and wage labour was still one of the most important means of support. But by attempting to knit together a viable sustenance from a wide range of economic practices, unemployment, while not exactly welcome, nonetheless did not pose a fundamental threat to livelihood. Waged labour was but one form of work existing in this period and to be out of employment was not necessarily to be without work.

It also seems apparent that the areas of work, play, family, religion and community rather than being separate spheres formed an overlapping set of activities. The slack periods of the agrarian year were punctuated by religious feasts and festivals while the more intense periods were characterised by a communal effort by villagers to gather in the harvest (Thomas 1964,p.52-53). Many of these seasonal activities, rituals and customs were important sources of income in themselves, making it worthwhile leaving off waged work for one or more days at a time (Berg 1988,p.90). Lean periods were mitigated by a reliance on the various earnings (not necessarily financial) of other family members or on community handouts. Kumar (1984,p.193) states that most workers accepted that there would be temporary periods of unemployment in their trades and that agricultural work in particular depended on a wide range of circumstances seemingly outside of human control. Thus, in those periods of stress that were a natural and inevitable feature of the life of all pre-industrial communities, there was nothing particularly degrading about accepting support from the local community to which one belonged.

Furthermore, workers, when in employment, were not motivated solely by a concern to make money. Eighteenth century commentators are unanimous in the view that workers preferred leisure to increased income (Kumar 1984,p.197). When wages were high or prices low, workers cut down their number of hours of work as they were able to achieve the expected level of subsistence and comfort with less labour. Kumar (1988,p.150) quoting Arthur Young states 'everyone but an idiot knows that the lower classes must be kept poor or they will never be industrious'. Hence during the early years of the industrial revolution when employers set about to change working habits, they believed this could only be achieved by compulsion. Thus early industrialists attempted to impose a rigorous labour discipline on their employees by fines for absenteeism, a campaign against holidays and wakes and the payment of very low wages (Thomas 1964,p.61). Therefore control became paramount.

Work and industrialization

As industrialism progressed however, it undermined the various means of subsistence outside the formal economy. A man's being came to be increasingly defined by his work and his work was increasingly limited to his occupation in the formal money economy. Whereas previously the family, work and leisure were all inextricably interrelated activities, with the evolution of industrialism they increasingly emerged as distinct separate spheres. Industrialization brought in its wake a clear separation between work and home by transferring work from the home into first the factory and then later the office. As Kumar points out (1984,p.8), to be at work was henceforth to be in work, to be employed as a worker in the formal economy. All activities outside the formal work setting were devalued as non work. Thus woman's work in the home, which was formerly on a more or less equal footing with that of the man in the domestic economy, now came to be regarded as non work and as marginal to economic life.

This is not to say that other more traditional and less 'industrial' forms of work ceased to exist. Samuel (1977) states that hand technology, much of it involving work in the worker's own home continued to survive throughout the nineteenth century. Girls in domestic service continued to regard themselves as part of the family enterprise and regularly sent back much of their wages to their families. For both themselves and their families, movement into domestic service in the towns was no more than an extension or expansion of the traditional contribution of girls to the family income (Kumar 1984,p.206). Nonetheless, as industrialism progressed, work was transferred more and more into an increasingly limited setting and accorded greater value. It came to be seen as a blessing, as a means of achieving personal worth and fulfilment. It gave the individual a purpose in life, a place and an identity. Since employment entailed so many positive benefits, then its opposite unemployment could have nothing but negative consequences for the person concerned. With a person's whole identity increasingly associated with his occupation in the formal economy then clearly unemployment could have a devastating effect on his psychological well-being. As Aitken puts it:

> In many countries when people are asked who they are they will usually answer in terms of the job they do. We are a job-oriented culture: take away a person's job and you take away more than a livelihood (1979,p.100).

The psychological effects of unemployment

Lack of work and its detrimental effect on the psychological well being of the individual began to increasingly demand the attention of psychologists. Eisenberg and Lazarfield (1938) suggested that individuals go through a series of phases following unemployment. The initial response, as in bereavement, is one of shock and, depending on the circumstances, disbelief. During this phase, the worker maintains a certain degree of optimism, regards his loss as only temporary and tends to look at his new situation as if it were a long deserved holiday. This notion will be enhanced if he has received a considerable redundancy settlement. During this period, the unemployed person will set his hands and effort to long overdue improvement tasks. Through time however, the reality in all its harshness becomes unavoidable. The holiday feeling is over; money is running short; there are no more jobs to do around the house and the first attempts at job finding have been unsuccessful. The unemployed identity begins to slowly creep in. The day is spent in forced and meaningless leisure. The concept of time changes drastically and days seem to fly past with nothing to distinguish them by. In spite of this 'forced' inactivity the unemployed person will feel exhausted and spend a considerable period of the day in bed. The final state is described by Eisenberg and Lazarfield as the 'broken state' where the person involved experiences a general feeling of inferiority, submissiveness and inability to provide sufficiently for himself or his family.

Marsden and Duff (1982) in a more recent study vividly report the experiences of the workless and their families. In close marriages, when the husband becomes unemployed, he tries to shield his wife from the impact and will only be frank about the seriousness of the situation when he is not in his wife's company. This sheltering extends to his children who are 'not supposed to know' but his attempts are often futile and in fact he feels devalued in their eyes. In marriages where couples lead more independent lives, the increased time together starts petty arguments. Through time many marriages actually break up or show evidence of violence among the partners or towards the children. The financial strain could be more tolerable if the wife found a job but this did not necessarily happen as most men had an overwhelming fear of permanent role change.

These studies, together with her own study of Marienthal, leads Marie Jahoda (1979,p.494) to suggest that employment performs several positive functions for the individual in society. Firstly, it imposes a time structure on the waking day. Secondly, it involves regularly shared experiences and contacts with people outside the family. Thirdly, employment links an indivdual to goals and purposes which transcend his own. Fourthly, employment defines aspects of status and identity and finally it enforces activity.

However, there are three main problems with these various approaches. Firstly, they fail to grasp the extent to which unemployment is normal and accepted in communities where the majority of the population find themselves in this position. As such the people concerned may not react to their situation as the classic theories assume they should. Secondly, most of these theories implicitly accept a definition of work which limits itself to employment in the formal economy. They fail to acknowledge that industrialism while undermining alternative forms of work outside the formal economy did not wipe them out completely (the most obvious example being women's domestic work). They also fail to consider that in present day areas of long term widespread unemployment, other forms of work might emerge and begin to co-exist alongside formal employment or increasingly replace formal employment as a means of livelihood, subsistence or identity. Thirdly, if, as suggested here, work is primarily a social construct then we need to investigate the mechanisms through which its present limited definition is created and maintained and this leads us into the domain of ideology.

Work and ideology

Ashton (1986,p.115-121) argues that in contemporary Britain, only one definition of work tends to hold sway. This, he refers to as the middle class work ethic which consists of three elements. Firstly, it usually equates work with employment. Secondly, it justifies the unequal distribution of income on the basis that those who receive the highest rewards contribute the most to society. Thirdly, it still contains the idea that people should achieve self fulfilment through their work. Each individual is therefore encouraged to adhere to the appropriate values of hard work, self discipline and loyalty in order that they may obtain entry into jobs which will enable them to fulfil themselves. However, because this set of beliefs, like all ideologies, is not universally accepted and is likely to be contested by various groups such as the unskilled, women and ethnic minorities, then its main tenets have to be constantly asserted and reasserted through the major cultural institutions such as the educational system and the media.

One way this is achieved is through the circulation of myths. According to Ashton (1986,p.120), one of the main functions of myths is to maintain the commitment of the working population to the legitimacy of the system of distributing work and allocating rewards. Hence many tend to accept that humankind was born to work, that men should be the main wage earners, that profits are important because without them there would be no jobs and that unemployment was caused by those in work demanding wages that are too high. Part of this strategy also involves degrading and stigmatising those out of work. Thus the unemployed are regarded either as 'welfare scroungers' or 'work shy'. They lack any motivation to seek work and are unemployed in the first place due to their own personality failings or because they are receiving such generous aid from the state that they lack any incentive to pursue the openings the labour market has to offer.

Such an ideology also tends to undermine or ignore any work performed outside the formal economy. This has important consequences for how society views such work and for how individuals engaged in such work regard their activities. For example, housework is undervalued in the eyes of society and in the eyes of women themselves as is illustrated in the oft quoted statement 'Do you work?' 'No. I'm only a housewife'. This has important consequences for any methodology concerned with encompassing a wider range of activities under the heading of 'work' as individuals may engage in a whole range of relevant activities which they themselves may dismiss as non work.

The following chapters attempt to separate work from formal employment and to assess the relevance of the former wider definition in a working class area of high long term unemployment in Belfast. Such a step is by no means wholly novel. Sociologists are increasingly turning to the informal or hidden economy in order to redefine the nature and extent of work in the past and present and offer suggestions for the future. Consequently, this book is an effort to expand on previous research into the extent and significance of informal economies and assess the applicability and limitations of studies into informal work to the Newbury area of Belfast.

The informal economy

The term informal economy was first introduced in the context of work in developing societies (Hart 1973). Bromley and Gerry (1979), suggest that the phrase was used thereafter, as an umbrella term to describe ways of making a living outside the formal wage economy, either as an alternative to it, or as a means of supplementing income earned within it. Henry (1982,p.461) suggests that in addition to the terms informal economy and hidden economy, there are at least fifteen other labels which are attached to activities in this area. These include black, cash, underground, secondary, domestic, household, communal and alternative economy. Nonetheless, despite the profusion of labels, there are several recurring characteristics that can be utilized to provide a general definition. Firstly, the informal economy includes the production, consumption and trading of goods and services either for cash or kind or social rewards. Secondly, these activities are more likely to be part time rather than full time. Lastly, the activities are unofficial in the sense that they do not explicitly form part of the state accounting system and are not registered by its economic measurement techniques. Added to this general definition is the observation that most of these informal activities are usually small scale and locally based, taking place among relatives, friends, neighbours and acquaintances and may be legal, quasi-legal or illegal depending on whether cash or kind forms the medium of exchange.

Researchers into informal economies have developed two contrasting viewpoints. On the one hand, it is suggested that the informal economy has not only the potential to absorb unemployment in the formal economy, but also could play a positive role in overcoming present contradictions in the welfare state by counteracting public expenditure cuts. On the other hand, it is suggested that the informal economy mirrors the distortions of the formal one and thus excludes the more peripheral sectors of the labour market access to its limited resources or at best does little more than provide a survival mechanism for the poor.

Adherents of the first viewpoint (Pym 1980, Gappert & Knight 1982, Handy 1984) start from the premise that there are other routes to solving the problem of unemployment than merely the full employment of everyone in the formal economy. Gershuny and Pahl adopt such an approach in their early work. Although both authors have reformulated their initial ideas in later work, nonetheless I want to concentrate to some degree on this early work because as Howe (1986) points out their later work may have underestimated the extent of the informal economy in working class areas such as those in Belfast. Howe's view gets broad support from my own research which suggests that Gershuny and Pahl's earlier work might have more relevance here than the authors' later research indicated and suggests that a greater range of empirical work into this area is urgently needed.

I also intend to concentrate, in some detail, on the later work of Pahl (1984a) because according to Gallie (1985,p.522), Pahl's research on the Isle of Sheppey has been the most important research project on this theme in the British Isles, and has more than any other study raised major doubts about earlier views on the extent and significance of informal work.

The early work of Gershuny and Pahl on the informal economy

Gershuny (1978) begins with the observation that Bell's post-industrial society has failed to materialise. Bell suggested that society was in the process of moving towards a service economy in which the bulk of employment would be in the service sector of the economy, concerned with the production of non material commodities. Gershuny's research indicated, however, that while some service functions had expanded over recent decades, these were largely in the spheres of medicine and education, areas which largely depended on public finance. Other services which relied on the private purchasing power of households did not grow as fast as predicted and in some instances actually declined considerably as a proportion of public expenditure.

To Gershuny, the reason for this change is perfectly simple: instead of buying services, households are increasingly purchasing capital equipment, to which they add their own labour in the production of services. Thus, for example, instead of going to the laundry, individuals buy and use washing machines, instead of using public transport, individuals buy cars and drive them themselves and instead of going to the cinema, people buy televisions and later video recorders. Thus needs once satisfied in the public sphere are increasingly being satisfied in the private sphere. This growth in the household economy is faciliated by the rising cost of purchased services relative to the declining cost of 'domestic capital goods' (Gershuny 1983,p.35-38). The falling cost of capital makes it continuously easier for individuals to own their own tools which in turn makes 'own account' working more convenient and less easy to detect. As it becomes more economically rational for individuals to provide services informally, jobs are increasingly exported from the formal economy into the various sectors of the informal economy. This is further promoted by the high rates of taxation and the administrative costs of dealing with the official state which make it an increasingly attractive option for those still engaged in the formal economy to transfer all or more usually part of their activities into the underground economy.

Gershuny and Pahl (1980,p.7) go on to suggest that a deskilling of the workforce in the formal economy may be compensated by a re-skilling in the informal one. Individuals who in the past might have called in a variety of tradesmen to carry out home repairs or improvements are more willing to try to do the job for themselves. They are also assisted by the wide range of do-it-yourself books currently on the market. These books 'democratize skills in the informal economy' (1980,p.7). Thus as tradesmen who sell their skills put up their rates, they encourage those who might previously have purchased such skills to develop their own.

Pahl further suggests (1984b,p.183) that those groups which have resisted most effectively incorporation into the dominant values of industrial capitalism may find it easier to adjust to the problems imposed by the decline of formal employment in the years ahead more easily. He acknowledges that the poor have always been obliged to develop a social economy and this informal support system may become increasingly valued as the recession deepens and unemployment rises. On the other hand, the 'new working class' or the middle class of the public and private housing estates who have not needed such support mechanisms in the past may be more seriously disadvantaged.

However, relations between the formal and informal economy may well be more problematic than outlined so far. The informal economy is liable to mirror the distortions and inequalities of the formal economy. Indeed, Gershuny and Pahl, even in their earlier work did not suggest that the informal economy could provide a utopia of socially functional unemployment. They accept that rather than being able to choose work strategies, particular social groups such as women, ethnic groups, the low status and the unskilled may be forced to accept unemployment. These groups are the ones least likely to be able to plug into rewarding informal activities. Thus the informal economy could emerge as a sort of dual economy with its relationship with the formal economy based on dependency and exploitation similar to the dual economies encountered in the developing world. At the same time, however, Gershuny and Pahl suggest that positive government action could extend the range of genuine options open to people. Appropriate policies could be introduced to control the inevitable expansion of the informal economy by encouraging its most desirable features and mitigating the less desirable.

Pahl suggests that (1985,p.249) if the state played a positive role in promoting the desirable aspects of this hidden economy then many benefits will accrue. Informal work may provide a seedbed for the establishment of small capitalist enterprises; it may allow people to practice skills which are not available to them in the formal economy; it may provide cheap training for a reserve army of workers; it may serve as an element of social control as if people are engaged in work in the informal economy then they are less likely to vent their frustration on mainstream society; it may save the state expenditure when for example the care of the elderly is taken over by kin rather than welfare institutions or at the very least it may provide a valuable coping strategy for the poor.

The Isle of Sheppey survey

Pahl's pilot survey (1984a) of work outside employment on the Isle of Sheppey in 1977 backed up his initial theories on the growing development of the informal economy. His pilot interviews confirmed that informal work on the Isle of Sheppey was widespread and extensive. Pahl (1984a) states, however, that by the time he was in a position to quantify informal communal work, approximately five years later, 'it had all but disappeared'. There was a drastic increase in registered unemployment and as surplus money dried up, so also did the opportunities for making extra money. People no longer had the spare cash to pay neighbours and friends for doing odd jobs. They became suspicious of one another and if anyone among the unemployed seemed to have money to spare they were 'shopped' to the local Social Security Office. The unemployed interviewed in 1982 were unhappy and dejected and quite unlike the competent, jovial respondents Pahl had interviewed five years earlier.

Pahl's pilot studies also initially backed up the conventional expectation that a household doing less in one sphere will do more in another. In other words, less time in employment would mean more time for work in the household economy. Indeed, despite the apparent decline in informal work outside the household, Pahl's later survey revealed an astonishing amount of work being carried out inside the household. However, since this work was 'private, inward-looking and concerned with domestic comfort then it does little to generate growth or provide communal support or benefits' (Pahl 1985,p.260). Rather, this informal work was largely structured around attempts by multiple earner households to add to their home comforts by concentrating their spare time, energy and resources into upgrading their homes. Very little work was carried out within the community. Of the forty one tasks most likely to be done on the Island, such as painting and decorating the house, fixing the car, getting shopping done; a mere 2 per cent of the complete range of tasks were carried out by people outside the household. Rather most tasks were carried out within households by members of households. This contrasts starkly with Ferman et al's study in Detroit (Henry 1981,p.26), where 60 per cent of household services were secured through the 'social economy' by friends, relatives and workmates without any monetary payment.

Out of the 730 respondents interviewed during Pahl's survey, a mere 27 acknowledged working on their own account for extra money. When this group were analysed further, Pahl found that they were sharply differentiated in terms of gender and employment status. Eleven men and sixteen women responded that they did engage in own account work for extra money. Of the eleven men, only one was unemployed. Of the sixteen women, eight were full time housewives. In other words, out of the entire Sheppey sample, only one unemployed man and eight unemployed women were engaged in any form of work 'on the side' for which payment was made.

Employment status and gender were interrelated in the explanation put forward to account for this low numerical rate of activity. Unemployment breeds suspicion. Activities which were once invisible were now subjected to scrutiny by jealous neighbours intent on finding out if cash changes hands. If this was the case, then the unemployed 'culprit' was reported to welfare benefit personnel. Society evaluates men's work and women's work differently, however, and this effects the opportunities open to men and women to engage in extra work 'on the side'. Men were most likely to engage in tasks which could have a price such as minor repairs, carpentry and decorating. Women, on the other hand, were most likely to engage in caring work in the community, such as shopping for others, babysitting and so on. While this work may be highly visible, it is not generally recognised as paid work and was therefore not subjected to the same scrutiny.

The analysis of survey results showed a positive correlation between number of earners and amount of domestic work done. In other words employment status was the key to participation in all forms of work both in the formal and informal economy (Pahl & Wallace 1985,p.222). The more employed adults there are in a relatively affluent household, the more work will be done. Pahl argues that work outside employment needs more than time, it needs tools, equipment, materials and social contacts. Households where most family members are unemployed have not got the money to buy the resources necessary to engage in do-it-yourself projects nor the money to go to pubs where potential employment contacts are made.

Pahl's interviews (1984a) describe the despair of men living in their own homes, with their own tools, with time on their hands and with urgent decorating jobs staring them in the face but without the money to buy the paint. He concludes that rather than expanding, the informal economy has passed its peak and ironically only offers opportunities to those least in need of them. Rather a household's position in the formal economy determines its position in the informal economy. To Pahl, only households with multiple wage earners engage in Gershuny's self service economy. Moreover, since such work is aimed almost exclusively at improving domestic comfort then it does little to stimulate further opportunity for work in the informal economy nor does it provide any communal mechanisms to ease the burden for those on the periphery of both the formal and informal economy.

Informal work and locality variations

From his work on the Isle of Sheppey, Pahl concludes:

> while it is true that no one locale can be said to be typical of the aggregation of locales that makes up a society, nevertheless, the processes at work (on the Isle of Sheppey) are certainly likely to apply universally and are therefore, generalizable (1987b,p.42).

However, what I want to argue here is that this approach underestimates the way particular social structures and localities shape, foster and constrain informal economic activities. Duncan Gallie, in a major book published in 1985, calling for 'New Approaches to Economic Life' suggests that studies on the effects of unemployment on the individual may not have given enough consideration to the importance of prior regional differences or the character of local networks, for the experience of social isolation. Gallie (1985,p.527) asks for more attention to focus on whether communities vary significantly in their efforts to stimulate activity among the unemployed and if so, do such efforts make much difference?

In relation to informal work, Gallie points out that existing studies which have revealed rather unimpressive levels of informal work have focused on areas of rising unemployment such as Sheppey and South Wales (although it must be added that Harris (1987) and Morris (1984) found higher rates of participation in paid informal work than did Pahl on the Isle of Sheppey). Alternatively, Gallie suggests (1985,p.522) that the 'most probable location of the growth of widespread informal work will be in areas of catastrophic economic collapse where the possibility of re-insertion into normal economic activity appears particularly remote'. Hence Gallie calls for future studies of informal work to focus on the long term unemployed living in such areas. People living in these areas may have had less exposure to dominant norms about work, employment and unemployment. Abrams (Bulmer 1986,p.93) makes a similar point in relation to the significance of reciprocity in any given locale. He argues that reciprocity flourishes in 'relatively isolated, relatively closed and relatively threatened social milieux with highly homogeneous populations where information and trust are high and where resources for satisfying needs in other ways are low'. This book is partly a response to Gallie's call for more research on areas of long term unemployment.

Informal economic activity in Newbury

The Newbury estate where this research is based is in West Belfast which is arguably the most economically stagnant urban area of the UK. Moreover, as the chapter on the formation of the community will outline, considerable statistical evidence indicates that the Newbury estate is perhaps the most depressed area within the overall region of West Belfast, with consistently high levels of long term unemployment among males in the area. Hence the area provides fertile testing ground for assessing the view that informal economic activity is by and large closed to the unemployed. Preliminary research indicated that not only was informal economic activity widespread in Newbury, but that it was accessible to the very groups found to be excluded in Pahl's later research. Hence Gershuny and Pahl's (1980) earlier observation that the informal economy can especially be exploited by the poor because they have been obliged to develop an informal support system and because they have resisted most effectively incorporation into the dominant values of industrial capitalism seemed a more appropriate hypothesis. This study describes a community which has responded in various ways to the economic crises and chronic unemployment which has faced the area almost from its inception. It is an area where almost every household participates in varying degrees in informal economic practices. This is partly because of the persistence of extended families and of wider kinship ties, partly because the area was ostracized from the surrounding areas and therefore had to develop its own internal mechanisms and partly because of the political situation in Northern Ireland. This is not to say, however, that poverty and hardship no longer exist. Rather it is to suggest that their effect is mitigated through various individual, family and community responses.

In Pahl's research on the Isle of Sheppey, the level of unemployment in 1983 was estimated to be 20 per cent. In other words, those unemployed were in a minority in relation to the rest of the eligible population. This led to a situation whereby those with the greatest access to resources in the formal economy also had greater access to resources in the informal economy. This also meant that the unemployed were faced first hand with the inherent inequalities embedded in both the formal and informal economy and hence became depressed and disillusioned. The Newbury estate in West Belfast however, has always had to face chronic unemployment. In 1958, just eight years after the estate was built, a study by Dorita Field revealed that 50 per cent of the male heads of households (HOH's) in the sample studied were unemployed while various studies since then have revealed persistently high levels of unemployment. It is an area where as one resident put it, 'Those with jobs stick out like sore thumbs'. Hence for most of the male occupants of Newbury, the 'normality' of full time formal employment has not been established. Unemployment is the norm and has been the norm for several decades. This does not mean that the residents of Newbury do not want to work or do not work. Rather they have accepted that for various reasons (to be discussed later) formal employment has been closed off to them and as a result they have reformulated their attitudes towards work, employment and unemployment. The dole (unemployment benefit) is viewed as a necessary but inadequate means of 'getting by' that has to be supplemented by engaging in various forms of 'work on the side' either for cash or kind or simply for prestige. Such economic activity is nothing to be ashamed of nor has it to be hidden from communal view. This is partly because so many inhabitants of the estate are, to varying degrees engaged in informal activities, that this lessens the likelihood of any one individual being reported to the welfare authorities. Furthermore, since the area is regarded as a Provisional IRA stronghold, this also reduces the possibility of detection, as Department of Health and Social Security (DHSS) investigators are unlikely to hang around the estate. The research indicates that informal economic activity appears to be above all dependent on social sanctions for its operation and that membership of a strong social network is vital as informal activity operates within a myriad of prior associations and personal ties (Ferman and Berndt 1981).

Research into informal economic activity in Northern Ireland

Perhaps the most comprehensive account of informal economic activity in Northern Ireland is the work of Leo Howe (1990). According to Harding and Jenkins (1988,p.103), Howe has produced the only rigorous community based study of informal economic activity in Northern Ireland which is comparable to research in Great Britain. Howe's data centres on a number of unstructured interviews with twenty unemployed males in a working class Catholic estate and twenty unemployed males in a working class Protestant estate. His intention is to demonstrate the differences between unemployed Catholics and unemployed Protestants in their level of involvement in the 'black economy' in Belfast (1990,p.14). Howe argues that because of the disparities between Catholic and Protestant unemployment rates, the inequalities in job opportunities for the two religious groups and their different attitudes to the Northern Ireland state, then it might be reasonable to suppose that each group would react differently to the experience of unemployment (1990,p.34). To illustrate this, Howe states that it is necessary to situate individuals in their local contexts, implying that locality has a major influence in providing opportunities for engaging in paid informal economic activity.

The two locales Howe's research focused on were chosen because of their similar geographical features. Both estates were on the outskirts of Belfast and each was roughly the same distance from the City Centre. Both had similar amenities, a mediocre bus service, a local primary school, local churches, a small number of shops and nearby green areas and parks (1990,p.34). The Catholic estate, Mallon Park, was located in West Belfast while the Protestant estate, Eastlough, was located in East Belfast.

However, both estates were very different when the occupants of each area were taken into consideration. Eastlough was more socially fragmented than Mallon Park. No community associations existed in Eastlough and residents barely knew their neighbours. By contrast, Mallon Park boasted several community organisations and people knew a great deal about their co-residents (1990,p.37). The residents of Mallon Park were also much younger than the residents of Eastlough. More importantly, in Eastlough unemployment was about half that of Mallon Park (1990,p.40). However, in discussing these two areas Howe gives us scant information about each estate. Rather, each locality is discussed with reference to the opportunity structures and labour markets of West Belfast and East Belfast as a whole. Hence we know nothing about the individual histories of either Eastlough or Mallon Park. Nor are we given any information on when Eastlough or Mallon Park was built or on how long residents lived in each area.

In Chapter Three, I intend to suggest that West Belfast is by no means a homogeneous area. Rather the area is sharply divided into respectable and disreputable estates by the occupants themselves and outside organisations. The distinction is of crucial importance for understanding the extent and significance of informal economic strategies. Moreover, one of the key arguments of the book is that differences in the level and duration of unemployment is essential for explaining differing levels of participation in paid informal economic activity. Jenkins states (Harding and Jenkins 1989,p.127) that his research in a different Protestant area in Belfast revealed a greater incidence of ‘doing the double’ than Howe’s data suggested. It may be that differences in the level and duration of unemployment in the two Protestant areas may help explain the different levels of involvement in ‘doing the double’.

On the other hand, there is much to recommend in Howe’s study. He effectively demonstrates that Protestants in Eastlough tend to view unemployment as a temporary setback whereas Catholics in Mallon Park tend to view it as an on going situation. This is based on their realistic assessment of local labour markets and opportunity structures. Howe suggests that there are more opportunities open to Catholics to ‘do the double’ but warns that the young, the old, the unskilled and those with few contacts are unlikely to find openings. Moreover ‘doing the double’ is characterised by irregularity, insecurity and lack of safety (1990,p.64). This type of informal economic activity also attracts very low wages and as such can never by viewed as a realistic alternative to legitimate employment. The income derived from such work is a supplement and not a replacement to benefit income (1990,p.64)

Howe’s research also casts doubt on two points made by Pahl in relation to his research in the Isle of Sheppey. Pahl (1984a) argued that the unemployed were too poor to work informally for two main reasons. Firstly, they cannot go to the pub where potential informal employment contacts are made and secondly, they do not have the money to buy the tools necessary to engage in paid informal work. Howe’s data (1990,p.98) indicated that the pub was the least likely place to secure paid informal work contacts. He further points out that many tradesmen acquire their tools when in formal employment, hence, on becoming unemployed, they can continue to utilise these tools to carry out informal paid work. Howe also suggests that many jobs do not require tools such as child minding and shop work. He concludes (1990,p.99) that Pahl’s study of Sheppey is particularly patchy on the mediating social and cultural processes embedded in specific localities. Howe argues that these need to be taken into consideration in order to understand the diverse world of the unemployed and the differing opportunities and constraints facing them.

Informal economic activity and the importance of locality

The importance of locality is further underlined by Morris (1990) in a study of the social networks and social segregation of the long term unemployed living in Hartlepool in the North East of England. Morris suggests that the clustering of the unemployed, together with the tendency for unemployment to be repeated in particular families, serves to separate them from informal contacts with the world of work. On the other hand, she suggests that within specific housing estates with very high concentrations of unemployment, elaborate networks of mutual aid will develop. Moreover, her research uncovered higher levels of male participation in informal work, than Pahl's Isle of Sheppey study, although the type of employment available was typically an occasional day or week's work for a contractor nearing the end of a job. There were also limited opportunities for self employment involving canvassing homes for repair work or scouring tips and factory sites for scrap metal. While Morris argues that these opportunities for informal work are short term, unpredictable and undertaken in considerable fear and anxiety, nonetheless these earning opportunities, together with the variety of ways in which social networks operate as a channel for informal aid can be a significant influence on the manner in which a household deals with unemployment. In emphasising the importance of locality differences, Morris states:

> locality differences require more systematic investigation and involve complexity that make blanket comparison inappropriate. The key focus would seem to be the local social setting - how generally familiar is the experience of unemployment, what traditions of mutual aid exist and what alternative sources of social identity are available (1990,p.56).

These studies suggest that in order to reach anywhere near an adequate understanding of informal economies, we need a case by case study approach. Such an approach may help dispel the notion that there is any such thing as a typical informal economy. Rather, such an approach may well promote the view that informal economies differ depending on the particular locales in which they are set. Thus informal economic activity may display different features in poor working class communities as opposed to middle class communities, in urban as opposed to rural settings, among the long term unemployed as opposed to the recent unemployed. As Edgell and Hart put it:

> The diversity of formal work is more than matched by the diversity of informal work, therefore theories about the social significance of particular types of informal work in specific societies would seem to

be more appropriate than theories about informal work in general (1988,p.13).

The state and informal economic strategies

On the other hand, I do not want to suggest that Newbury exists out on a limb and is not comparable to anywhere else. Certainly the peculiar nature of the Northern Ireland State and the 'troubles' have fostered, and at times stifled, informal economic activity in the estate. Informal economic strategies do not exist in a vacuum. Economics and politics are inextricably interrelated and this becomes very obvious when considering a politically sensitive area such as Northern Ireland. In outlining the formation of Newbury estate, I will illustrate how the political system influenced the development and image of the estate and also encouraged or hindered the growth of informal economic strategies. The 'house-shops' discussed in Chapter 6 are a direct legacy of the 'troubles'. The scope to engage in some forms of shady economic activity outlined in Chapter 8, also owe their origins to the post-1969 breakdown of law and order. Among some residents, there is a highly developed awareness of the inadequacies of the formal system and this lessens their vulnerability to be stigmatised as unemployed or unemployable. For some, this leads to participation in informal economic activity for the sheer pleasure of 'beating the system'. For the activities that cross the line of legality, detection by the formal system is difficult due to the visible 'republican' nature of the estate and this reduces residents' anxieties about the possibility of being caught. In other instances, state involvement in hindering informal activity is clearly evident. Attempts to stifle the development of informal community work were at their most obvious in the Government's handling of Newbury Industrial Estate (see Chapter 3).

The fact that some informal economic activities are concerned with evading regulation by the State, in itself, makes informal economic strategies as much a political as an economic phenomenon. As Harding and Jenkins (1989,p.41) point out, most irregular economic activity is not, as a practice, in itself illegal. Rather the circumstances in which it is practiced render it illegal. Redclift and Mingione (1985,p.4) argue that it is important to see informal activities as political options and not simply as solutions to individual subsistence problems or household survival. Weiss (1987), from an analysis of informal economies in Italy, argues that informal economies are political creations rooted in features of social structure which have been shaped and sustained by the state. She concludes (1987,p.231) that it is frequently the need to circumvent the inadequacies of the state that throws citizens back on informal support systems. Hence, rather than displacing the need for informal networks, the very organisation of the state has sustained and enlarged the space for their operation.

The failure of the formal economy to provide jobs for the residents of Newbury and indeed other estates throughout West Belfast has fostered informal economic activity. The particular marginalisation of Newbury estate has further enhanced informal practices. However, while the state undoubtedly has influenced participation in informal economic activity, it has not politicized many of my respondents. Individuals and households constituted a community burdened with hardship and poverty, attempting by whatever means available to lessen the rigours of its harsh existence. Hardship and poverty, in many instances, overrode political awareness. In this respect, the data, in many ways is comparable to the work on the household strategies of the poor outlined by Stack (1974), Dow (1977), Gaughan and Ferman (1987) and Lowenthal (1981). As Gaughan and Ferman (1987,p.20), point out, 'the continuing importance of informal social links involving kinship, neighbourhood and friendship remains a crucial factor in understanding the informal economy'. The research illustrates how stability of residence, duration of unemployment, social homogeneity, extensive friendship and kinship networks and low levels of access to external resources are all conducive to the development of informal economic strategies.

Problems with terminology: formal/informal economy, work/employment

Before leaving this chapter, I want to mention some of the problems associated with the terms formal and informal economy, and work and employment and outline the distinctions I intend to adopt here. Firstly, the term, informal economy, is notorious for the variety of meanings attached to it. Its usage is almost as hazardous as that of the term community. The informal economy has been variously described as providing a means of survival for the poor, compensating for the failures of the formal economy, helping to solve unemployment problems, providing a means of gaining access to cheap goods and services, and providing a seedbed for the development of eventual small scale enterprises. To Feige (1977), the informal economy describes all unreported and unmeasured economic activity falling outside the scope of a nation's techniques for monitoring the economy. For Portes (1981), the informal economy refers to all income producing activities outside formal sector wages and social security. Others (Smith 1986, Mattera 1985) make distinctions between activities that are merely unmeasured and those that are concealed in order to evade taxation and other regulations, while Henry and Mars (1978) distinguish between activities that merely escape regulation and others that are more overtly illegal. In all these cases, informality is defined in relation to formality and the very diversity of informal work is rarely utilised to question the supposed homogeneity of the formal sector. Rather, it is naively assumed that economic life falls into two distinct categories, formal or informal. This distinction between formality/informality has led some researchers to develop a dichotomous theoretical framework in relation to the formal/informal economy. Shankland (1984,p.188), for example, outlines what he sees as the mutually exclusive characteristics of each sector and views the relationship between the two as benign. This artifical separation of economic sectors has created significant obstacles to our understanding of this whole area.

Other researchers anxious to emphasise the unity of the economic system have adopted a sub-economies model. Edgell and Hart (1988) suggest that the basic approach used has been to outline a three economies model of work comprising the formal, informal and domestic economies. Again a wide variety of terms have been used to distinguish between different types of formal and informal work. Ferman and Berndt (1981) use the terms regular, irregular and social economic activity while Rose (1985) distinguishes between the official, unofficial and domestic economies. Other researchers have adopted this threefold model but have introduced a variety of sub-sectors. Hence Gershuny and Pahl (1981) subdivided the social economy into household and communal types of informal economic activity while Henry (1981) developed a six-fold model based on distinctions between legal, extra-legal and illegal activities. Other researchers have developed a fascination for colours. Hence Davis (1985) distinguishes between the black and blue economies while Handy (1984) distinguishes between the white, black, mauve and grey economies. This profusion of terms and definitions leads Banerjee (1981) to view the informal economy as an exceedingly 'elusive concept' while Edgell and Hart agree that there is little consensus on the conceptualisation of the informal economy.

These criticisms are discussed by Harding and Jenkins (1989) in their book on 'The Myth of the Hidden Economy'. They argue that the phrase, informal economy, has entered into the careless usage of everyday conversation and has little usefulness beyond drawing attention to the fact that while some economic activities are taken into account by the state in the compilation of annual accounts, others are not. Harding and Jenkins (1989,p.178-179) present three basic criticisms of the 'myth of the hidden economy'. Firstly, they argue that the distinction between formality and informality is not clear cut nor unambiguous. Secondly, they apply this criticism to the distinction between economic and non economic activities and to distinctions between work and employment. Thirdly, following on from these criticisms, they suggest that attempts to establish the value of the hidden economy have been misguided and unreliable.

Harding and Jenkins (1989,p.175-179) stress that the key to understanding the relationship between formality and informality lies in adopting a historical perspective. They argue that the notion of formality emerged as a result of a historical process in which the development of writing and information technology interacted with the rise of bureaucracy and the modern state. These two broad developments created and encouraged the monitoring, accounting and control of economic activity. It is within this context that distinctions between formality and informality began to emerge. Hence Harding and Jenkins state that the bureaucratic and organisational control and definition of economic activity should form the focus of any distinction between formality and informality. However, the authors warn that formality and informality may be very difficult to establish in practice. Formality and informality often co-exist. This can be illustrated by focusing on the extent to which formal organisations often utilise informal recruiting mechanisms to employ new staff (see Chapter Seven). Moreover, while state regulation is essential to distinguishing between formality and informality in the first place, nonetheless, this does not mean that informality should be characterised by the mere absence of formal regulation. Informality is a social condition in its own right with its own rules and conditions of social experience.

Harding and Jenkins (1989,p.10-14) also adopt a historical perspective in their discussion of the distinction between work and employment. They state that the development of capitalist social and economic relations resulted in a gradual distinction emerging between work and employment. This historical perspective is reflected in the work of Garraty (1978,p.103) who suggests that unemployment as a concept is a relatively new thing, even in Western industrial society. The word 'unemployed' did not appear in its modern meaning in the Oxford English Dictionary until the late 1880's and 'unemployment' was not a separate heading in Hansard until after the Boer War (Kumar 1988,p.164). Harding and Jenkins suggest that unemployment only becomes meaningful for those moving in an economy dominated by the employment relationship. This is because employment has become a technical term referring to a relationship between capital and labour. It is this relationship which differentiates employment from the concept of work. This relationship has rarely been taken into account by researchers into informal economic activity. Rather economic activity which is not recorded in official statistics and which operates in the absence of adminstrative monitoring and control is referred to by the term 'informal work' regardless of whether or not such activity is conditioned by an employment relationship. Harding and Jenkins suggest that what is or what is not work can only be determined by looking at the specific social relations within which it is embedded. Some informal economic activities may exhibit an employment relationship and thus should be defined, not simply as informal work, but as informal employment.

The following chapters will focus on the various informal economic activities utilised by the residents of Newbury estate to gain access to scarce goods and services. These activities do not fall neatly into the realm of full time employment, part time employment or self employment in the formal economy. These three types of employment are discussed briefly in Chapter Three and lie outside the main scope of the book. They are distinguished by the following three features. Firstly, the participants in each of these three aspects of employment define themselves as either employed full time, part time or self employed. Secondly, the state officially categorises the participants in a similar way, as either full time, part time or self employed workers. Thirdly, researchers investigating work, employment and unemployment in Newbury have focused on these three types of formal employment as representing all forms of work in Newbury. The activities discussed in this book from Chapter Four onwards lack one or more of these characteristics of formal employment. However, I do not intend to argue that each of the activities examined henceforth are uniformly informal. Rather the economic activities outlined in the following chapters will display varying degrees of formality and informality. Moreover, while some of these activities will fall clearly into the realm of either informal work or informal employment, others will occupy the grey area between these two categories.

Chapter Four focuses on self servicing households in Newbury. Here, the emphasis is on the extent to which households rely on the internal labour of their members to provide a range of goods and services rather than purchasing these from external sources. The activities outlined in this chapter are defined as informal work as no employment relationship exists between the producers and consumers of these goods and services.

Chapter Five is concerned with reciprocal transactions in Newbury. The activities described in this chapter will be referred to as informal work as the relationships surrounding these activities are qualitatively different from the employment relationship. The activities outlined in this chapter are embedded in complex social relationships and the transactions themselves are surrounded by the norms of reciprocity. However, this does not necessarily mean that the profit motive is absent from these transactions. While repayment may be deferred for a long period and may be in kind rather than cash, nonetheless, the chapter will illustrate that male motivations for engaging in reciprocal transactions are often tinged with economic rationality.

Chapter Six concentrates on community economic enterprises. Participants in this range of activities utilise their labour power to provide a commodity or service to others in the community for money. Most of the activities outlined in this chapter can be described as community self employment. Here a money relationship exists between the producer of the goods or service and the customer. However, this relationship is qualitatively different from that which exists between employer and employee. The various activities discussed in this chapter will form a continuum between formality and informality. The sample includes a discussion of women who work as catalogue sales agents. These women work in a self employed capacity for a formal organisation. The catalogue sales company accounts for these women in their business records but it is up to the women themselves to declare their earnings to the tax authorities or to the DHSS. None of the women I spoke to felt it necessary to declare their earnings.

Others operate trading outlets from their homes. These 'house-shops' operate without the knowledge of the local housing authority and the participants do not officially declare their trading activities. Others are involved in producing a diverse range of goods and services, mostly for community members, although in a few cases the customer is a formal organisation. Again, depending on the social relationships involved, these activities will fluctuate between formality and informality. The participants in Chapter Six fall into two main categories. Firstly, those who claim some form of welfare benefit or are married and their spouses claim some form of welfare benefit. These people define themselves and are classified in terms of their welfare benefit category or as housewives. The second group consists of a small number of people who are employed in a full time or part time capacity in the formal economy. This group define themselves and are categorised in terms of their formal employment. As a result the economic activities outlined in this chapter remain largely invisible. Furthermore, in terms of the participants' perceptions of these economic activities, many of the respondents, like Cragg and Dawson's (1981,p.21) homeworkers did not regard themselves as really 'having jobs' and hence they felt under no obligation to declare their additional income for income tax or benefit purposes.

Chapter Seven will focus on informal wage labourers. These people offically defined themselves as either unemployed, sick/disabled or retired. Furthermore this group are defined by the state in this way. Previous research in Newbury has also tended to accept uncritically these definitions. All of this group are employed informally by formally registered individuals and organisations. None of this group declare their earnings in case it affects their benefit entitlements. The relation of informal wage labourers to state regulation may be further illustrated by looking at the way in which they are paid. All of the sample are paid in cash and all of the sample state that they have never received a pay slip or written record of payment. The ways in which the individuals and organisations who informally employ this group deal with their own bookkeeping in order to conceal or account for this activity is outside the scope of this study.

Chapter Eight deals with shady economic transactions in Newbury. Here the emphasis is on the trading in stolen goods and the economic aspects of joy-riding. The chapter will look at fiddling connected to informal employment and outline how the low wages attached to informal employment provides a justification for engaging in fiddling. The chapter will also focus on a small number of individuals who steal from shops in the city centre of Belfast.

While each of the following chapters will deal with specific economic activities nonetheless no individual chapter is exclusive from the others. Rather a considerable degree of overlap and interdependence is evident. Edgell and Hart (1988,p.8) argue that many of the typologies of informal economic activity convey a false sense of clarity. The book will illustrate how one household and indeed one individual may be engaged in a whole range of different types of informal economic activities. Attention will also be paid to actors' accounts and perceptions of what they are doing. This means that certain activities may be discussed in more than one chapter. Women's knitting practices, for example, will be discussed in relation to community entrepreneurship, self servicing households and community reciprocity. Hence the production of the activity does not allocate it to a specific informal category but rather the way in which the product is distributed and consumed.

Many of the activities outlined in the following chapters have already been dealt with extensively by researchers into informal economies who tend to portray them as separate from the formal economy. Such an approach ignores the possiblity that distinctions between the formal and informal economy may be blurred rather than clearcut. Because of the conceptual difficulties embedded in the term, informal economy, I intend to utilise the term informal economic strategies/activities to refer to the various economic practices outlined henceforth. Moreover, in order the underline the interpenetration of the formal and informal economy, most chapters will conclude with a short discussion on the connection between the two sectors.

2 Methodology: Investigating a sensitive topic in a politically sensitive locality

> The government makes the absurd assumption in household surveys that everyone always tells the truth.....This is sheer unwillingness to face reality...... Those collecting unemployment benefits while actually working for cash know that it is illegal......Why should they admit illegal activities to an official agency? (Gutmann 1985,p.7)

This quote by Gutmann illustrates one of the most difficult problems embedded in studying informal economic activity. Since some aspects of informal work are illegal, how likely are respondents to admit to such activities? This leads Gutmann to suggest that informal economic activity is best analysed through indirect methods of measurement that do not involve interviews or direct data collection. In the first part of this chapter, I critically assess some of these indirect measurement approaches and then go on to discuss the combination of survey and combination of the survey and ethnographic method was utilised by Ferman and Berndt (1981) in Detroit and by Pahl and Wallace (1985) in their research in the Isle of Sheppey. I was initially critical of this approach and adopted it with some reluctance. The reasons for my hesitation and the modifications I introduced will be discussed. Finally, the ethical issues arising from studying a sensitive topic in a politically sensitive locality will be considered.

Measuring the unmeasurable

Economic analysts of informal economic activity have been mainly concerned with attempts to estimate the volume or value of informal work in monetary terms. Economic interest in informal work flourished after the publication of 'The Subterranean Economy' by Peter Gutmann in 1977. Two aspects of Gutmann's article caught the attention of academics and politicans (Thomas 1990,p.621). Firstly, Gutmann proposed a simple procedure for measuring the size of the underground economy that could be applied to easily obtainable data. Secondly, the estimates of the size of the underground economy Gutmann produced, were dramatic and well publicised. Instead of looking at the amount of cash in circulation, Gutmann examined the composition of the money supply, that is the ratio of currency to current accounts (Harding and Jenkins 1989,p.57). Gutmann assumed that there was no subterranean economy in the United States during the period 1937-1941. This was because taxation levels were so low during this period that tax evasion seemed unnecessary. Gutmann took this period as the baseline norm and measured subsequent changes in the ratio between currency and current accounts. To Gutmann increases in the ratio were indicative of an increase in informal economic activity. Using this method, Gutmann estimated that the subterranean economy in the United States in 1976 amount to appromimately $176.

However, as Thomas points out (1990,p.626), the choice of the base year in which it was assumed that the underground economy did not exist is an arbitrary one. Consequently, changing the base year can produce quite dramatic effects on the estimated size of the underground economy. Thomas quotes research by Mathews and Mathews and Rastogi, in the United Kingdom, which indicated that when the base year was changed the size of the informal economy increased from 0.5 per cent to nearly 12 per cent of GDP in 1969.

This indirect measurement approach has been used, with some modifications by Feige (1981) who calculated that informal economic activity represented 33 per cent of GNP and by Tanzi (1982) who arrived at a much more conservative estimate of 4.4 per cent of GNP. Portes and Sassen-Koob (1987,p.42) suggest that despite the similarity of method, these economic estimates vary wildly and this casts their validity in serious doubt.

Other measurement approaches on the extent of informal economic activity have focused on the involvement of the labour force in informal economic activity and on discrepancies between income and expenditure reported on household surveys. The first approach is motivated by the observation that while participation rates in the formal labour market have fallen over time in a number of countries, output has nonetheless increased faster than could be accounted for by increased productivity (Thomas 1990,p.628). Two general conclusions emerge from studies into labour market participation in informal work. Firstly, the observation that it is mainly small firms and the self employed who operate in the informal economy and secondly, that the construction, retail and service industries offer most scope for such activities. However, estimates regarding the percentages of the labour force participation again vary wildly from 3 to 35 per cent of a nation's labour force (Smith 1986).

The second approach concerns discrepancies between income and expenditure. The underlying assumption here, is that while people may well try to hide their 'real' income when interviewed in government surveys, they will not be as concerned to conceal their expenditure. Discrepancies between spending and income were analysed by Dilnot and Morris (Thomas 1990) using Family Expenditure Survey data. They concluded that between 10 to 15 per cent of households might have some form of concealed income but that the total amount involved was not large representing only about 2 to 3 per cent of GNP. They also suggested that the self employed were the group most likely to conceal their true income. These conclusions are echoed by Smith (1986) who also suggests that the self employed have more scope to engage in informal economic activity.

The divergent conclusions these various studies have reached in their attempts to measure the extent of informal economic activity levels leads Mattera (1985) to question the possibility of measuring accurately the 'unmeasurable'. The primary concerns of most of the studies mentioned so far, are with the size of the informal economy and hence leave many issues of interest to sociologists, unanswered. Little attention has been paid to who is involved in informal economic activity (apart from the generalisation that the self employed have greater scope to engage in informal economy activity) and how or why certain individuals, households or localities 'choose' to operate in informal economic activity.

The problems with surveys of informal work

The most perceptive sociological accounts of informal economic activity have used a variety of research methods to provide a comprehensive account of the social significance of such work. Ferman and Berndt's study (1981) of informal work among households in Detroit combined a survey and ethnographic approach. Howe (1987) utilised participant observation, in depth interviewing and data on local labour market opportunities derived largely from surveys in each area investigated. Pahl and Wallace (Redclift and Mingione 1985) built up extensive knowledge of the Isle of Sheppey through participant observation and semi structured interviewing, before commencing a survey of the area. Pahl and Wallace (Allen 1986,p.131) also conducted follow up interviews with selected households in order to describe the actual patterns of work of the unemployed. During the early period of the research when I was reviewing these studies, I was sceptical about the possibility of a survey generating data about informal paid work. If money for goods or services changes hands and is not recorded, then the activity may be illegal. This begs the question, how likely are people to admit to actions which strictly speaking are illegal? Pahl (1984) was particularly conscious of this problem in his Isle of Sheppey survey. The survey revealed that 27 people out of 730 undertook some form of work 'on the side' for which payment was made. When the 27 respondents who acknowledged that they got extra money informally were analysed further, some striking contrasts emerged. Of the eleven men, ten were in full time employment. Only one was unemployed. Of the sixteen women, eight were full time housewives.

Pahl was aware that he could have been misled by his respondents who may have avoided being explicit about activities they may know are not quite straight. The responses gained credibility, however, by other documented responses which indicated that exactly 27 people admitted paying others for doing informal work. Whilst this latter finding does make Pahl's conclusions more justifiable, nonetheless I felt that he may have underestimated the different moral connotations attached to 'doing the double' compared to 'moonlighting'. To hold two jobs in order to maintain one's family spending budget may be regarded as quite an enterprising way of adding to one's household income. To claim unemployment benefit and engage in own account work for extra money may be regarded as parasitic. The media tends to have a fondness for publicising stories about 'benefit scroungers' caught 'doing the double' and also for covering extensively the latest government's efforts to root out 'benefit swindlers'. When Norman Tebitt was Employment Secretary (during the time of the Isle of Sheppey survey), he formed special 'hit squads' to crack down on fraudulent claims which were estimated to cost the taxpayer over £300 million per year. Ten strong teams of investigators were sent to various parts of the country to supplement teams of investigators already in the field. Their aim was (Society Today November 1983) 'to root out those now claiming dole payments while working on their own account and not declaring their income'. I felt that society's evaluation of these people and the emotive terms used by the media in describing them such as 'scrounger' or 'swindler' would impede the likelihood of an individual 'owning up' to such activity, especially if using the methodologies of survey research.

Moreover, the estate had provided a focus for a considerable amount of research especially since the 'troubles' of 1969 and this presented added difficulties. As one resident sarcastically put it:

> Newbury has become a goldfish bowl where you observe people in it. There has been more PhD's done here per square mile. If you want to

> do a PhD, you go here or to Divis Flats. What you should be concentrating on is the extent to which this estate provides an informal economy for the academic world.

Much of this research has involved the survey method and has concentrated, by and large, on the psychological effects of unemployment or the 'troubles' on the residents of Newbury estate. These researchers are not confined to the British Isles. Every summer, I am told, at least one or two foreign students turn up on the residents' doorsteps asking questions about the effects of the 'troubles' on day to day living on the estate. These students begin their surveys by offering the residents platitudes such as 'I hope you get your freedom' and then proceed to ask them a range of questions concerning the impact of the 'troubles' on their everyday lives. These researchers are generally regarded with amusement. Others are regarded with suspicion. I have been told, on more than one occasion, of a student researching the impact of different army tactics on the residents of the estate who now works as part of an army intelligence unit operating in Northern Ireland. Taylor (1988) argues that, at various times, researchers have been forced into hiding or have had to leave Northern Ireland, due to fears (usually unfounded, it should be said) that research materials were finding their way to the security forces. Hence, bearing in mind the sensitive nature of the topic and the sensitive nature of the estate itself, I felt that a questionnaire which asked about controversial issues such as 'doing the double', especially when put by a stranger would not only be unreliable because of the reluctance of respondents to give truthful answers but also could be a potentially dangerous activity. Rather, I felt that qualitative research based on participant observation and extensive unstructured and semi structured interviews were best suited to my purposes. Qualitative methods have special qualities for dealing with controversial topics in sensitive locations as they entail a gradual and progressive contact with respondents which is sustained over a long period, allowing a rapport to be established slowly with respondents (Brewer 1990).

However, as the research developed, it became apparent that qualitative methods by themselves were not sufficient to generate meaningful data about informal work in Newbury. Hence, after one year in the field, I decided to carry out a survey of the area. My reasons for this change of heart will be discussed below. As Wax has observed:

> Rigid adherence to any method....may, for the fieldworker, become like confinement in a cage......if he finds himself in a field situation where he is limited by a particular method....he will do well to slip through the bars and try to find out what is really going on (1971,p.10).

Gaining access

At its most basic, access involves gaining permission to do a piece of research in a particular social setting or institution. Access is an essential prerequisite in the research process. Yet, access is by no means a straightforward procedure, particularly if the research concerns a community or locality. In many research settings, access is negotiated with a gatekeeper, a gatekeeper being a person who has the power to grant or withold access to people or situations for the purposes of research (Bogdan and Taylor 1975). However, in a community, no gatekeeper, in the sense of an individual occupying a paramount position exists. Rather in such settings, there are multiple points of entry that require a continuous process of negotiation and re-negotiation throughout the research (Geer 1970). Hence in such situations, access is often gained by befriending a number of individuals within the locality who will then act as quarantors in order to assist the researcher to gain access to the wider community.

Access to Newbury estate was facilitated by my employment, one night per week, in a local community school in the district. I was working in the community school for one year before the decision to do research was made. Hence, I already had contacts in, and knowledge of, the setting in which the research was conducted. Working in the community school went far beyond turning up one night per week to teach a class. The conscientious tutor was expected to attend the meetings of local community associations, attend various local social functions and take his or her class (which usually consisted of members of the estate) off to Donegal for study weekends. Since the community school was also a charitable association, the conscientious tutor was expected to assist in raising funds by taking part in sponsored walks and collecting money during the various 'flag-days' organised by the community house committee. By taking part in all these ventures, I managed to build up several contacts within the estate.

Moreover, the community school was a key focal point in the estate. The community school was housed in a ordinary three bedroom house occupied by a radical priest who lived in the district. The house served as a meeting place for many of the residents of the estate who utilised the premises as a drop in centre. During the early part of the research, I engaged in participant observation by spending as much time as possible in the community school. Being a teacher enabled me to blend into the everyday life of the community school and gave me an opportunity to observe the residents of the estate in everyday interaction with each other. Often I would initiate conversations on unemployment and informal work and was able to gain an insight into how these issues were regarded by the residents of the estate. Teaching in the school enabled me to develop trust and establish relationships with several residents of the area who were able to act as key informants.

The use of key informants

The usage of key informants in sociology was made famous by Whyte's study of Street Corner Society (1955) where Whyte's key informant Doc, became as well known as the study itself. Other examples include Liebow (1967) who gained access to a group of black street corner men through Tally, Patrick (1973) who utilised Tim to gain access to studying a Glasgow street gang and Nichols and Beynon (1977) who suggest that their study of factory life was strongly influenced by accounts provided by five men. Key informants can play a major role in community research by helping the researcher to learn about the core features of the setting under study. Van Maanen (1981) suggests that sociologists need to establish relationships with a number of informants as it is doubtful whether individual informants are acquainted with all aspects of a cultural setting. He suggests therefore, that researchers need to find informants who have knowledge about specialised interests and concerns in a social setting. I interviewed and tape recorded detailed conversations with five key notables from Newbury estate. Some of these people were among the first residents of the estate and all had played a key role in the history of the area. Through these five informants I was able to build up a detailed knowledge of the background to the estate and the accounts provided by these respondents were checked against each other and where possible by reference to documentary sources.

Documentary sources

The five key informants mentioned above provided much of the material for the following chapter on the formation of the estate. These people were able to provide me with important dates in the history of the estate. These accounts were checked against newspaper reports of the period. When analysing newspaper accounts of key events in the history of the estate, I focused on Belfast's two main daily newspapers, The Irish News and The Newsletter. It was necessary to refer to each paper as each cater for a different audience and tend to portray a partial view of events in Northern Ireland. The Irish News caters for a largely Catholic readership while The Newsletter caters for a largely Protestant readership.

The community school where I was employed also housed a small local library on the top floor. Here documentary sources relating to the history of the estate were kept. The collection included newspaper articles relating to the estate, letters written to newspapers by members of the estate or about residents of the estate, written reports and personal recollections. I was granted unlimited access to the library and was able to verify verbal accounts provided by my informants, often by referring to more than one documentary source.

Letters in particular proved indispensable to the research. As Allport (Plummer 1983) points out, letters are always written for an audience and reveal much about how the two parties involved view each other. Letters can shed light on different kinds of social relationships and can complement data obtained in interviews. All in all, the documentary sources of information utilised throughout the study played an integral part in investigating interaction between the residents of Newbury and the wider society, and how both parties regarded each other.

Snowball sampling

My initial intention was to gain access to the wider society of Newbury by utilising the contacts I had already made in the estate. Through these informants, I intended to gain access to the wider social pattern by interviewing their social networks and associates in a snowball pattern. While snowball sampling throws up problems of representativeness, nonetheless, I felt that this was the only way I would be able to gain meaningful data on informal work. Throughout my period of working in the community school, I heard countless 'stories' of how various bureaucrats, particularly 'dole-busters' had gained information on the work patterns of the unemployed in Newbury by pretending to be researchers carrying out door to door interviews. These 'stories' were related to me with such frequency that they further increased my misgivings about the survey method. The contacts I had made so far in the estate expressed their willingness to pass me through their social networks. However, after adopting this approach for one year, I decided to supplement the methodology by carrying out a survey of the area.

I became unhappy with the snowball technique for several reasons. Firstly, the method proved very time consuming. Long periods lapsed between respondents expressing their willingness to pass me through their social networks and these contacts materialising. I don't feel I was deliberately fobbed off by my initial contacts. Rather I just came low on their list of priorities and hence several weeks would pass before interviews with any of their associates would emerge.

Moreover, often when arrangements were made to meet the associates of my initial contacts, the respondents failed to turn up. For example, on three separate occasions, arrangements were made to interview three women who worked informally as contract cleaners. The interviews were arranged through one of my key informants. The women were reluctant to be interviewed in their own homes, so it was decided that I should meet them in the local leisure centre. On the first occasion, the women turned up one day early for the interviews. On the second occasion, one of the women's sons became ill and all three decided not to turn up; while on the third occasion the women failed to turn up and I was eventually told by my key informant that they had changed their minds about being interviewed.

Other informants who had expressed their willingness to pass me through their social networks reported back to me that their contacts were unwilling to be interviewed. My informants tended to blame the formality of making a definite appointment to see me as the major reason for the unwillingness of their associates to be interviewed. This attitude was aptly expressed by one informant who told me:

> If you'd have just called to the door like, I'm sure they would have let you in no problem. But they are very reluctant to make definite arrangments.

Even when interviews were arranged, often the setting was the community school rather than the respondents' households. It seemed logical to my contacts that the community school should serve as an interview base and they stated that this would enhance the willingness of their associates to talk to me as anonymity would be assured. However, I felt that often these interviews took place in artifical settings and valuable data was lost by separating respondents from their household environment.

Furthermore, although I emphasised to my initial contacts, that I was interested in all forms of informal work, through time I came to be more narrowly defined as 'the girl who wants to talk to people who do the double'. As a result the snowball sampling technique tended to generate data, only on the more dubious forms of informal work.

As time progressed, I became increasingly dissatisfied with the quality of the data I was collecting. Sample sizes were very small. Respondents were interviewed, often in isolation from their households and the wider community. Data was only collected on informal paid work and this left many questions unanswered. What about households who are unable to gain access to informal paid work? How do they get by? What other types of informal work exist in the estate? Is involvement in informal work influenced by gender, life cycle or other variables? In order to try and answer these, and other questions, I decided to carry out a survey of the area.

The combination of ethnography and survey approach

Up until recently, sociologists have been preoccupied with the qualitative versus quantitative debate, although it has become increasingly acceptable to employ a wide variety of research methods within a study (McNeill 1985). As with the terminology used to describe the informal economy, the combination of qualitative and quantitative methods attracts a wide variety of labels. The combination of both approaches has been variously called, combined operations (Stacey 1969), triangulation (Denzin 1970), mixed strategies (Douglas 1976) and multiple strategies (Burgess 1982). According to Bryman:

> an ethnographer carries out a survey in order to fill some gaps in his or her knowledge of a community, group, organisation or whatever, because the gaps cannot be readily filled in by a reliance on participant observation or unstructured interviewing alone (1988,p.137).

A number of advantages can be gained by combining research methods. The integration of ethnographic and survey methods can contribute to a better overall understanding of the research topic. Both approaches can provide a crosscheck for each other, enabling researchers to have greater confidence in common findings (Sieber 1982,p177).

As I mentioned earlier, I became dissatisfied with the usage of qualitative methods in isolation. I felt that the qualitative approach used prior to the survey, though valuable in itself, was merely scratching the surface of the range of informal work in Newbury. On the other hand, the qualitative work before the implementation of the survey had other benefits. Hanging around and informally interviewing subjects in the community school enabled me to identify relevant issues which could be utilised in the questionnaire. By the time the survey was being carried out, I had built up an extensive knowledge about Newbury and had established relationships with many key figures in the area. I was able to exploit this information and these relationships in order to gain the trust and confidence of the respondents interviewed during the survey

While a questionnaire was used throughout the survey, flexibility was the keynote of the interviews. Throughout the process, I had to make a number of pragmatic compromises which departed from the textbook portrayal of ideal research practice. Brewer (1990,p.592) suggests that when the research involves sensitive locations and/or topics, the pragmatic compromises tend to increase in number and in the magnitude of the departure from ideal practice.

The survey

I contacted the Northern Ireland Housing Executive (NIHE) who gave me a detailed breakdown of their housing stock in Newbury. The housing total in the area was 660 dwellings. From the information supplied by the NIHE, I selected every fourth address to make up a total sample of 165 households. Despite my initial reservations, I had little problem in gaining access to households in the estate. All in all, I gained access to 150 dwellings, hence the refusal rate was just under 10 per cent. Where possible, I interviewed both husband and wife in households containing married couples. Where this proved difficult, either spouse was asked about the structural characteristics of their partner. In all, I obtained information on 118 males and 124 females in the 150 households surveyed.

I told all respondents that I was using a pseudonym for the estate and that while this would enhance anonymity, I could give no guarantees that the location would remain secret. I also gave assurances that pseudonyms would be used to describe all persons mentioned in the study. Hence individual identities would remain anonymous, except perhaps to other residents in the estate. Thus no space existed on the questionnaires for the names and addresses of respondents and this was illustrated to each household. This proved important as on several occasions I was stopped and searched by army patrols in the area, in full view of the residents of the estate.

I also decided to omit direct questions on 'doing the double' from the questionnaire. Rather I hoped to introduce this topic casually during my interaction with the respondents. As I mentioned earlier, no gatekeeper exists for the area. Rather access had to be continually negotiated and renegotiated with several competing groups. I felt that if the questionnaire was scrutinised by any of these groups, or by my respondents, then the presence of one or two 'offensive' questions would jeopardise the whole research project. After all, I was not interested in 'doing the double' in isolation. Moreover I remained doubtful about the possibility of households responding to direct questions on involvement in working while claiming benefits. Rather I hoped to build up a rapport with my respondents and introduce the subject where I felt the opportunity was ripe. Brannen (1988,p.553) suggests that researchers into sensitive topics need to tread warily, particularly at the beginning of interviews and not reveal all their hand at the outset. She further states that it is important not to prejudge the research problem by labelling it or defining its boundaries too closely, respondents may thereby define the problem in their own terms. Hence, in relation to this study, while all interviews were structured by an interview schedule, the natural progression of the conversation dictated the final nature of the interview.

The interviewing proved to be a very time consuming process. When interviewing, my intention was to allow the research topic to emerge gradually in its own terms. This often meant that respondents would become totally absorbed in talking about their own lives. Often the issues covered were not directly related to my research interests. In these circumstances, my inclination was not to interrupt. As a result, often respondents would give away telling information about themselves which was sometimes at odds with earlier responses, especially those given in answer to direct questions. For example, in Chapter Five, I discuss female involvement in reciprocal favours. Most of the female respondents replied 'No' when asked directly whether or not they ever did favours for others. Their widespread participation only emerged during informal conversations rather than as responses to direct questions.

Moreover, during the conversations, I wanted to adopt as unobtrusive a role as possible. Therefore I felt that writing down everything that was said would interrupt the natural flow of the conversations. Hence while responses to direct questions were noted, conversations were generally trusted to memory. Rather only key words and phrases were jotted down. Interruptions in the interview, were often utilised to write down quotes or other relevant information. Thus while respondents were making tea or answering the door or whatever, I used these periods to write feverishly. Furthermore, often I pretended to be much slower in taking down replies to direct questions to enable me to write down key parts of the informal conversations. Usually interviews were only carried out one at a time. Once the interview ended, I left the estate to immediately write down the informal conversation. Again this meant that the process was very time consuming. Interviews lasting three or four hours were not uncommon and this was followed by a number of hours spent recalling conversations. As a result the survey took a full six months to complete and during this time I visited the estate on a daily basis.

Doing the survey was also an emotionally exhausting experience. I was well aware that the area had already been the setting for several surveys and that among many residents there was a feeling that survey research was useless, representing merely a form of exploitation by the investigator for his/her gain or for the gain of the institutions and powers they serve. Moreover I was also aware that there was a highly developed suspicion of outside investigators and their motives. Hence wandering into peoples' homes and asking them a series of sometimes sensitive questions was something I viewed with trepidation. As it turned out, there were very few occasions when doors were slammed in my face. Rather people welcomed me into their homes and rapport was easily established.

In gaining access to households and obtaining information, I was greatly assisted by the fact that I originally came from a Catholic working class estate in West Belfast, situated about two miles from Newbury. Burton (1978) illustrates how the process of 'telling' permeates social relationships among Catholics and Protestants in Belfast. 'Telling' is the pattern of signs and cues by which religious ascription is arrived at in the everyday interactions of Protestants and Catholics. It is based on the social significance attached to, among other things, name, face, dress, area of residence and school attended. Burton (1978,p.56) argues that, in particular, the area one lives in, is of paramount importance for the Belfast working class. Hence interviews were often preceded by attempts by respondents to pry into my background. Once it was established that I was 'one of them', trust and confidence was easily secured. The usefulness of coming from the same background as one's respondents has been outlined by Nukunya when he says:

> Many a time informants were met who admitted, this is a thing we normally don't divulge to outsiders but since it is you, we shall give you all the necessary help (1969,p.19).

On the other hand, this relationship placed greater responsibility on the researcher and intensified the ethical issues concerned with studying both a sensitive topic in a politically sensitive area.

Ethical problems

I have argued that some aspects of informal work strategies are illegal. This begs the question, have I the right to examine these activities and what implications will my findings have for the residents of the estate? I can only justify my interest in this topic by stating that I was interested in informal work strategies in general and not in the black economy in isolation. Moreover, I was interested in examining 'myths' already commonly held. The two most commonly held 'myths' regarding this topic are that the people of Newbury do not want to work because they are too lazy or because they are making so much 'doing the double' that to work formally 'wouldn't pay them'. The research indicates that the people of Newbury do want to work but, for various reasons, have often been denied the opportunity. Also, 'working on the side' is, in most cases, little more than a supplement to inadequate welfare benefits and because of its unpredictable nature, is rarely a compensation for formal employment.

The implications of studying such a sensitive locality is more problematic. Throughout this research, I have used pseudonyms in order to facilitate anonymity and confidentiality. I believe however, that a detailed historical account of the estate is essential to understanding current informal work strategies. This means that people familiar with West Belfast may well recognise the identity of the estate. Barnes (1979,p.137) argues that a pseudonym usually only offers a partial disguise. Most individuals are able to recognise themselves and through time one's colleagues come to share the secret of where the research was based. However, Barnes argues that even if a disguise is transparent, it may still serve a useful purpose. It may shield the area from casual reproach. Identities remain uncertain and ambigious and this may provide some useful protection if a powerful outsider tries to use the research as evidence against the respondents (Barnes 1979,p.138).

There is no easy solution to this problem. I have discussed this with some of my informants who are willing to co-operate because the estate has such a 'bad name' anyway and 'I might as well set the record straight'. But the implications go beyond the mere identification of the area. If parts of the research are quoted out of context, then the research may well end up feeding the myths it is testing. Moreover, in the context of Northern Ireland, some of my observations may well provide certain groups with excellent propaganda material. Propagandists interested in scoring a political point are unlikely to pay much attention to the wider theoretical distinction I am making between work and employment. Rainwater and Pittman's (1966,p.361) reflection on their study of a controversial housing project argue that publication of results can be a major problem. People's bigotry can be inflamed by what they read, and the results can be interpreted by members of the public in whatever way they want. Again, there is no easy answer to these problems. All the researcher can do is continually reflect on the issues involved and continually consider and reconsider what to include, what to exclude, what to disguise and what to make public.

It has been suggested that if the researcher makes it clear at the outset what he/she intends to do and how he/she intends to use any information obtained, then this will prevent ethical problems arising. With constant contact, however, the relationship between researcher and subject is bound to change in that the subject becomes less and less guarded. Moreover, if the researcher is regarded by his/her respondents as 'one of them', then this may dilute the respondents' awareness of being researched. While, on the one hand, the researcher depends on such an occurrence, the problem remains, to what extent should he/she take advantage of it. I have already faced this dilemma by being present at several conversations and witness to several events, where my status as a researcher and observer has been temporarily forgotten. Very careful deliberation and soul searching was required before I decided whether or not to use this information. At the end of the day, I can only reiterate Bronfenbrenner's remark:

> The only safe way to avoid violating principles of professional ethics is to refrain from doing social research altogether (1952,p453).

3 The formation of a 'dreadful enclosure'

> Certain milieux gather reputations for moral inferiority, squalor, violence and social pathology, and consequently they objectify the fantasy of the dreadful enclosure (Walter 1976,p.155).

It is one of the main arguments of this book that space is central to the development of informal economic strategies. The ways in which actors accept, reject or manipulate the limits of their space has important consequences for the development of paid and unpaid informal economic activity. Often people on the margins of society have to find alternative ways of 'making out'. Their decisions to engage in informal economic activity may not emerge from autonomous choice but stem from necessity. In the first section of the chapter, I will focus on the emergence and development of the negative image of Newbury estate and illustrate how this negative image affected the residents' inner perceptions of themselves and each other. A focus on the negative image of the area is crucial for understanding the residents' attitudes to formal and informal economic practices. This will be followed by an overview of the residents attitudes to, and experience of, work, employment and unemployment. The final section of the chapter will focus on the extent and significance of informal economic activity in the area.

The establishment of the estate

On the surface, Newbury is a grim, depressing Catholic estate in West Belfast. Its streets, which house a flourishing population of children and dogs are thickly carpeted with stones, broken glass and litter. Houses are built in a circular pattern with the shops located in the centre which is known as the Bullring. As was common at the time in similar estates, very little attention was given to environmental provision. No provision existed for off street car parking on the estate and no space was set aside for play purposes or general spaces for the planting of trees and shrubs and so on.

From the 1960's, the deep rooted socio-economic problems of the estate as indeed those of the whole district became increasingly visible. The eruption of the sectarian troubles in the late 1960's expanded the complexity of the problems and have had a lasting effect on the area. The drabness of the estate is now mitigated somewhat by the colourful wall murals which adorn almost every end gable wall and which starkly proclaim the inhabitants' political persuasions. One such mural depicting three IRA men with rifles raised, defiantly declares 'Our Day Will Come'. The lack of amenities for young people, combined with general dilapidation, absence of 'normal' policing and the attraction of paramilitary involvement has led to an increase of vandalism and anarchy in the estate. The inhabitants of the estate have had a very strained relationship with the security forces. Many of the estate's inhabitants were interned in 1971 and many more have been imprisoned since. Local residents estimate that every one of the 660 houses in the estate have been searched by the British Army, some of them several times.

In an official report carried out into areas of special need in Belfast in 1974 by Boal et al, Newbury was constantly top of the range of negative indicators which stretched from overcrowded households to mental handicap. Perhaps not surprisingly, Newbury also topped the list for unemployment. Yet, Newbury could have been a pleasant place to live in. It was the first estate to be built in Northern Ireland in the post-war period. It occupies a magnificent setting nestling at the foot of a mountain with panoramic views over the city of Belfast. At the time of its construction it seemed very progressive to rehouse people up in the clear air near the mountain. However, the estate was conceived, designed and built over a remarkably short period of time, using new and cheap methods of construction to meet urgent housing needs and stands today as an example of how an estate should not be built.

The consequences of the failure over the years to build public housing in Belfast and indeed throughout Northern Ireland came to a head immediately after the 2nd World War. This failure has been attributed to sectarian reasons but to Wiener (1975,p.27) a more likely hypothesis was that the Belfast Corporation simply reflected the class interests of the ruling party and lacked any due concern for the needs of working class people in general. This view is shared by Bew et al (1979) who suggests that the Unionist Cabinet at that time fitted almost perfectly Marx 'executive committee for managing the common affairs of the whole bourgeoise'. As in England, however, the 2nd World War raised awareness about social problems and an increasing number of working class Unionists began to complain about the standard of social services that the Unionist Government was providing. Such dissatisfaction was reflected in the growing support for the Northern Ireland Labour Party which was able to mobilise around a number of issues such as health, housing and the Province's high infant mortality rate. This dissatisfaction also led to growing demands for recognition that the Province had a right to parity in social services with England. The Unionist Cabinet gradually came to the conclusion that to maintain working class Protestant support, they needed to implement welfare reforms. This set in motion a number of inquiries, which in the housing field were made more urgent by the effects of the 2nd world war bombings which destroyed 3200 dwellings and damaged 50,000 more (Birrell 1971,p82). A 1943 survey (Birrell 1971:Table 3.2) found that throughout the Province 71 per cent of dwellings required repairs and that in Belfast itself, one fifth of all existing dwellings were unfit for habitation. A 1944 Interim Housing Report declared of the 104,470 houses surveyed, that only 13 per cent needed no repair work done. The Report recommended that there should be large scale slum clearances, new legislation modelled on English lines and an increase in the house building programme (Cmd. 224:1944 HMSO).

In response to such surveys, in housing and other welfare areas, a Ministry of Health and Local Government was established in 1944 and in 1945 an Act was passed setting up a new body, the Northern Ireland Housing Trust, with the task of building houses to supplement the effort of local authorities. The Act also increased subsidies to local authorities for working class housing. Two years later, plans to build a mixed Protestant/Catholic estate to be called 'Newbury' on the western outskirts of the city were discussed by the Belfast Corporation and a fifty six acre site was acquired. Within a year, plans for 436 houses to be built on the lower part of the site had been drawn up. However, after revision of the plans by the Ministry of Housing and Local Government, 501 mostly three bedroom houses constructed of cheaper 'no fines concrete' rather than traditional red brick were crammed on to the site with a further 159 'orlit block' houses being built shortly afterwards in the upper part of the estate.

The houses were badly laid out and designed with most bathrooms situated next to the front door. Moreover, along one side of most streets, living rooms were located at the front of the house, while along the other side, living rooms were located at the back of the house. This made it difficult to establish visual contact with ones' neighbours. The occupants of one side of the street looked out on to their back gardens while the occupants of the other side of the street looked out on to their neighbours' back gardens. This layout promoted feelings of isolation and loneliness. Inadequate shopping facilities also existed on the estate. The block of six shops that were situated in the centre of

Newbury, were built a couple of years after the first phase of houses, seemingly as an afterthought. These factors together with a total disregard for social amenities ensured that the estate would face a difficult future.

Nonetheless, in the immediate post-war years with housing in Belfast in such an apalling state, many people were extremely anxious to be rehoused in the neat cream houses with a generous strip of garden. So much so, that within a few years of its construction, a major housing scandal emerged whereby prospective tenants anxious to avoid long waiting lists were prepared to pay substantial amounts of money for 'keys' to houses on the estate. The scandal which became known as the 'Copeland Key Inquiry' made front page headlines in local newspapers in May 1953 and dominated front page headlines for several months.

The scandal concerned a public inquiry into allegations of irregularities in the allocation of houses by the Belfast Corporation. Persons wishing to avoid lengthy waiting lists for accommodation paid 'key money' to an ex-employee of the Belfast Corporation and in turn were placed at the top of the housing waiting list and a short time later offered accommodation in Newbury.

The case is an important one in the formation of the estate, for several reasons. Firstly, the anxious behaviour of prospective tenants to be housed on the estate contrasts starkly with the later behaviour of residents who would have gone to almost the same lengths to be rehoused away from the estate. Secondly, the episode was to pave the way for the strained relations the inhabitants of the estate were to have with outside formal institutions. There was a widespread feeling among the residents of the estate at the time, that the public inquiry was little more than a cover up operation. The burden of responsibility had been placed on the shoulders of the ex-employee of the Belfast Corporation and on the tenants who had purchased keys while those in positions of authority had emerged 'scot-free'. This sense of injustice was exacerbated further by the Council's subsequent drive in the aftermath of the Inquiry to evict all those tenants who had paid 'key money' for their houses. Apart from being regarded as a face saving device which diverted attention away from the reasons why applicants had to resort to such measures in the first place, the decision created a lot of ill feeling and suspicion in Newbury for many years to come because only a handful of those alleged to have paid 'key money' had actually come forward to give evidence at the Inquiry and these people were to end up being victimized while many others who had resorted to the same tactics were able to remain in their existing accommodation.

The emergence of the negative image of the estate

It is ironic to find that a mere four years later, Newbury, which was regarded as such a desirable estate that people were prepared to pay substantial sums of money for keys, was to be recommended to Dorita Field for her 'Study of Unsatisfactory Tenants' in 1958. It is all too easy to assume that something catastrophic happened in the intervening years. However, a more likely explanation is that the inherent problems in the layout and design of the estate and the fact that no social provision existed whatsoever, finally manifested themselves in the neglected surroundings. People from all over Belfast were brought together and housed on the estate. Most were total strangers and no provision existed at all whereby they could get to know each other. There were no schools, no churches, no bus service to the estate, no focal point whatsoever whereby the residents could come into frequent contact with each other.

By an unfortunate coincidence the Ministry ordered the closure of a number of temporary war time hutments just at the time the Newbury estate was being completed. Forced to find accommodation for the inhabitants quickly, the Estates Committee rehoused a number of the occupants in Newbury. Many of these people had originally squatted in the hutments and were widely believed to be dirty and unable to manage their children, their money or their homes (Spencer 1973). Hence Newbury began its existence with a number of 'problem families'. The Copeland Key Inquiry referred to earlier did little to enhance any kind of community spirit. The subsequent evictions caused much bitterness. Apathy and resentment grew and was reflected in a growing disregard for the surrounding environment. Dorita Field described the physical condition of the estate as follows:

> The general appearance of the estate is most depressing. The roads and paths are always strewn with paper, metalscrap and glass. The shop frontages are very dirty and the broken ventilators under each shop look like gaping holes in the wall (1958,p.10).

It soon became a liability to have a Newbury address. The estate began to get a bad name with traders, rent collectors, employers and the police. The media, always anxious for a story, readily attributed the misbehaviour of residents in surrounding estates to Newbury. Rather than people joining waiting lists to be rehoused in the estate, many now wanted to be rehoused elsewhere. A local survey revealed that approximately 12,000 people went through 600 houses in the area in the first fourteen years of its existence (Doolan 1982,p.21). Again this did little to enhance community development. According to my key informants, those who could have contributed positively to the estate's development left at the earliest opportunity and this further reinforced the inadequacy of those who remained.

Community attempts to change the image of the estate

Nonetheless, some of those who remained decided to do something positive to change the image of the estate. In 1963 a group of tenants formed the Newbury Tenants' Association (NTA). One major factor held responsible for the general apathy and vandalism that existed in the estate was the absence of any social amenities. The NTA therefore decided to approach the Church authorities to gain permission to use the facilities of the two newly built local primary schools to hold social functions and bingo sessions. This would give the tenants of the estate an opportunity to relax and socialise with fellow residents. It was also planned to utilize any money made from these social gatherings to build a proper community centre. These efforts by the NTA were not wholly successful. The majority of the residents of the estate were unused to socialising and initially at these social gatherings, fights broke out and this did little to foster any community development. As such events became commonplace, however, the residents learned to settle their disagreements in a more amicable manner and gradually some sense of community identity and loyalty did emerge.

Nonetheless, such internal efforts did little to alter the outside image of the estate. In despair, some of the Committee members turned for advice to a local businessman, sympathetic with the problems of the estate. He suggested that the NTA should employ a Public Relations Consultant and agreed to subsidise the cost of employing such a person. By this time (1967) the NTA had amassed £6,000 from the various social functions that had taken place. The Public Relations Consultant suggested that this money should be invested in City Council Bonds as a gesture of goodwill and commitment to the future of the city of Belfast. Local newspapers were contacted and the members of the NTA duly had their photograph taken with the Lord Mayor of Belfast handing over a cheque for £6,000 with the caption 'Newbury Does Care About the City of Belfast'.

An appeal fund was set up to raise money for a new community centre and throughout this period it did seem that a more positive view of Newbury was emerging. Sir Graham Larmor, head of the Appeals Committee stated (Irish News 12th Oct. 1967) that the NTA's efforts were 'a wonderful demonstration of self help which he hoped would commend itself to others in Northern Ireland'. The NTA began to act as intermediary between the tenants and the various local bureaucracies. They consistently approached the Belfast Corporation to urge them to carry out improvements on the estate. The NTA's efforts attracted the attention of the Child Poverty Action Group of Northern Ireland (CPAGNI) who decided to set up their first social action centre on the estate. The CPAGNI, confronted with several of the residents' main problems in the area of marriage, hire purchase and credit facilities, poor housing conditions and unemployment, felt that an Advice Centre was desperately needed to help the tenants articulate and perhaps remedy their most pressing grievances. A branch of the Citizens Advice Bureau (CAB) was set up in the local primary school. The CAB operated on only one night per week and yet by the end of the first year, they had dealt with a staggering 500 cases. Their main discovery was that people on public assistance were not getting all the benefits they were entitled to. This lack of awareness regarding eligibility for benefit was also highlighted in a study carried out in 1983 (Upper Springfield Resource Centre) and brings into question two commonly held myths: that the unemployed don't want to work because they are gaining so much from the Welfare State and that Catholics, because of their lack of allegiance to the British State, are abusing the Welfare State in order to 'bleed the state dry'.

These efforts by the NTA had little impact on the day to day lives of the majority of the residents of the estate. Many of the NTA's practical solutions to the problems of the estate were thwarted by bureaucratic red tape and led to a general opinion that future appeals to public authorities would be utterly useless. In desperation, the NTA invited a range of professionals from 'all walks of life', doctors, teachers, clergy, academics, social workers and journalists to the area to highlight their grievances and ask advice on what action could be taken. It was hoped that from this discussion, a document could be drawn up which could be signed by all those present and then utilized to pressurize the local authorities into taking some remedial action. Two representatives from Queen's University Belfast, Social Studies Department, were invited to the meeting and they proposed that the tenants should undertake an in-depth survey of the area in conjunction with the Social Studies Department of the University in order to highlight problems relating to the social and physical environment of the estate. A house to house survey was initiated in the early 1970's and the final report was compiled by Spencer (1973).

The survey had two main objectives: firstly, to stimulate external statutory and voluntary bodies to take action that would improve conditions on the estate, and secondly, to help and encourage residents to take corrective action 'from the inside'. When the Report was finally published, it confirmed the worst fears of the residents of the area. Male unemployment was more than three times the Belfast total for 1971 while female unemployment was more than double the Belfast total. Overcrowding was also prevalent. In 1969, a report by the Building and Design Partnership (BDP) (Spencer 1973,p.51) had expressed concern at low public housing densities in the outer estates and had recommended minimum standards of 43 persons per acre. In Newbury, because families were so large the population density was more than twice the BDP minimum in 1966 and almost twice in 1971. The Report also uncovered a higher than average sickness rate among adult males. The Report had only limited results, however. By the mid 1970's the 'troubles' in Northern Ireland were firmly entrenched making residents of areas like Newbury more suspicious than ever of outside institutions. Moreover, with the emergence of paramilitary organizations, the NTA had long since ceased to be the unopposed representatives of the residents of the estate.

The accidental or deliberate creation of a problem estate

It remains a matter of contention whether the disreputable image of the estate occurred by accident or design. There have been innumerable discussions in many different contexts about 'unsatisfactory tenants' and in Great Britain, public policy is said to come down in favour of distributing such families widely so that there is no concentration of them in any one area. Dispersal among good neighbours, it is suggested, can have a positive educational effect on less reputable families and many families have in such circumstances improved themselves enormously. However, Nicholson points out that:

> the plan of scattering families known to be difficult throughout the community, in the hope that standards will be raised, overlooks the tendency for those with like standards and interests to group themselves together anyhow wherever they are housed (1961,p.133).

This observation is shared by Roger Wilson (1964,p.14) who suggests that tenants with comparatively low economic status may want to live beside neighbours who are 'not too fussy' so that they will not be judged too harshly for their own inherent incapabilities. Such attitudes place too much emphasis on 'blaming the victim' and ignore the alternative housing strategy of concentrating such families into a few estates so as to insulate the majority from their influence.

It is very difficult to gain concrete evidence to support the view that the Belfast Corporation had a 'Newbury type' in mind when allocating houses on the estate. The public are denied access to past housing records probably because the allocation of houses under the Stormont Regime is still a very sensitive issue. The majority of older tenants on the estate, however, are convinced that such a policy was practiced. Most argue that the area was used as a 'dumping ground' for problem families and any whose categorisation was in doubt, were promised another house away from the estate if and when they proved their worth. The high turnover of tenants during the first fourteen years of the estate's existence referred to earlier, provides some evidence for this viewpoint. Comments scattered throughout the 25 annual reports of the Northern Ireland Housing Trust (Birrell 1971,p.125) provide some evidence to indicate that the Housing Trust deliberately selected better off tenants not only on financial grounds but on certain social grounds and left the remainder to be rehoused by the Belfast Corporation.

As I had worked in the Northern Ireland Housing Trust, prior to its amalgamation with the Belfast Corporation to form the Northern Ireland Housing Executive, I was personally aware of how carefully prospective tenants were vetted before they were allocated a Housing Trust house. One Housing Manager's criteria was a crisp clean cloth on the dining table. She continually informed the Housing Visitors under her supervision that it was the strongest proof she had found yet to indicate high overall standards throughout the dwelling. A common utterance among Housing Visitors returning from vetting prospective tenants was 'No, they're unsuitable, they're Corporation stock'.

Tony Spencer (1973) argues that while most cities in Britain have their problem estates, in the Northern Ireland context, the existence and development of estates such as Newbury had a political role to play that made them useful to both sides. The Protestant side could use them as 'permanent visible evidence of the laziness, dirtiness and destructiveness of the Catholic republican minority'. The Catholic side, on the other hand, could use them as 'permanent visible evidence of prejudice, discrimination, neglect and incompetence on the part of the Protestant Unionist majority'. Such a viewpoint, however, underestimates the extent to which estates such as Newbury were shunned by the 'more respectable' Catholic working class.

The significance of territory

Territory has always been important in Northern Ireland. Boal (1972) has carried out surveys to examine territoriality in parts of Belfast. His results indicate a high degree of segregation not only in the places where people live but in their everyday social habits. The first area he selected was 98 per cent Catholic and the second 99 per cent Protestant. Although both these areas were situated side by side, each was insulated from the other. The inhabitants of each area attended different churches, read different newspapers, supported different sports and sent their children to different schools. Boal sums up these observations by saying 'the cumulative evidence indicates the presence of two very distinct territories'. While polarization between Catholic and Protestant is extensive in some urban areas, Boal also provides evidence to indicate a high degree of polarization between working class and middle class Protestants. In 1968, a comparative study between two neighbouring Protestant estates in Belfast, one comprising Council housing and the other expensive private residences was carried out by Boal (1971). Contact between the two areas was found to be as low as that between the Protestant and Catholic working class estates mentioned earlier. This led Boal to conclude that 'socio-economically based territories exist that are every bit as sharply divided as the more publicised religious territories of Belfast'.

Other writers have suggested that territory determines the extent to which the inhabitants of Belfast are affected by the Northern Ireland 'troubles'. As Harold Jackson put it:

> let us be quite clear, the problem is one of the working class. There have been no riots in the prosperous areas of.......Belfast (1971,p171).

Similarly Rolston (1979) in discussing the impact of the 'troubles' on the residents of Belfast, argues that one does not need to resort to such drastic measures as emigration to escape the 'troubles' in Northern Ireland. The middle class can and do escape any impact both geographically and socially while remaining. As Rolston puts it:

> the middle class in Belfast need not have more than the slightest contact with the violence. Given the nature of present mass communications, it is possible to know as much in New York as in parts of Belfast about what a riot is like (1979,p.42).

Respectable and disreputable Catholics

This emphasis on the importance of territory between Catholic and Protestant in Northern Ireland or between working class and middle class underestimates the importance of territory within the Catholic working class. Newbury estate was shunned, not only by the Protestant working class, not only by the middle class but also by the 'respectable' Catholic working class. Why was this the case? The Catholic working class in Belfast was in a disadvantaged position in general terms. Catholics generally experienced the lowest socio-economic status and the highest unemployment. It is easier to accept inferior conditions, however, if you can point to someone worse off than yourself. Such was the function that areas such as Newbury played. As one Newbury resident told me:

> I myself never believed any one working class area was better than

> another. I lived down the Lower Falls and I never saw anything to glorify there. I watched my mother struggling to make ends meet and I saw no glory in that. Yet, my ma was a classic victim of this myth that Newbury was a bad estate. It was a veil for her own situation.

Catholic disaffection towards the state only became visible from the late 1960's onwards. However, the potential for such disaffection to rear its head simmered beneath the surface for many years. Whyte (1983) reviewing fifty years of Stormont rule states that the most striking aspect of the whole period is that the regime managed to survive so long. One reason rarely contemplated may be due to the existence and development of areas such as Newbury. It is naive to assume that 'myths' regarding 'dirty, lazy Catholics who don't want to work' only existed in the consciousness of the 'other sort'. Myths generate their own truths about the world and gradually become part of everyday taken for granted common sense. Hence, myths regarding the base qualities of certain Catholic working class members permeated the consciousness of Catholics generally and were reinforced by the existence of areas such as Newbury.

I grew up in a Catholic working class slum area situated about two miles from Newbury estate. I was reared on stories about the 'savages' of Newbury who were so uncivilised that they didn't know what a bath was to be used for, so they stored coal in it, while they kept a variety of animals ranging from pigs and chickens to horses and donkeys in their coal sheds. No one ever entered into the estate to check the accuracy of such statements. Rather media coverage of the estate and everyday tittle-tattle kept such myths alive.

Under Stormont, the Unionist Party was able to establish its hegemony over the Protestant working class and prevent any united working class action by ensuring that the Protestant working class were marginally better off than their Catholic counterparts. Another aspect of this strategy was to make a distinction between 'respectable' and 'disreputable' Catholics. Such a tactic prolonged the existence of the Stormont Regime. The 'respectable' Catholics received limited gains from the Stormont system which were to satisfy their needs in the short term but, in the long term, paved the way for the development of the Civil Rights Campaign. More importantly, the 'disreputable' Catholics (many of whom were unemployed) formed a large reservoir of passive supporters for any movement which would rise to voice their frustration. Hence, this reservoir could be effectively mobilised by the Republican Movement in the late 1960's and early 1970's to tackle the very foundation of the state.

Influence of the negative image of Newbury on formal employment opportunities

While this detailed outline of the development of the negative image of Newbury may be regarded as peripheral to the main concerns of the research, nonetheless, one of the most recurring instances throughout the survey was the frequency with which respondents mentioned their awareness of the negative image of the estate. Usually this was without any prompting on my part. Rather this awareness was referred to by respondents during general conversations regarding work, employment and unemployment. The constant references to outsiders' lack of awareness of the positive attributes of the estate indicates how important this neglect is to the residents of the area and justifies the detailed inclusion here. This negative image of the area affected the residents' chances of obtaining formal employment and provided the impetus to embark on a wide range of informal economic practices.

While Newbury is not more deprived than that of many of Belfast's public estates and certainly it is no worse than other estates in its immediate surroundings, nonetheless, the residents believe that they have been, and continue to be, singled out for particular negative attention. Moreover, they believe that this negative image has precluded their opportunities for formal employment. Many of the residents are convinced that their address goes against them on job application forms. This is particularly the case for residents who live in Newbury Road or Newbury Avenue as it makes it impossible to disguise their address. Residents tell me that when they apply for jobs, they will often use the address of friends and relatives who live in more ambiguously named streets or who live outside the area altogether. Some residents state that it was only when they employed this tactic, that they began to get replies to job applications, previous applications being ignored. One respondent stated that during one job interview, the interviewer quizzed him about where exactly his address was. When the respondent admitted he lived in Newbury, the interviewer asked him if he had a criminal record. The respondent said that he found it difficult to persuade the interviewer that he had no such record, the interviewer stating that he had never met anyone from Newbury who did not have a criminal record. During the survey, the unemployed respondents were asked what factors they felt would go against them obtaining formal employment. In each group the majority placed address above other potential structural drawbacks such as gender and religion.

Formal employment and unemployment in Newbury

It is against this background that I wish to focus on formal employment and unemployment in the Newbury area of Belfast. The residents of the Newbury estate have been doubly disadvantaged in the employment market. Firstly, they have been disadvantaged in general terms by being Catholics living in the west of the City of Belfast and secondly, they have been disadvantaged in particular by having a Newbury address. Employment has always been a scarce resource in West Belfast and demand has always exceeded supply. Thus, any employer faced with numerous applicants would be more likely to employ 'respectable' workers with 'respectable' addresses rather than employing someone with the dubious distinction of coming from Newbury estate.

Numerous studies have consistently illustrated an above average unemployment rate for the Newbury area. In Dorita Field's Study of Unsatisfactory Tenants (1958), 50 per cent of her sample of male householders were unemployed. In October 1970, the headmaster of the local secondary school carried out a survey into the occupational status of the fathers of the boys who attended the school and found that 47 per cent of the boy's fathers were unemployed. Spencer's survey published in 1973 found 38 per cent of all males were in the various categories of unemployment. Newbury also topped Boal et al's study of 97 Areas of Special Need (1974) with an unemployment rate of 33.3 per cent among economically active males. According to the 1978 Northern Ireland Housing Executive Household Survey, 48.7 per cent of the economically active heads-of-household (HOH's) for the electoral district of which Newbury is a part, were unemployed. Doherty's study of unemployment in the Belfast urban area concluded (1977,p.259) that Newbury had the 'unfortunate distinction of being the peak unemployment area in both 1966 and 1971 with one in three of its economically active males out of work'. While a study carried out by McAuley in 1986 discovered a staggering 78 per cent of economically active male HOH'S in the various categories of unemployment.

Male formal employment

My own survey of the area was carried out during January to July 1989. Information was obtained on 103 males and 114 females living in 150 households. In 93 cases, households were occupied by married couples. In the remaining 57 cases, households were headed by a single, divorced or widowed adult. Of the 103 male respondents, only 27, 26 per cent of the sample, were in formal employment. Fifteen of those in formal employment, had been employed in the same job for over ten years. Four of those in formal employment, had been in their job for less than one year. Twenty of those in formal employment, worked in unskilled manual occupations. Seventeen were employed in jobs located in West Belfast, three worked in the City Centre of Belfast and four had occupations that entailed travelling within Belfast. Only three were employed in areas outside West Belfast and the City Centre. The concentration of employment in these two areas will be returned to later.

Female formal employment

Of the 114 females, 25, 22 per cent of the sample, worked in formal employment. Of this group, the majority, 19, worked part time. Wives' occupational status closely matched that of their husbands. Ten of the females formally employed, also had husbands in formal employment. The remaining thirteen of the females in formal employment had husbands who qualified for some form of welfare benefit. Five females had husbands who qualified for Invalidity Benefit, while four had husbands who received a Retirement Pension. More generous allowances for spouses' earnings are accorded to males receiving these types of welfare benefits compared to the regulations concerning Income Support (Supplementary Benefit up until April 1988). Hence females in low paid, part time employment with husbands in these categories can take home their earnings intact, without it affecting their spouses' benefit entitlements. This means that wives with husbands in these categories can continue to seek, at least part time formal employment, whereas, women whose husbands qualify for Income Support face more severe restrictions on earnings and hence may have to focus their attention on informal employment. This issue will be returned to in Chapter Seven.

Only four of the 25 women who worked formally had a husband who qualified for Income Support. Two of this group have informed the Department of Health and Social Security (DHSS) that they were separated, although both secretly continue to live with their husbands. The respondents state that this ploy was necessitated by current welfare benefits legislation and the separation was regarded as a means of escaping the severe penalties on their formal earnings.

Attitudes of the formally employed to the unemployed

Many of those in formal employment in Newbury are employed in low paid, low status jobs. How then do they view their unemployed neighbours on welfare benefit 'handouts'? Field (1977) noted, during a survey carried out in Liverpool, the bitter feelings expressed by those on low wages towards their unemployed neighbours, who they often thought, albeit wrongly, enjoyed higher standards of living. Marsden et al (1982) noted that at each upturn of unemployment throughout the 1970's, there was a corresponding increase in negative attitudes towards the unemployed fuelled by the perceived erosion of differentials between the unemployed and those in low paid formal employment. During the survey, the formally employed were asked to compare their wages with their perception of what they might receive in welfare benefits and state whether they thought their wages would be higher, lower or the same as welfare benefits. The majority of males, 19, felt that their wages from formal employment were significantly higher than what they would receive in welfare benefits. Seven felt that their income would be about the same but stated that they preferred to work for a living than cope with the boredom and frustration of unemployment. Only one respondent, felt that his wages were lower than what he would qualify for on welfare benefit.

None of the females felt that their wages were lower than welfare benefit entitlements. Seven of the sample believed that the family income would be about the same if they were not in formal employment, while the majority, 18, of the sample believed that their income was much higher than it would be, if the family depended totally on welfare benefits.

Hence, few of the formally employed felt that they would be better off 'on the dole' than working formally. This view is borne out by research carried out by Hill et al in 1973. In the three areas of England covered by the survey, the unemployed were living on little more than what could only be classed as subsistence incomes. Hill found no evidence to support the view that the unemployed choose to remain out of work because they find it more lucrative than working. Similarly Smith (1980) found that only 3 per cent of unemployed men were receiving more in benefits than they had earned in previous jobs, even though the majority of those jobs had been low paid.

Throughout this book, I will be focusing on the various ways in which the unemployed in Newbury attempt to cope with poverty and unemployment. Some of these responses generate the unemployed additional income but it must be stressed that this income is a supplement to, and not a replacement for, welfare benefits. Indeed, the inadequacy of welfare benefit allowances provides a major motivation for seeking ways to increase income. Although, simultaneously, the welfare benefits' system provides formal enterprises with justification for paying exploitative wages to those willing to work 'off the record'. The formally employed in Newbury are well aware that some of the unemployed bolster their income by working informally but they feel that the opportunities are too sporadic and unpredictable to be considered as a viable alternative to secure formal employment.

Male unemployment

Seventy six males, 74 per cent of the sample, were officially classified as not working. Forty four were unemployed, fourteen qualified for Invalidity Benefit and eighteen were classified as retired. Thirteen of the eighteen men classified as retired, had been receiving Supplementary Benefit prior to reaching the qualifying age for an Old Age Pension. The fourteen respondents qualifying for Invalidity payments illustrate the strong connection between poverty and ill health. Twelve of this sample had been claiming Invalidity Benefit for over five years. Seven of the sample had transferred from Supplementary Benefit to Invalidity Benefit due to the deterioration of their health. Five of this group had been unemployed for over ten years before making this transfer.

Of the forty four males categorised as unemployed and eligible for work, 5 had been unemployed for under 5 years, 20 had been unemployed for between five to ten years, while 19 had been unemployed for over 10 years. While many males blame their lack of occupational success on their address and to a lesser extent, their religion, there are other structural reasons which can be put forward to partially explain their occupational misfortunes. Only one of the unemployed males, for example, held any educational qualifications. Indeed only 4 males from the total sample of 103 held any educational qualifications.

Only nine of the unemployed males had ever undertaken any form of occupational training or served an apprenticeship. The remainder of the sample had never received any formal occupational training since leaving school. The results from the overall sample were little better. Out of the 103 males interviewed, only twenty one, 20 per cent of the sample had any kind of formal job training experience.

These disadvantages are compounded by the unwillingness of most of the unemployed to seek formal employment outside what they perceived to be, 'safe areas'. Even those already in formal employment tended to mainly work in either West Belfast or the City Centre. Most of unemployed respondents stated that these were the only two areas where they would seek job vacancies. Only seven of the unemployed males interviewed stated that they would be willing to work outside these areas. These attitudes have become firmly entrenched since the outbreak of the 'troubles' in 1969.

Female unemployment

Women's occupational status was more difficult to categorise. Only eight, of the 89 women not formally employed were registered as unemployed. Twenty two were classified as retired, while the remainder, 59, were classified as housewives. However, the distinctions between women classified as unemployed and women classified as housewives had more to do with social security regulations than the women's individual decisions to either seek employment or remain at home. Many of the housewives interviewed expressed a desire to find employment but were not registered as unemployed because there was no financial incentive to do so.

The females in the sample displayed the same lack of educational and occupational training as the males. Out of the total sample of 114 females, only 8, 7 per cent of the sample, held any form of educational qualifications while only 7, 6 per cent of the sample, had ever undertaken any formal occupational training. The women seeking employment were unwilling to go outside West Belfast and the City Centre of Belfast. They were also adversely affected by the occupational status of their husbands. If husbands were unemployed, this precluded the likelihood of women seeking formal employment compelling them to focus their attention on informal economic activity. This issue will be returned to in Chapter Seven.

Unemployment: a common experience

The negative image of Newbury estate, the structural characteristics of the inhabitants and their unwillingness to seek employment oustide West Belfast and the City Centre has resulted in unemployment being a constant feature of life on the estate. Even those currently in formal employment have not been immune from unemployment. Nineteen of the males who work formally have been unemployed at some stage in their lives. For ten of this group, the period spent in unemployment exceeded five years. Hence in Newbury, unemployment is a collective rather than an individual experience. Hardly any individual has escaped its effects and this largely dilutes differences between those currently employed and the unemployed. While the rest of the book will focus on informal economic activity, it is important to stress here, that the various types of informal economic strategies practised by the inhabitants of the estate largely take place with the assent and in some cases, co-operation of those formally employed. Occupational identity is relatively unimportant to most inhabitants of the estate. All residents are concerned with coping with the hardships associated with everyday living and will use whatever opportunities are available to ease the rigors of poverty. For some these opportunities will present themselves through formal employment. For others, the opportunities will exist outside formal employment. Other identities are more important to many inhabitants. The formally employed and the unemployed are fellow Catholics, fellow republicans. Each has suffered from the negative labelling of the estate and this has enhanced community solidarity.

Informal economic strategies in Newbury

Up to now I have focused on the negative image of the Newbury estate and how this image persisted even though some of the residents went to great lengths to improve the image of the area. This image in turn adversely affected the residents' attempts to obtain formal employment. This inability to secure formal employment is reflected in the various studies of the area referred to earlier and by the survey data discussed above. Of course this concentration on formal employment is to some extent misplaced as informal economic strategies are as old as the estate itself. Concentration on formal employment in isolation ignores the existence and vitality of the various informal institutions prevalent in the area. Concentration on the negative social, economic, and psychological effects of unemployment ignores the complexity and diversity of human responses to their situation. The Newbury estate is an area of informal economic practices. These practices either complement or undermine their formal counterparts. By paying attention to these strategies, I do not intend to sweep the considerable social problems the estate faces under the carpet. The area is one of multiple disadvantages and no informal economic strategy, no matter how developed, can ever wipe out this deprivation. Rather my intention is to focus on a whole range of informal economic practices implemented by the residents of the area in their efforts to make ends meet. These informal economic strategies have been ignored in the wide variety of surveys that have been carried out in the area. These surveys have equated work with employment and painted bleak pictures of Newbury as a 'workless community'.

In reviewing the extent and significance of informal economic activity in Newbury, it is necessary to distinguish between the pre-1969 and the post-1969 period, as the 'troubles' were to have an important impact on informal economic strategies in the estate. Thus in the remainder of this chapter, I intend firstly, to briefly discuss the informal economic strategies of the residents of the estate prior to the outbreak of the 'troubles' in 1969, when Newbury resembled any other poor working class marginalized community. I then intend to focus in more detail on the effect 1969 had on the residents' attempts to provide for their own needs. This account is largely based on oral histories by my key informants. Finally, I intend to briefly discuss the post-1969 period. This section will pave the way for the remainder of the chapters in the book which will focus on the variety of informal economic strategies currently prevalent in the area.

Informal economic strategies prior to 1969

The following account is based on tape recorded interviews with three of the five key informants. While these three accounts were similar, nonetheless, other than checking each statement against the other, it is difficult to establish the accuracy of these accounts, particularly after such a long time period. Moreover, since each of these three informants are actively involved in promoting a better image of Newbury estate, then their accounts may well romanticize the past. During my employment in the community school, I asked the older residents who utilised the school to reflect on the past history of the estate. These informal conversations backed up some aspects of the data provided by the three key informants.

Throughout the 1950's and 1960's, most of the unemployed residents of the Newbury estate believed that their situation was mainly due to their own inherent incapacities. While pockets of unemployment did exist in Belfast during these two decades, nonetheless, there was a widespread general belief that you could get a job if you really tried. It may not have been the job you really wanted or felt really suited for, but if you weren't too fussy, employment could be found. However, even when the residents of Newbury weren't too fussy, it wasn't enough to wipe out the liability of having a Newbury address. Faced with one rejection after another, many of the unemployed stopped looking for formal employment believing in advance that their address would go against them. This perceived apathy was regarded by outsiders as further proof that the residents of Newbury were basically lazy and didn't want to work. This outside attitude in turn reinforced the negative self image held by many of the residents of the estate.

Throughout this period, limited opportunities for informal economic activity did exist. The construction industry, in particular provided an avenue for informal employment for some of the men in the district. Having a 'disreputable' address did not prove as great a liability for informal employment. No formal employment contracts existed and if someone did prove to be unsuitable, they were simply told not to turn up the next day. Employment was seasonal, unpredictable and very low paid. Employers in this field were by and large very small concerns whose survival depended on the availability of this cheap labour. Men with large families to support needed some additional income to supplement unemployment benefit and were in no position to negotiate fair wages or proper working conditions. It is difficult to estimate accurately the percentage of men from the district active in this way. There are no records kept nor figures published on the number of people economically active outside formal employment. All I can do is surmise from talks with these older residents that opportunities for limited employment in this field did exist, although the proportion of residents employed in this way would be impossible to quantify, especially two decades later.

For those unable to participate in paid informal employment, ways of 'getting by' centred on the household economy. Through a variety of techniques, many households were able to stretch out, or at times supplement, the benefits received from the state. Women specialized in knitting cardigans, making clothes, cushion covers, curtains etc. and after they had satisfied their own family's internal needs, these products were exchanged with neighbours and wider kin for payment in cash or kind. Nothing was ever wasted. Clothes were passed down from one family member to another and then handed over to neighbours or wider kin to repeat the passing down process. When these clothes finally outlived their usefulness, they were then sold, for a small sum, to the rag man who visited the estate two or three times each week. Shoes had a similar fate. Once they reached a state where they were no longer serviceable, they ended their days on the back of the fire providing extra warmth to a family who had ran out of fuel. The burning of fuel was also often supplemented by the burning of potato skins and vegetable peelings prolonging the day when additional fuel would have to be purchased. Families who did not make use of potato peelings in this way would leave them aside for the young boys who called daily to collect such offerings and who would sell the potato peelings to families in less fortunate circumstances for a few pence pocket money.

The making and selling of sticks for the fire also provided an opportunity to make a 'few shillings'. Young boys from the district would travel many miles around the fruit shops in their own and surrounding areas collecting used orange and apple crates. These crates were in turn chopped up into 'one penny and two penny' bundles. The boys would then 'go around the doors' selling these sticks in their own and surrounding districts. The money made from these ventures was a crucial supplement to many households.

Such activities did little to reduce the harsh effects of poverty facing many households. Most families lived on a hand to mouth basis and, as a result, most bills usually could not be paid on time. When families were threatened with court action, they had to try and borrow money to get them out of their pressing difficulties. However, the reputation of the inhabitants as bad debtors and the fact that most of them possessed no assets meant that formal lending agencies were unlikely to agree to the advancement of a loan and this paved the way for 'loan sharks' to operate in the estate charging exorbitant rates. These 'loan sharks', aware of the residents' frequent incapacity to pay, often confiscated Family Allowance Books. Residents of the estate tell me that it was a common occurrence for the car of a 'loan shark' to be parked outside the local Post Office on Family Allowance pay out day while he handed out Family Allowance books to his various clients who in turn would go into the

Post Office and cash the appropriate order and hand the money and the book back to the 'loan shark'. Borrowing money in this fashion very rarely enabled people to get back on their feet again and set in motion a policy of robbing Peter to pay Paul that characterised family budgeting.

These various economic activities did little to enhance the individual self image of the residents of the estate. Those who were informally employed kept quiet about their involvement and were acutely aware that they weren't considered good enough for formal employment. Those who worked in the household dismissed their activities as non work. Rather these activities were regarded as ineffectual survival mechanisms for coping with the harsher effects of poverty and unworthy to be placed beside 'real work'. The Newbury Tenants' Association did try throughout the 1960's to rectify the bad image of the estate but many people within the estate itself accorded some legitimacy to the stereotypical image of the lazy, feckless Newbury tenant. Many families in the estate appeared to be poor organizers, bad budgeters and few had proved their worth to outside institutions. While to many tenants on the estate, these negative characteristics were often exaggerated, nonetheless they appeared to have some validity and in the absence of adequate formal opportunities, no one could be certain that their situation was not the result of their own inherent incapabilities.

The impact of the troubles

All this changed in 1969 when the 'troubles' erupted in Northern Ireland. The conflict is usually referred to in terms of political and economic disaster leading to tremendous social and moral erosion, thus providing overwhelming evidence of its dysfunctionality. However, it is possible to point to three ways in which the conflict could be regarded as functional to areas like Newbury. First of all, blame for the apathy, deprivation and destruction that existed on the estate could be transferred from the shoulders of the residents to the shoulders of the Stormont Government. The whole situation prevalent on the estate was to become politicized. The Government could be blamed not only for political and economic malpractices but for every social problem that the residents encountered. No longer would the residents accept so easily explanations that focused on individual deficiencies. Prior to 1969, the residents of the estate (like many other working class Catholic estates) had little interest in politics. The stress and strain of everyday living was to consume most of their energies. This is not to say that prior to 1969, the residents of the estate were totally ignorant of Government malpractices or were completely unaware that their disadvantaged position was in some way due to the fact that they were Catholic. But again, this was only part of the explanation. The people from Newbury were disadvantaged not just because they were Catholic but because they were Newbury Catholics. The distinction is important. It meant that, prior to 1969, laying the blame at the foot of the Stormont Government would have been regarded as 'passing the buck' by the more respectable Catholics. Once the whole area of Protestant/Catholic disparities became politicized in 1969, however, Newbury could jump on the bandwagon, 'find for the first time widespread outside sympathy for their deprivation and in turn become willing fodder for the radical groups that were emerging' (Tape-recorded interview with key informant: January 15th 1988).

Secondly, the outbreak of the troubles in 1969 was to lead to the development of a whole range of what Beals calls cultural revitalisation movements. To Beals these movements are:

> deliberate organized conscious efforts by members of a society to construct a more satisfying culture....They are the reactions of people to stress and disillusionment resulting from contact with a dominant culture (1967,p.237-238).

These movements centred around revitalising Irish history, language and culture and were to have two main effects. Firstly, they were to provide people with a means to hit back at a mainstream culture that had kept them on the periphery. For example, considerable emphasis was placed on learning how to converse in Irish and classes in local community centres flourished, instilling in people a sense of power when they could speak a language alien to that of the status quo. Secondly, this revitalisation was to provide areas like Newbury with new opportunities for work expecially since internment in 1971. For example, many of those interned in 1971 passed their time in prison by making a whole range of Irish cultural artefacts varying from Irish harps to thatched cottages to plaques proclaiming Republican victory. Many of those interned had been unemployed and in prison with so much time at their disposal, they had learned to develop skills with their hands they never realised they possessed. At first these artefacts were given to families and friends as keepsakes but gradually these souvenirs found a wider market, many ending up as far away as America. In the initial years of the 'troubles', such souvenirs were sold for quite substantial sums supplementing the income of many prisoners' families.

A flourishing trade also emerged in framing handkerchiefs embroidered by the prisoners in Long Kesh. These handkerchiefs carried personal messages and greetings to friends and relatives 'on the outside' and depicted various republican slogans and imagery. A number of small lucrative businesses emerged on the estate (as on other working class Catholic estates) concerned with framing these handkerchiefs. Even if an individual did not have a relative or friend 'inside' Long Kesh, they could still place an order for a handkerchief containing a personal message, at a number of houses in the district. Orders poured in, making money for prisoners on the inside and those who framed the pictures on the outside. Indeed one small picture framing business still survives on the estate today, although it now deals with the more mundane framing of family photographic souvenirs.

Thirdly, and most importantly, the conflict resulted in the community map in many areas of Belfast having to be re-drawn. Attacked, intimidated or simply frightened, many families who once lived in areas predominantly inhabited by people of the opposite sectarian identification fled for security to live 'amongst their own kind'. According to Darby (1986,p.58), in the months of August and September 1969 a total of at least 3570 families were displaced in the County Borough of Belfast, mostly from the West and North West of the city. An analysis of 1820 cases of families which appeared on official lists revealed that 83 per cent of those who moved were Catholic. Another period of population movement occurred following the introduction of internment on 9th August 1971. A Community Relations Commission Research Unit (Darby and Morris 1974) recorded that 2069 families had been forced to abandon their homes during the rest of the month of August. Most were Catholic and crowded into the already over populated areas of West Belfast.

The mass population movement was to have important consequences for the Newbury area of Belfast. Many of the people who fled their homes during this period surged into the Newbury estate. To facilitate this movement, local community organizations usurped the functions of formal organizations who were unable to cope with this mass onslaught by finding emergency accommodation for these evacuees and providing them with food and other immediate basic needs. This community response demanded considerable organisational skills and instilled in a number of people the realisation that they had the ability to mobilize, co-ordinate and successfully carry through a plan of action. This was to have considerable positive effects on the residents' self esteem. Although by this stage, most of the residents had already transferred the burden of responsibility for the deprivation and disadvantages the area faced on to the shoulders of the Stormont State, the absence of opportunities whereby they could prove their newly acquired worth meant that many residents still held niggling doubts as to their own personal abilities. These uncertainties were removed when the community stepped into the vacuum created by the inabilities of formal organizations to respond to the emergency created by the mass evacuations from 1969-1971.

The organizational capabilities of the community that came to the fore during this period awakened in many residents a new faith in their own abilities to overcome the disadvantages the area faced. This was the period when a range of experts from 'all walks of life' were invited into the district to advise, help and co-ordinate the community action programmes that were unfolding. As mentioned earlier, this led to co-operation between Queen's University Belfast and the local Tenant's Association. In the Report (Spencer: 1973) which followed, there was a meticulous assessment of the living conditions of the area, with recommendations about what should be done to improve conditions. Although the recommendations were treated with scant regard by public authorities, other effects came from Spencer's surveys. The main one was that the people inside the estate began to have a new appreciation of their own ability to describe, remedy and reason about their problems.

The sense of power and increasing autonomy the community was experiencing was further reinforced by the emergence of 'no-go' areas in the aftermath of internment whereby Catholic areas barricaded themselves in and began to administer themselves from within. The Ulster Workers Council strike of 1974 had a similar effect, amenities were cut off and people had to fall back on their own resources. This led to an awakening in the minds of some of the residents that people could quite effectively administer their own lives without the state regulating and controlling their activities.

The period also led to a mushrooming of small informal co-operatives which in their initial stages paralleled the observation of positive forecasters of the informal economy that informal economic activity could provide a seedbed for the establishment of small capitalist enterprises. Once these concerns attempted to formalise their operations however, the harsh realities of commercial inexperience and powerlessness of the residents became increasingly visible.

I want to present initially a purely descriptive account of some of these developments and then highlight the main implications these projects have for informal economic activity in Newbury generally.

One of the first co-operatives to emerge was Newbury Enterprises founded in 1970. One of the instigators behind the setting up of the co-operative stated its purpose was 'to convince the people that they have it in their own hands to create work and manage their own affairs'. The project was funded by local people with some help from outside well wishers in the belief that industry could be founded on already existing local skills. The initial most obvious domestic skill was that of hand knitting. This knitting had taken place on a loosely commercial basis in approximately twenty women's homes over the previous year. Newbury Enterprises decided to co-ordinate and develop this hand knitting home industry in order to make it a more viable and profitable commercial concern. Second hand knitting machines were purchased and placed in a house rented from the Belfast Corporation. The aging machines and their need to be constantly overhauled gave a job to the maintenance man who lived in the district but were a great liability in such a competitive industry. In other parts of Ireland, knitted goods industries, which were organized along more efficient lines were working with a profit margin of as little as 2½ per cent. To enter this kind of world required extremely efficient production, little or no wastage, keen marketing and very good management. For a young emerging co-operative this was a very difficult programme. Shortage of money, leading to shortage of staff meant that the manager had to go out selling as well as taking charge of the factory. This way of working simply could not produce the marketing efficiency and economy required in an industry of this kind. Yet, remarkably, Newbury Enterprises survived for nearly ten years. By that time, however, enthusiasm alone could no longer prolong the co-operative's existence and the inefficient production methods and marketing inexperience of the workers led to the co-operative's terminal decline.

Newbury Enterprises also attempted to establish a locally controlled light engineering industry which had two main aims; firstly, to bring limited employment to young males in the area and secondly, to encourage industrialists to recognise the potential of the district in this field. Twelve young men from the district undertook a six week course in wood turning and metal work conducted voluntarily at the local secondary school and on completion of the course started work in converted premises on the site of a former Belfast Corporation maintenance yard (destroyed during the 'troubles') in the district. The men were paid by the Committee who arranged for the sale of the goods they produced ranging from table lamps to wrought iron gates. The Project also gave part time employment to another twenty women in the district working at home making lamp shades (Irish News 29.7.71). Initially the Project had limited success. People from the area, proud of the Project's development, felt morally obligated to buy the end products in the Craft Centre set up in the district to display Newbury Enterprises output. Once these initial orders were fulfilled, however, lack of resources and inadequate marketing contacts brought major difficulties to the Project. Moreover, the women working from their homes had large families of eight, nine or ten children and the consistent effort and discipline required for this home work brought marital problems. Increasingly, many felt that the small financial return gained was not enough to compensate for the enormous social sacrifices they had to make. The Project received its dying kick when the Craft Centre set up to display the co-operative's products was destroyed by vandals.

Another small enterprise, Newbury Pictures, was set up in 1973, shortly after Newbury Enterprises began. Pictures were produced by the blockmounting process - a base of wood is covered with a sheet of adhesive, a print is placed on top and then the whole item is covered with a laminated coating. Blockmounting had not yet been introduced in Belfast and so the co-operative had the advantage of providing a service which was not otherwise available. A range of 'old masters' from Goya to Constable were displayed and sold and orders poured in from inhabitants of the estate and outside shops and individuals. However, again, lack of managing and marketing experience brought long term difficulties. Eventually the business folded and was bought over by a successful dentist from a very prestigious part of Belfast, anxious to widen his horizons who relocated the industry in another more 'neutral' part of the town. The business is still in existence today and appears to be flourishing.

The last Project I wish to refer to is that of Newbury Industrial Estate. This development caused considerable controversy and is still referred to with much bitterness by the residents of the estate. When the Project finally collapsed, those involved issued a typewritten statement which is worth quoting at length because it indicates how strongly the residents feel about the failure of the Project and why many feel apathetic about future attempts to bring industry to the area.

> This paper draws attention to a policy of de-industrialization in West Belfast and its effect on job creation there. The charge is often made that the Government fails to industrialize this and other areas. That is not the whole truth. It also undermines and destroys efforts made by private citizens and community based groups to create industry for themselves...........We do not look on the financial and industrial disasters of Delorean, Strathearn and Mackies and others as unimportant. We recognise that the amount of money wasted in these and other ventures, discrimination in employment evident in some of them and the wrongness of Government policy have been scandalous. But the 'Newbury' Industrial Estate shows an aspect of the situation in West Belfast which is not generally recognised. In 1971, the 'Newbury' Industrial Estate was started by a group of community workers, members of trade unions, professional people etc. They bought land in the Newbury area and made it into an industrial estate. In spite of Government apathy and in many cases refusal to help, the industrial estate survived and four factories were created on the site, with inadequate Government financial help - there was ample room for many more. These factories remained open on the site along with a training unit which the Government eventually agreed to open in 1979. In that year the British Army entered the industrial estate, told the workers and management that they had two weeks in which to find other premises and by force occupied the whole industrial estate, thus closing four factories, putting people out of work, reducing the employment potential of the area still further and undermining yet another attempt by local people to create industry for themselves. This was the clearest example yet of the policy of de-industrialization.

> It was also the most cynical act of government in relation to industry that local residents had seen even in West Belfast. But even more cynical was the use to which the industrial estate was put. It was made into a costly and formidable army barracks and has been used as such ever since. Once again it was made clear that any attempt to persuade the Government to create industry in the area was going to fail but also that any attempt to create industry ourselves was going to be undermined and destroyed, if necessary by force.

It is very difficult to reconcile this intervention by the Army with the need to find a military base in the area. Certainly there are clear strategic reasons that can be put forward to account for the army's actions. The Industrial Estate is situated on a slightly elevated site overlooking several Catholic 'republican strongholds'. Moreover, the site is surrounded by waste ground making it almost impossible for 'hostile groups' to approach the army base undetected. Yet, it is debatable whether the taking over of the Industrial Estate was motivated by military reasons alone. While the reasons may not be as vicious as those outlined by community groups in the area, nonetheless one can suggest that the existence of an industrial project planned and developed solely through autonomous community action is an acute embarrassment to a Government whose own industrial policies to bring industry to the area so publicly failed. This is not to say that the Government never responds to community development programmes. It often does. In doing so, however, it attempts to gain a foothold into these developments and is able to exert some control. Groups who are willing to accept some measure of constraint imposed on their autonomy in return for financial assistance can do quite well out of Government grants. On the other hand, groups who want to maintain their autonomy intact and rely on the Government merely for financial back up are less likely to succeed.

While the situation peculiar to Northern Ireland undoubtedly influenced the development of some of these projects, nonetheless these case histories contain some relevance to informal economic activities generally. They make it difficult to sustain the positive image of informal economic activity as a seedbed for the establishment of small capitalist enterprises. Rather they indicate that informal economic practices best survive when they provide a range of goods and services not otherwise available. Thus the men and women in their homes making knitted goods, rugs and lamp shades could sell their goods cheaply to friends and neighbours. These people made a small return which supplemented inadequate state benefits but barely compensated for the effort involved in the making of the products. Dreams to expand on these home skills and make them more viable commercial concerns succeeded initially because the co-operatives could exploit the community network who felt morally obligated to make some initial purchases from the co-operatives. In this way, the response of the community mirrors Davis' (1985) observation that people can be exploited through their social networks. Davis suggests that this is at its most blatant in selling parties like Tupperware and home agent catalogues and perfume distribution. Once these initial orders are fulfilled however, most of the projects do not have the resources, the efficiency and the expertise in management and marketing techniques to make them viable competitors in the capitalist market.

The aftermath of the troubles

Today, Newbury has regained its image as a 'dreadful enclosure'. For a brief period, at the beginning of the 'troubles', Newbury was able to jump on the bandwagon proclaiming Catholic grievances and gain some outside sympathy. Today, it seems to be regarded by the residents in more 'respectable' areas, as master of its own fate. Past attempts by the community to bring industry and employment to the area have by and large been forgotten. The intervention by the Army into the Newbury Industrial Estate was a seven day wonder, the memory of which remains only in the minds of the residents of the estate. The struggle to establish small co-operatives seems no longer evident. Yet this is not to say that Newbury can now be regarded as a 'workless community'. Informal economic practices still survive and have expanded beyond the realms of production and consumption to include a whole range of cultural and community activities. Indeed community activists from Newbury estate can grasp more readily than academics the obvious distinction between work and employment as the following tape recorded conversation I had with one key informant illustrates:

> When talking about unemployment, I don't know anybody unemployed. I think that's the first thing you've got to define. What I mean is I don't know anybody who is not working regardless of how employment/unemployment is defined. Let's put it this way, if you define it as waged employment then you run into difficulties over definition. Although you have mass unemployment of HOH's. I think the last survey was 78 per cent, people are not getting a wage, fair enough, but they are no longer victims of the stigma that once was attached to the unemployed because they see themselves as part of a general thing, a massive thing. But there is an alternative economy certainly. People develop their own economy. There is barter and exchange in operation all the time. You have a home economy. You've people using knitting machines. It starts off with their own

members of their house, then the neighbour across the street will supply wool. They will be paid, for example, in cigarettes or a couple of shillings. People who have certain skills develop them. If she's good at fixing a dress, she progresses from fixing her own dresses to fixing the dresses of other people and within that you have a limited barter and exchange going on and that's a very vital aspect of life here. My own wife does her own knitting for the family on a machine. Another example would be sticks for firewood. The old things that people did has now taken on a new dimension. Whereas before it was for pin money, kids doing it during the summer, now you have adults doing it. We have our own waste disposal team. Empty lager tins are collected for their aluminium content. You have a whole team start at five o'clock in the morning and go around the estate picking up empty larger tins with sacks. You've 'doing the double' although with the recession in the building trade that's more or less banjaxed. You have your own internal civil service has developed. You have people within the community who have leadership roles, that is, they will deal on behalf of tenants of the estate with various bureaucracies. You're not paid for it but where the benefit comes from as far as I see it, is that you are helping people do their own thing and that's a form of training going on. You have an exchange of skills. You have skill sharing. These people aren't paid but they are working. (Tape-Recorded Interview: Feb. 2nd. 1988)

The remainder of the book will expand on the points raised in this interview by exploring the various types of informal economic strategies that exist on the estate. It is hoped that each of the chapters will provide an overall picture of the diversity of informal economic activity within Newbury. An underlying theme of the book will be an attempt to show how the structural disadvantages of the residents stem primarily from factors emanating from outside the area and beyond the control of the residents, rather than from their own inadequacies. When the conditions of poverty, deprivation and unemployment become established in a particular area and when the outside society is not prepared to tackle the base inequalities which are at the root of these problems, then the way is paved for the development and acceptance of informal economic strategies.

4 Self servicing households

The economic value of work done in the household has been greatly underrated. We are only now beginning to realise that, if work done in the household was counted, its value would greatly affect the size of GNP. Gershuny (1987,p.49) suggests that unpaid work in the household sector, using manufactured goods and materials, substitutes for what might previously have been paid service employment. Advances in technology have ushered in new patterns of self provisioning which in turn have led to a new relationship between formal and informal economic activity. In this chapter, I intend to focus on attempts by some households in Newbury to reduce household costs by engaging in household production in order to supply household needs directly with unpaid family labour. The extent of unpaid work carried out within households is so wide ranging that a full systematic account of all forms of household work was outside the scope of the study. Instead, for the purpose of manageability, I choose to concentrate on three basic aspects of household self sufficiency; family needs, household and car maintenance. An exhaustive study of all the possible forms of activity that could fall within each of these categories was not contemplated. Instead, I focused on a selection of activities specific to each category in order to give some indication of the extent to which the working class households of Newbury substituted formal commodities and services by producing similar commodities and services using household labour.

Housework, en masse is a primary example of informal work. Many of the household duties which are defined stereotypically as housework and which women perform at no charge in their own homes can be easily marketed in the formal economy. Many substitutions between formal employment and household work are possible, A household could, for example, employ someone to do the cooking and the washing up or to clean the house. Depending on one's financial circumstances, the choice between household production and an alternative from the formal economy involves a fairly straightforward decision between performing certain activities oneself or employing someone else to perform broadly similar activities instead. Given the deprived nature of the Newbury estate and the employment status of most of the residents, employing someone to undertake mainstream housekeeping duties was not a realistic option for most of the residents. Hence, the study focused on a number of specific activities where it was felt an alternative between formal/informal substitution was more readily available. The first two, home baking and home brewing relate to domestic consumption of food and drink. The second two, dressmaking and knitting refer to family clothing patterns. The cutting of household members' hair is focused on next. This service is widely available both formally and informally within the estate (See Chapter Six). The cleaning of outside windows is also considered as this refers to an aspect of housework where an alternative is readily and reasonably cheaply available by those involved in community economic enterprises. The final set of activities to be considered relates to car and home maintenance.

Home baking

Bread is an integral part of most people's daily diet, while continuous Family Expenditure studies indicate significant amounts of money being spent by most households on cakes and other pastry products. Instead of purchasing these commodities from formal sources, households can easily purchase basic ingredients and turn these raw materials into consumable products utilising household labour. In 34 households, 23 per cent of the sample, at least one family member engaged in weekly home baking. In three of these households, baking was done for people outside the immediate family, while in two households baking was an income generating activity. The remaining 29 households baked for family members only.

Reviewing the range of tasks focused on throughout this chapter, there appeared to be three main factors which influenced whether or not a family choose to domestically produce rather than purchase goods. Firstly, the relative cost of home production vis-a-vis market prices; secondly, the family's perception of the quality of home production in relation to the quality of market goods and thirdly, the inner satisfaction that could be gained from doing a certain task for oneself.

As far as home baking was concerned, the second and third factors were the most important. The majority of households believed that their baking was superior to similar commodities which could be purchased in local shops. In

32 households, a range of pastry products including cakes and buns were made. While in eight households, bread was also made on a weekly basis. Most home bakers stated that they derived a sense of pleasure from this activity and this, rather than saving money was their primary motivation. While some households stated that home baking often could turn out to be cheaper than buying formally produced pastry products, this was only a secondary consideration. In only one household was cost cutting the main reason for substituting home baking for similar formally produced products. In this case, the householder was a single parent with three young children. The householder baked wholemeal bread every two to three days and the family's bread consumption was satisfied solely by internal means. The householder states that wholemeal bread requires minimal ingredients, just flour and water, and these can easily and cheaply be transformed into finished products. She states that her growing family's consumption of bread is quite high and the only way she can satisfy their appetites is by supplying this product informally.

Gender, rather than employment status was the main structural feature influencing whether or not a household engaged in home baking. Baking was primarily a female activity. In 31 cases, 91 per cent of the sample, baking was carried out by a female. In the remaining three cases, 9 per cent of the sample, baking was done by a male. Home baking was seen by the women as an essential component of housework. Twenty two of these women also engaged in dressmaking and knitting for family needs. These were activities associated with being a 'competent' housewife. Viewing their housewife role in this way resulted in the women engaging in home baking primarily to illustrate their aptitude as housekeepers to their extended family network, rather than as a cost cutting venture.

Home brewing

Much coverage has been given to Pahl's (1984) observation that one reason why the unemployed cannot gain access to informal employment is that they do not have the money to go to the pub to buy a drink and this is where many potential informal employment contacts are made. The drinking of alcohol is a primary feature of modern living and socialising and if the unemployed cannot afford to purchase alcohol in formal establishments, then might they find substitutes for this formal commodity by engaging in home brewing?

The survey of 150 households in the Newbury estate revealed very low levels of this form of substitution. In only seven households (5 per cent), did a household member engage in home brewing. One household made wine only, three households made beer only, while the remaining three made both. While home baking was primarily a female activity, home brewing was predominately a male one. In all seven households, this activity was performed by a male. In six cases, the male was unemployed, while in the seventh household the male was retired. However, the low number of cases make it difficult to establish a positive correlation between employment status and this form of substitution. Instead, we can focus on the threefold classification mentioned earlier (price, quality, satisfaction), to assess why some households were motivated to engage in this form of substitution and others were not.

As regards the first, the price of substituted commodities vis-a-vis their formal counterparts, significant savings could be made through home production, as the heavy excise duty on alcoholic drinks could be immediately eliminated. These potential savings were reduced somewhat by the initial high costs of engaging in home brewing. Apart from purchasing the home brewing kit, separate containers and other sterilising equipment are often needed. Moreover, there is no immediate return on one's capital outlay. Instead the brewer has to wait several weeks or months for the beer to ferment or the wine to mature. These factors reduced the individual's awareness of being involved in a cost cutting exercise.

The second point refers to the quality of home production vis-a-vis similar formal products. Several of the homebakers mentioned above, stated that their homebaking was better than similar products which could be purchased from formal sources and this was one of the motivating factors influencing their decision to engage in home production. The best claim the home brewers made was that their product was 'as good as' products that could be purchased from formal establishments. In no case, did an individual claim that their home substitution product excelled that produced formally. Instead, the home brewers focused on the satisfaction that could be gained from making one's own wine or beer and this was the principal reason why they decided to engage in home brewing.

Moreover, home brewing was not regarded as a substitution for formally produced similar products but rather as a supplement to them. To focus on substitution here, is to misrepresent the whole notion of consuming alcohol. Drinking wine and beer was seen primarily as a social activity. The quality of alcohol was enhanced by the surroundings in which it was consumed and the company one was in. In the Newbury estate, there were two main drinking clubs that were largely frequented by unemployed males. An unemployed man could spend the entire day in one of the clubs, playing snooker or pool, and perhaps only buy one pint of beer. Not having enough money to buy another pint or 'stand a round' is an embarrassment only if one's companions are in a more comfortable financial situation. In an area of widespread unemployment where everyone's financial situation is precarious, an individual's meagre alcohol consumption does not present a problem for himself, his social circle or the staff of the drinking clubs. Hence the seven formally inactive men who engaged in home brewing did so mainly for the pleasure. The final product was an addition to, and not a replacement for, formally produced similar commodities.

Intra familial knitting distribution

Knitting was quite an extensive internal family activity. In forty nine households, 33 per cent of the sample, at least one family member engaged in knitting. All forty nine households were involved in this activity to fulfil internal family needs, although as the chapter on community economic enterprises will illustrate, some had turned this family practice into an income generating activity. Those who had monetarised this ability had developed and enhanced their skill by working in the family economy. It was often only after an extensive period of satisfying internal family needs, that the transition to the money economy was made.

Within the family clothing economy, knitting was organised along very clear gender lines. Mothers were particularly active knitting for small children. Everyone involved in this task were mothers or had been mothers of young children. Knitting had been largely organised around catering for the clothing needs of young children. The willingness of a recipient to wear a knitted item of clothing was directly related to age. Pre-teenage children were the group most actively catered for. Here items of clothing were knit for school and leisure needs and there was little difference in the provision between the sexes, with the exception of jumpers being knitted more frequently for boys and cardigans for girls. Once the children reached their teenage years, knitting was solely to fulfil school needs and centred on knitting school jumpers and cardigans. At this age, children preferred to formally shop for leisure or casual wear rather than accept home made garments. Once the children left school altogether, their clothing needs were no longer satisfied in the household economy. This did not necessarily mean that the household knitter became redundant by this stage. Instead, what usually happened was that the recipient of the knitted products changed. In fifteen of the forty nine households that engaged in home knitting, the knitter was over fifty years of age. These fifteen respondents had grown up families and had ceased to knit for their children's needs. Instead, their efforts were now concentrated on knitting jumpers and cardigans for their husbands.

Two factors can be put forward to account for this change in household knitting distribution. Firstly, when children are young and resources scarce, children's clothing needs take precedence over those of husbands. The family's expenditure on wool and the mother's labour time is devoted to satisfying growing children's needs, particularly in relation to the supply of often compulsory school uniforms. As children grow older and their demands for household knitted items diminish, then attention can be focused on satisfying husbands' needs. Secondly, younger married men appear more unwilling to wear home knitted products. Several of the women interviewed stated that their husbands were generally unenthusiastic about wearing the end products of their knitting activities, preferring instead to wear similar items purchased from formal establishments. This preference for formally purchased items tended to diminish as the males got older. As their age increased, their knitted clothing needs were more likely to be satisfied within the family domestic economy. As one woman told me:

> Do you see that jumper that he's wearing. I done it. He wouldn't have wore that a lot of years ago. He wouldn't have been seen dead in it. But do you see now, he never has my jumpers off him.

The threefold classification, (price, quality and satisfaction) mentioned earlier can be utilised to assess why the substitution between formal and informal knitted products takes place. As regards price, most households stated that it was much cheaper to engage in home production of knitted commodities rather than purchase similar items from formal establishments. This was particularly the case in relation to school uniforms. Wool was relatively cheap and was often bought in bulk between a number of households or from the nuns in the area. Moreover, most households stated that the quality was far superior than similar items that could be purchased from formal sources. 'Washes better and lasts longer' were the two most frequent comments. The superior quality of hand knitted garments was also frequently cited by the older members of the sample. Heavier garments tended to be knitted for the older members of the sample. The main emphasis here, tended to be on warmth. Several respondents stated that hand knitted cardigans provided the greatest protection against chilly winter months and could act as a substitute coat on warm summer evenings. As one lady stated:

> Feel the weight of that? That would cost you a packet if you were to try and buy it in a proper shop.

Hand knitting was also considered as a pleasurable activity by the bulk of the respondents. Knitting often accompanied chatting to friends, neighbours and relatives. Tea would be made. Conversation would centre around knitting patterns and ideas and then progress to local gossip. Knitting provided the background whereby some of the women could emphasise their common identity. For those who did not join informal knitting circles, knitting was usually done in the evenings and was accompanied by the watching of television. As one woman said:

> You don't feel you've wasted your whole night in front of the box. At least you have something to show for it.

Dressmaking

Dressmaking was a less frequent household activity than knitting. In only thirteen households, 9 per cent of the sample, was dressmaking a significant internal activity. Two main reasons can be put forward to account for this. Firstly, dressmaking requires more skill than hand knitting. Ten of the thirteen respondents who engaged in dressmaking had at one stage undertaken a short course on stitching or had at some stage in their lives been employed as a stitcher. The women who engaged in hand knitting by contrast had never had any kind of formal training. Secondly, there is more capital outlay attached to dressmaking compared to knitting. Knitters have the option of either knitting by hand or machine, so at a basic level the only tools required to engage in home knitting are a pair of knitting needles. Dressmaking on the other hand was rarely undertaken without the use of a proper machine. While costs may be reduced by purchasing a second hand machine, nonetheless the initial financial outlay may act as a deterrent against more households contemplating this form of substitution.

The thirteen households who did engage in dressmaking stated that considerable savings could be made from supplying these commodities through the family economy. Again, as with the knitting, the recipients tended to be mainly young children. As age increased, so did preference for formal clothing products. Six of these households utilised their skills to make money by charging their friends, neighbours or relatives for dressmaking services. Outside the household, more specialised garments were made such as christening robes and wedding dresses. Five of the households also utilised their dressmaking skills to make household fabric furnishings. The most common articles made were cushion covers and matching curtains. Less occasionally duvet covers were made. Here again, the saving of money was the primary motivation for engaging in this activity. As one respondent told me:

> Look, I made the cushions and curtains you see here in the living room and I've made curtains for the whole house. I also made that fancy covering for the pelmet. I went down to Anderson and McAuley's and

nearly had a heart attack when I saw what they were charging for covering pelmets. I said to hell with that, I'll do it myself.

The quality of the garments and household furnishings depended on the level of skill of the dressmaker. The six households who engaged in dressmaking for money were all highly qualified and all felt that their products were much superior to similar products which could be purchased from formal establishments. The remaining respondents had mixed views regarding the quality of their work. Three believed that the quality was superior, three believed that the quality was 'as good as' while the final respondent stated that the quality was inferior but admitted that this was the only way she could ensure that her children were adequately clothed.

The pleasure or satisfaction to be derived from engaging in this activity was also linked to the skill of the performer. The more highly skilled the dressmaker, the more pleasure was gained from the work. This was mainly because the highly skilled dressmakers often designed their own garments rather than simply following patterns. While this creativity was often channelled into money making activities, nonetheless the originality was also applied to supplying internal family needs. This innovative aspect of the highly skilled dressmakers' work enhanced the satisfaction they derived from practicing their skills both within the household and within the community.

Intra familial hairdressing

Table 4.1
Formal and informal hairdressers

	No. of Households	Percentage
Formal establishment within estate	60	40.0%
Formal establishment outside estate	27	18.0%
Friend, neighbour or relative	40	26.7%
ACE worker *	11	7.3%
Internal family member	12	8.0%
Totals:	150	100%

* ACE = Action For Community Employment. This is a government sponsored scheme aimed at giving one year employment experience to people unemployed for over one year.

The above table represents a breakdown of who cuts the hair of the residents of the estate. From the table, we can see that the bulk of households in the estate get their hair cut in a formal hairdressing establishment either inside or outside the estate. Just over a quarter of the sample relied on either a friend, neighbour or relative working informally to provide this service. These people usually charge rates below that charged in formal establishments. Moreover, rates are often negotiable depending on one's social circumstances and one's relationship with the informal hairdresser (See Chapter Six). The ACE scheme which operates in the area employs a part time hairdresser to cut the hair of pensioners free of charge. Hence, various opportunities exist within and outside the estate for household members to have their hair cut by hairdressers working either formally or informally. Nonetheless, twelve households in the sample choose to rely on an internal family member to provide this service. In all twelve households, the person who cut hair had no formal training as a hairdresser. Furthermore, in each of the twelve households, this task was performed by a female.

Motivations to provide this service internally varied between saving money to a general reluctance to have the task performed by either a formal or informal hairdresser. In five of the twelve households, the recipients of the internal service were elderly. The task was generally performed by an adult daughter still living at home. The decision to substitute for a service that was widely available both formally and informally was not so much to do with saving money as with a general unwillingness to either travel to a hairdressing establishment or to allow a 'stranger' into the house. In the remaining seven households, the saving of money was the primary motivation for substituting for this activity. In all seven households, the male head was unemployed or unable to work. Providing for this need internally was another way of saving scarce family income.

The quality of the substitution was felt by all respondents to be inferior. This is illustrated by the selective recipients of this informal service. In the five households where daughters cut elderly parents' hair, the daughters themselves went to a formal hairdressing establishment either on or off the estate to have their own hair cut and styled. Elderly parents' hair was basically just kept short and no styling of the hair was attempted. In the remaining seven households, children were the main recipients of this internal service. Each of these seven households had between two and seven children under the age of twelve and all these children had their hair cut by the mother in the household. Furthermore, in five cases the male head of household also had his hair cut by the wife. Again the cutting of hair was practical, being kept short and again no styling was attempted. However, in each of these seven households, the female respondent went to a formal hairdressing establishment to have her own hair cut and styled. This decision was due to the perceived inability of informal haircutters to do anything more than keep hair short. Little satisfaction was derived from engaging in this task. The activity was merely seen as a cost cutting exercise. By substituting for this service, these families could prevent a further draw on vital household income.

The cleaning of outside windows

The cleaning of outside windows provides a source of income for some of the unemployed males living in the district (See Chapter Six). A standard charge of 80p is made for this service. Hence households in the area have a direct choice between performing this activity themselves and keeping the 80p or paying for this service to be performed by someone outside their household. Most households employed an informal window cleaner to clean the outside of their windows. This was the pattern in 95 households, 63 per cent of the sample. In a further 14 households, 9 per cent, outside windows were cleaned by a relative while in the remaining 41 households, 27 per cent, windows were cleaned by a family member. In these 41 households, windows were cleaned mainly by a female member of the household, usually the wife. In only five households, were outside windows cleaned by a male; in the remaining 36 cases, outside windows were cleaned by a female. This contrasts starkly with the pattern of cleaning windows for which a charge is made. Once a price is placed on the service, it becomes a male activity. Once the direct economic value of the task is removed, it transfers to becoming a predominately female activity.

Most households who cleaned their own windows did so solely to save the 80p which they felt could be better spent elsewhere. Paying someone a weekly sum for an activity that could easily be carried out by a household member using existing household materials was a luxury these households felt they could ill afford. In all but three of the 41 households, this was the primary motivating factor influencing the households' decision to substitute internally for a service that could easily be purchased externally. In three cases, the main motivating factor for performing this service for oneself was the quality of the external service on offer. These three households were not satisfied with the standard of the service provided by the informal window cleaners and thus undertook the activity themselves. Little personal satisfaction was gained from cleaning windows. Even the three households who were unhappy with the quality of the external service, viewed the cleaning of outside windows as a necessary chore rather than a satisfying activity. While the households which performed this activity to save money viewed window cleaning as another chore to be added to the burdensome task of housework.

Car maintenance

Only twenty five households, 17 per cent of the sample, were the owners of a car. Car ownership was directly related to either formal or informal employment. In thirteen of the twenty five households, the male head was in full time formal employment. While in a further nine households, the male head was in informal employment. Only two out of the twenty five car owners relied on a garage to repair or maintain their car. The majority of car owners, nineteen households, relied on a friend, neighbour or relative to fix their car when necessary. In the remaining four households, car repairs were undertaken by an internal family member. In one of these four households, the male head was in full time formal employment, while in the other three the male head of household worked informally. Two worked informally as motor mechanics and the third was employed as an informal labourer in the construction industry. The two households where an inexperienced family member carried out car repairs were motivated not so much by the desire to save money but because they enjoyed, as both put it, 'tinkering about with cars'.

Household maintenance

Household maintenance was closely bound up with ownership and non ownership of property. The Newbury estate was built by the Belfast Corporation in the immediate post-war period and transferred to the the Northern Ireland Housing Executive (NIHE) in 1972. The NIHE is now responsible for all council estates in Northern Ireland. During the past decade, as with other council estates in the mainland, the residents of Newbury were given the option of buying their rented accommodation. Prices were negotiable depending on length of residency and the only qualifying stipulation was that the male head of household or his wife should be in full time formal employment. This has been a major barrier to most households in the estate. With unemployment so high, most households were not in a position to make a decision about whether to buy their property or remain tenants. Out of the 150 households surveyed, only 10 per cent had bought their own homes. In each of these fifteen households, the male head was in full time formal employment at the time of purchase. At the time of the interviews, nine were still formally employed and one was temporarily unemployed. The latter respondent works on fixed term contracts and finds himself occasionally out of work between contracts. He has been employed in this way for the past twelve years and states that he is never out of work for more than six months at a time. Six of the nine men who were still in formal employment at the time of the survey also had wives in either full time or part time formal employment.

Ownership of property is a crucial factor that needs to be taken into account when evaluating the extent to which households utilise their own labour power to upgrade or maintain their dwelling. For the majority of households who rent their house, the NIHE is responsible for the structural maintenance of the dwelling. All tenants are basically responsible for, is to keep the dwelling in good decorative order. Moreover, this responsibility is only a tacit one. Any major repairs are undertaken by the housing body. The NIHE also engage in periodic improvements of the dwellings, both internally and externally. For example, over the last decade, most households have been supplied with central heating to replace coal fires. At the time of the survey, the NIHE were embarking on a major renovation and environmental improvement scheme. House exteriors were being repainted and rotten wooden fences were being replaced by red brick walls.

The NIHE also engage in minor internal repairs to dwellings following a tenant's complaint. Repairs may be serious or trivial, ranging from fixing a faulty electrical socket to replacing a window catch or door handle. Community groups in the estate will take down details of tenants' complaints and pass them on to the NIHE. They will also act as intermediaries between the residents of the estate and personnel of the NIHE. Sinn Fein has a caravan parked in the estate two mornings per week and also fulfils this function. Since complaints are so easily reported due to the high profile of community and political groups in the area and since the NIHE will undertake these repairs, free of charge, there is little incentive for households in rented accommodation to substitute for formal maintenance services. Hence the only significant substitutions in this area lie in painting and decorating and repairing electrical consumer durables. In other words, services which lie outside the NIHE's jurisdiction.

Painting and decorating

For most households, painting and decorating was done on a yearly basis, usually around Christmas time. Eighty seven households, 58 per cent of the sample, had at least one room in the house painted or decorated during the preceding year. In thirty households, 20 per cent of the sample, painting and decorating was carried out between one to two years prior to the survey. In the remaining thirty three households, 22 per cent of the sample, no painting or decorating had been carried out during the two years prior to the survey.

While there were several households where the occupants told me they could not afford paint or wallpaper, for the majority of residents, money for decorating materials did not appear to be an insurmountable problem. The cheapest paint and wallpaper were bought often during seasonal sales. Often living rooms were papered with heavy embossed paper which then only required yearly coats of paint to look like new again. Painting and decorating is largely a labour intensive task and thus the greatest cost attached to this activity is the purchase of labour power if the service is carried out by a worker in the formal economy. Hence most households performed this service internally relying on indigenous household labour. Table 4.2 represents a breakdown of who carries out painting and decorating within households in the estate:

Table 4.2
Family labour and household painting and decorating

Work Done By	No of Households	Percentage
Husband mainly	65	43.3%
Wife mainly	13	8.7%
Husband & wife	4	2.7%
Husband & friends	3	2.0%
Neighbour	4	2.7%
Relative	34	22.7%
ACE worker	27	18.0%
Totals:	150	100.0%

From the above table, we can see that in 82 households, 55 per cent of cases, painting and decorating was done by an internal family member, either the husband or wife or both. When we focus on the breakdown of the task by sex, it becomes apparent that painting and decorating is primarily a male activity. The selection and purchase of paint and wallpaper was mainly done by females but the actual activity was carried out by males. This sexual division of labour was clear when focusing on the other groups who carried out the task. Where the activity was performed by a neighbour or relative, the person was in all cases a male. In the three households where the husband was assisted by friends, the friends were male. The ACE scheme employs a number of 'environmental workers' to carry out physical improvements to the estate. These environmental workers are usually young males between the ages of 16-25. At the time of the survey, the ACE scheme employed thirty such workers and the number has risen substantially since the research was carried out. The environmental workers' main duties were to provide a free painting and papering service to pensioners and single parents who live on the estate.

The sexual division of labour is further underlined when examining the thirteen households where the activity was carried out by a female. In over half, seven cases, the main reason for the task being carried out by a female was because no male was present in the household. These seven households were headed by female single parents who were unaware of the ACE scheme in operation in the area.

Not one household in the estate utilised a formally registered tradesman to carry out decorating. Where a friend, neighbour or relative carried out the task or assisted with the task, often no payment was made. The service was usually done as a favour and this aspect of the data will be outlined in more detail in the next chapter. Where a charge was made, it was well below the market value of the labour input and was usually performed by someone who worked informally.

Electrical repairs

This section refers to the maintenance of electrical domestic durables such as television sets and washing machines. For the majority of households, any other electrical work such as faulty sockets or the rewiring of the dwelling is the responsibility of the NIHE. All households in the survey were asked who they were likely to contact in the event of an electrical product developing a fault. The most common electrical durables present in most households were television and video sets and washing machines. Hence the responses referred mainly to these items.

The following table represents a breakdown of the responses:

Table 4.3
Repair of electrical products

	No. of Households	Percentage
Rental company	77	51.3%
Under guarantee	7	4.7%
Someone from newspaper ad.	17	11.3%
Relative	9	6.0%
Friend	5	3.3%
Neighbour	22	14.7%
Internal family member	13	8.7%
Totals	150	100%

Most households, 51 per cent of the sample, rented television and video sets rather than buying them. Hence if the product developed a fault, then it was up to the rental company to rectify the fault. A further seven households, 5 per cent, bought electrical items with a guarantee. Again, if a fault developed during the guarantee, then the company from where the item was purchased was responsible for fixing the fault. Seventeen households, 11 per cent, relied on someone from the classified advertisements in the paper to fix electrical faults. In all seventeen cases, the person was contacted through a local newspaper published in West Belfast, rather than through any of Belfast's three main daily newspapers. In thirty six cases, 24 per cent of the sample, a friend, neighbour or relative would repair faults in electrical durables. While in thirteen cases, someone within the household would repair defective electrical products.

In only one of these thirteen households was the male head in full time formal employment, working as an electrician. In the remaining twelve households, the male head was either unemployed or retired. In all thirteen households, electrical work was carried out by a male. In each of the households where the male had no formal employment, none had any formal training as an electrician. The rest of this section will focus on these twelve households.

For each of these twelve households, the saving of money was the primary motivation for engaging in this form of substitution. Each respondent stated that they did not know anyone informally who could carry out electrical repairs and they could not afford to employ the services of a formally employed electrician. In four cases, respondents borrowed do-it-yourself books from the local library and studied these to develop elementary electrical skills. As one respondent stated:

> I've a lot of time on my hands. I read a lot. I've taught myself a lot of things. If anything electrical breaks down, I can fiddle about and fix it. I've actually become quite good.

and another:

> We have to do things for ourselves. We've no option. The library is my main source of information. I get what I want there and then tackle anything.

Gershuny and Pahl (1980) recognised the potential of do-it-yourself books in their early work when they stated that such books 'democratise skills in the informal economy' but in later work Pahl (1984) goes on to argue that such skills are more likely to be developed by those in formal employment. This is because informal work needs more than time, it needs the money to buy tools and materials. This approach ignores the possiblity that tools like do-it-yourself books can be borrowed rather than purchased from formal sources. Most electrical repair work requires minimal materials and often the only main tool that is required is a screwdriver.

As regards the quality of the substitution, none of the respondents regarded their electrical skills as equal or superior to those that could be formally purchased. All felt that electrical work was highly skilled and the best they could do was cope with elementary household repairs. This is reflected in the language used by the respondents to describe this activity. 'I can fiddle about' or 'I can tinker about' were the two most common phrases used. None of the respondents felt competent enough to market their skills either formally or informally. Rather such skills were reserved solely for household substitution, although two interviewees who used the library occasionally attempted repairs for friends, neighbours or relatives as favours. Finally, there was often a feeling of achievement gained from this form of substitution. All respondents stated that they derived high levels of personal satisfaction from successfully repairing an electrical fault.

Improvements to dwellings

As mentioned earlier, improvements to dwellings were directly related to ownership of property. Fifteen households had purchased their dwelling from the NIHE and all these households had improvements carried out to their property. A further two households had bought their property from the NIHE and then sold it back again. These two households occupied the Orlit houses which are described in Chapter Three. The houses were made from inferior building materials and have caused considerable contention throughout the years, between the various housing authorities and the residents of the estate. When the NIHE embarked on their policy of selling rented accommodation to their tenants, their internal surveyor stated that the Orlit houses were suitable for purchase. A small number of households in the estate who occupied Orlit dwellings decided to purchase their accommodation. However, after a period of about two years, the houses were discovered to be sinking. An inquiry into the purchase of the dwellings stated that the sale should not have gone forward. As a result, the NIHE decided to re-purchase the dwellings. During the period of ownership, these two households carried out major improvements to their dwellings. The NIHE still has to reach a decision on the long term implications for the Orlit dwellings.

All seventeen of the male HOH's discussed so far in this section had been employed at the time of the purchase of their dwelling. The most common improvements carried out were the replacement of doors and windows and the installation of a new bathroom suite. While only three of these households relied on a firm to carry out these improvements, nonetheless, in no case was the work carried out by an internal family member. Rather most households here relied on friends, neighbours and relatives to carry out this work. This was the pattern adopted by fourteen of the seventeen households. In some cases, a charge was made for performing these services but always below the price charged by formal establishments or workers. In other cases, the services were performed as favours, with a tacit agreement being made between the parties to return the favours at some future, usually unspecified, date. This aspect of the data will be returned to in the next chapter.

A further nine households whose homes were owned by the NIHE also engaged in a variety of home improvements. In the seventeen cases discussed above the likelihood of improvements being carried out depended on property ownership and employment status of the male head of household. Improvements in the nine households living in rented accommodation were also related to employment, only this time, not to formal employment but to informal employment. In seven out of these nine households, the male head of household had experience of long term informal employment.

The data throws up several contrasts with Pahl's survey on the Isle of

Sheppey. In the latter, home improvements were most likely to be undertaken by those in full time formal employment. In Newbury, home improvements were also likely to be carried out by those in informal employment. When looking at motivation for substitution here, time seems to be a primary factor in determining whether a household will carry out home improvements using household labour or employ someone from outside the household. Those in full time formal employment had less surplus time on their hands to engage in this form of self provisioning. Hence the work was most likely to be undertaken by friends, neighbours or relatives either as favours or at reduced prices. Thus the cost was not too much of an offputting factor. For those in informal employment, work was much more sporadic and slack periods could be utilised to engage in home improvements.

The benefits of carrying out improvements in privately owned property are obvious. Improvements enhance the value of one's property and increase the possible return on one's investment. While outsiders may not be interested in buying a house in Newbury, there is limited internal demand. The majority of households in Newbury are related to at least one other household in the estate. In many cases, households were related to as many as ten to twelve other households. Newly married couples may not want to break the strong kinship ties that exist on the estate and since newly weds would not qualify for a NIHE house, they may prove potential customers for privately owned property. Moreover, the majority of those who purchased their dwellings lived on the outskirts of the estate where it was felt property would be easier to sell.

The financial benefits attached to improving rented accommodation are not as clear cut. The nine households who lived in rented accommodation and carried out improvements did so mainly to increase their own domestic comfort. The layout of the houses was felt by the majority of the residents in the estate to be highly unsatisfactory. The NIHE were seen to be slow to respond to complaints and tended to focus on repairs rather than improvements. Thus, these nine households decided to undertake improvements for themselves. The potential financial gain or loss on this work was not considered. In all cases the work was carried out without the knowledge or consent of the NIHE.

For the seven households where the male head engaged in informal employment, there was a further reason for engaging in home improvements. There was a limit to what these seven households felt they could do with their surplus income. Since the income was derived from working what many considered illegally, then it was felt to be too risky to place earnings in a bank or other financial institution. Furthermore, since one's informal employment often depended on one's neighbours, friends and relatives within the estate, then moving out of the area was highly unlikely. This could jeopardize one's chances of gaining future informal employment. Thus money earned from working informally was put into current consumption. This mostly involved purchasing a car, luxury consumer durables and upgrading one's house, regardless of ownership. It must be stressed though, that only a minority of households where members worked informally found themselves in this position. Often in these households, there were multiple informal workers. For most people who worked informally, the extra income was spent on necessities rather than luxuries.

The link between formal and informal production of goods and services

Throughout this chapter, the focus has been on the extent to which households in Newbury substitute for formal goods and services by utilising household labour. The usage of the term substitution needs to be clarified here. No single activity outlined in this chapter involved total substitution. The term, while useful for distinguishing between formal and informal goods and services and how they are produced, nonetheless undermines the subtle links between formal and informal economic activity. No informal self service mentioned in this chapter was totally autonomous from the formal economy. Rather the production of each good or service involved a continuous interchange between formal and informal economic activity. The general pattern was that previously outlined by Gershuny (1987). Materials were purchased from formal sources, informal labour was then added to transform the materials into final products or services. In some cases, once the initial materials were purchased, the good or service could be produced solely by informal means. Hence for making wine or beer, cleaning windows, painting and decorating; once formal purchases were complete, informal labour power was all that was necessary to finalise production.

For other activities, informal labour was not in itself enough to complete the transformation. Rather informal labour had to be utilised alongside formal usage of electricity. Thus, for example, the women who baked or engaged in knitting and dressmaking using machines could only perform their informal service by consuming formal electrical units. Even housework considered an archetypical example of informal work was not wholly autonomous from the formal economy. Apart from the cleaning of windows, all households in the estate could be regarded as self supporters in doing everyday housework. In no cases was a market alternative such as the employment of household help used. This, however, did not mean that housework was separate from the formal economy. To keep one's house in a hygienic state, cleaning materials and agents had to be continually purchased from formal sources while household durables such as washing machines and vacuum cleaners could only be utilised by plugging into a formal power supply.

The relationship between formal and informal production of goods and services by the households mentioned in this chapter was sometimes a competitive relationship and sometimes a complementary one. Often this was dependent on the composition and age structure of the household. This was particularly apparent when focusing on knitting, dressmaking and the cutting of family members' hair. Rather than households making a clear cut choice between producing these goods and services internally or purchasing them formally, there was a continuous process of selective substitution. Goods and services were often produced internally for the very young and very old members of households while those in between were more likely to have their needs satisfied by formal sources. In this way, the relationship between most households in the estate and the formal economy was a complementary one. Satisfying specific household members' needs by relying on internal sources, saved valuable income and enabled other members of the same households to purchase formal goods and services.

Summary

This chapter focused on the extent to which households in the Newbury estate engaged in self provisioning. The likelihood of a household engaging in self servicing was dependent on a number of factors. Whether or not the adults in each household were in formal employment had little impact on the household's decision to engage in self provisioning. Rather, the age structure and composition of the household were very important determinants influencing participation in self provisioning. This was particularly noticeable in relation to knitting, dressmaking and internal hairdressing. Families with dependent children were the group most likely to engage in household substitution. This held true for each of the activities mentioned in this chapter. The fewer dependent children in a particular household, the less likely that it would engage in self provisioning.

In assessing why households decided to engage in self servicing, I concentrated on three main points, whether money could be saved by performing a service or producing a good informally, the differences in quality between formal and informal goods and services and whether any satisfaction could be gained from engaging in household self provisioning. These three points provided the background against which the substitution between formal and informal goods and services was assessed. In some cases, the saving of money was the primary motivation for making use of internal family labour. This was particularly true for the cleaning of outside windows and painting and decorating. Often the superior quality of informal products was emphasised. This was mainly the case for the provision of goods rather than services. Unemployed individuals in particular, also stressed that some form of satisfaction could be derived from utilising family labour to produce goods and services. Motivations rarely related to just one of these factors but more usually to an amalgamation of two or three. Employment status was important only in relation to DIY improvements and car maintenance. The likelihood of owning a car or having the resources to engage in home improvements was directly related to formal and informal paid employment. However, those in full time formal employment were least likely to maintain their own cars or engage in household improvements drawing on household labour. This was mainly due to time which was a scarcer resource for those in full time formal employment than for those in informal employment. Gender differences were also important in relation to which member of self servicing households were likely to do which task. Males tended to focus on traditional male areas of work, being responsible mainly for home improvements, electrical repairs, painting and decorating and the making of wine and beer. Females were concentrated in the traditional female activities of knitting dressmaking and home baking.

5 Social economic transactions and community self help networks

> The habit of share and share alike is easily understandable in a community where everyone is likely to find himself in difficulties.... for it is scarcity and not sufficiency that makes people generous.....He who is in need today receives help from him who may bc in need tomorrow (Evans Pritchard 1940,p.210).

In the last chapter, I focused on self servicing households and treated the household as the unit of analysis. This reflects the growing shift of research attention away from work as an individual activity, undertaken in a variety of contexts, towards the household as the unit of production (Harding and Jenkins 1989,p.29). Gershuny (1983) for example, has focused on self servicing within households while Pahl (1984a) has concentrated on distinctions between multiple earner and no earner households. In both these studies, households have been largely treated as collections of individuals engaged in the process of production and consumption. The communities in which households are located have been considered relatively unimportant as a source of informal economic activity. Pahl in particular argues that informal work is largely structured around attempts by multiple earner households to add to their home comforts by concentrating their spare time and energy into upgrading their homes. His survey data on the Isle of Sheppey revealed that very little work was carried out within the community. Of the forty one tasks most likely to be done on the island, such as painting and decorating the house, fixing the car and getting the shopping done, a mere two per cent of the complete range of tasks were carried out within the community.

What I want to argue here is that ties of kinship and geographical propinquity between neighbours remain significant in certain types of locality and become immensely important during times of social and economic stress. Reciprocal favours between neighbours thrives among cohesive working class communities where resources for satisfying needs in other ways are low. In chapter Three, I outlined a brief history of Newbury estate from its inception in 1950. I pointed out some of the reasons why Newbury was ostracized from the wider working class society of West Belfast and thus had to fall back on internal resources. One way of utilising internal resources is by fostering notions of reciprocity. Reciprocity involves the mutual recognition of the obligation to give and receive. Newbury has developed an intricate system of reciprocity which in turn acts as a redistributive mechanism within the community. Participants in reciprocal relationships can derive some measure of security within a wider society which considers them as marginal occupants.

The issues discussed in this chapter relate to long standing theoretical debates about the applicability of market based notions of exchange to situations where social and economic relationships cannot easily be disentangled. Many of the commodities and services which are exchanged in Newbury lie outside market calculations of the value of the exchanges. Household labour and wider communal relationships provide the essential means of survival for many households. Goods and services are traded and swapped among many residents of the estate. Kinship and friendship relationships provide the vitality for these exchanges of goods and services. The chapter will focus on the various forms of reciprocal relationships that exist between households in the estate. Particular emphasis will be placed on the reciprocal relationships between relatives and non relatives. Men and women's participation in reciprocal arrangements will be assessed. The chapter will overlap to some degree with the analysis of activities mentioned in the last chapter. But here I am concerned with the surpluses of goods and services which feed into the wider economy.

Reciprocal obligations between neighbours

In Newbury estate, many households do not have sufficient income to meet their own needs nor do they always have the opportunity to engage in income producing economic activities, hence they are often compelled to create and maintain supportive relationships within their community. Out of these relationships emerge reciprocal transactions which bind households together and help cement the social relationships themselves. These reciprocal transactions symbolise the social and economic interdependence between the households involved. Such transactions take place mainly between neighbours and extended kin living within the estate. Here I want to concentrate on reciprocal transactions amongst non kin.

Most households in Newbury have had a long standing association with the area. Almost 75 per cent of the survey sample have been living in Newbury for over twenty years. Fifty per cent of the male heads of household between the ages of 26-40 had been born in Newbury. While 72 per cent of the females between the ages of 26-40 were also born in the estate. These long periods of residency in an area characterised by scarcity were conducive to the establishment of social support networks. These networks were typically forged between neighbours. Individual streets in Newbury could be regarded as individual communities. Support networks existed mainly within streets rather than across streets and it was not uncommon for people at the top of the estate not to know anyone at the bottom half, despite their length of residency and the smallness of the geographical area concerned.

All the households in the survey were asked whether they knew their neighbours, very well, quite well or not very well. 77 per cent replied that they knew their neighbours very well, 15 per cent replied that they knew their neighbours quite well and 7 per cent replied that they did not know their neighbours very well. Most of those who replied that they knew their neighbours quite well or not at all well, were recent residents in the estate or worked in full time formal employment. Households were also asked whether they felt that they could rely on their neighbours for help. 86 per cent stated that they could, 6 per cent stated that they could not and 8 per cent were not sure, as they had never experienced the need to rely on neighbours. Those who answered that they could rely on their neighbours for help were asked to give a specific example of help received from neighbours in the past. Most households relied on neighbours for a variety of general favours, with neighbourliness being more prevalent among females. The following are some examples of the responses received:

> I've the best of neighbours. The woman next door pays the society man for me. I can borrow from my neighbours and pay back whenever I can. When I'm sick, one would run and get the paper and a bap for me and another would maybe go to the chemist for my tablets.

> Oh yes, very much so. They are just like my family, my neighbours. They would sit up with you all night if they had to. My neighbours call in all the time and one always helps me out and when I need things, like you know when I'm a bit short and it's rough going, she always gives me things in through the back door so no one is the wiser.

> If they're going shopping, they always call to see if I want anything. If I need the kids looked after for a couple of hours, there's always

> somebody about. If I'm late up from the town and the kids are out of school and all, there's always somebody about to take them in.

Other respondents stated that they mainly relied on their neighbours during a time of crisis, particularly if there was an illness or death in a household. In these circumstances, the inhabitants of the street would come to the assistance of the household concerned. The reciprocal arrangements that came to the fore during the illness or death of a street member were mainly managed by females. The illness of a household member prompted neighbours to offer to look after young children while family members attended hospital or to help with household chores. This was particularly the case if the female head of household was taken into hospital. The following two quotes illustrate this:

> When the wife was taken into hospital, a different one would send me over my dinner at nights.

> Yes. It's a very close knit community. My wife wasn't well and was in hospital for a long time and the neighbours did my ironing and did bits of washing for the kids and cleaned the house for her getting out of hospital. They were great.

Street collections were often made if a member of a particular street died. The money was used to buy a wreath and the remainder was given to the family to 'tide them over' the crisis period. Two respondents I spoke to, stated that if a household member died at home, they were called upon to wash and prepare the dead body. The two females concerned had been performing this service for over twenty years and the tradition had been passed down to them from their parents. They travel throughout the estate and surrounding estates performing this task. They bring with them white linen cloths, 'blessed' candlesticks and other necessary religious emblems. Their services are often in demand, not as a substitute for intra household members' obligations in this respect, but because many households had no previous or at best very limited experience of death and recognised the expertise of the two women in knowing what traditional procedures should be adopted in 'laying out the dead'. The following quotes illustrate the depth of support that comes to the fore during the death of a street member:

> They (the neighbours) don't bother me and I don't bother them but do you see when he (her husband) was killed, you want to see the many were in this house. There was that many here that they were sitting on the stairs from top to bottom and the neighbours made tea, sandwiches, pots of stew, the lot.

As soon as there's a death, the street takes over and they don't leave you for the three days. We buy milk, make sandwiches, get wreaths and flowers and collect money and all.

There's always a collection if somebody in the street gets into trouble. If there's a death especially because then you need extra money. The collection is made immediately. You always give because next time it might be for you.

If there's a death, they gather like flies. Like I'll give you an example. The woman's a couple of doors up husband died last year. She kept a couple of cats and dogs and they stunk the whole place. To tell you the truth, she wasn't the cleanest of people and the place was stinking. Anyway, her husband died in hospital, sudden like, and he was to be released the next day and she was in a terrible state because of the house and all. Me and a couple of other neighbours went up to the house and spent the whole night cleaning and disinfecting it. We found a couple of rolls of wallpaper up the stairs and papered the living room where the corpse was going to be laid out.

Other households stated that the willingness of the inhabitants of individual streets to respond to this type of crisis depended on how the person died. If the person died as a result of feuding between republican extremist groups, then these collections and the traditional wake often did not take place, as the following two quotes illustrate:

Let's put it this way, if there's a death, they all rally round except of course if it's one of your own killed by another one of your own.

At a death everyone gathers round. That's the tradition here. But nowadays it depends on the circumstances. If the death is the result of in feuding then everyone is afraid to openly show any sympathy.

While many respondents stated that they did not bother with their neighbours on a day to day basis, nonetheless they felt a sense of security knowing that they could rely on their neighbours if the need arose. The following quotes typify the responses received:

You can keep yourself to yourself but be happy to know that they're there if you need them. They're always in the background ready to come to the fore if the need arises.

> I don't bother with them hardly at all but do you see if there was a sickness or a death, they'd all rally round. It's great knowing that.

The mutuality of these support systems was continually referred to by many respondents in answer to the question concerning the degree of neighbourliness. If someone in the street was sick or if there was a death, households helped out realising that they may be the recipients of the community support networks some time in the future. The interdependent relationship between households did not just apply to periods of crises but often included providing for everyday needs, such as shopping or babysitting for others. This mutuality of interests is reflected in the following two responses:

> My door is always open. Anybody can come here for anything and I know I could do the same. Babysitting, the lend of a few bob, a bit of trouble, you name it and I'll help them and they'll help me.

> Well, we ourselves have always an open door. Whoever comes here is never turned away. No questions are asked, just whatever is needed is given, should it be a loaf of bread or a loan of money. Its good to do this because you never know what the future might bring. You might be the one that has to go knocking on people's doors.

On the other hand, I don't want to paint too rosy an image of reciprocal support networks within the estate. The chapter on criminal activity will present a much more negative image of life within Newbury estate illustrating the complexity of community life and how mutual help and exploitation can co-exist. Moreover, willingness to help others may not be matched by ability to help others, hence many needs are not met. Furthermore, some of the older households in the sample questioned whether even the willingness to help one's neighbours was prevalent among the younger households in the estate. The following quotes typify this view:

> Years ago yes but not as much now. When my mother died everybody pulled together but the younger ones are not as helpful. Still it's alright I suppose.

> All the new ones coming and going all the time. They don't bother much with me. I'm too old for them.

> I'm sure they would but I don't really know. The problem is, all the

ones you really know well are dying off or moving into flats and the young ones don't bother the same.

Reciprocity among kin

While the mutual support relationships outlined in the previous section existed only within particular streets, aid relationships among extended kin were widespread throughout the whole area. These kinship relations are crucial for understanding community economic behaviour. All households in the survey were asked whether they were related to any other household. One hundred and seventeen households, 78 per cent of the sample, were related to at least one other household in the estate. Of these 117 households, 88, 75 per cent of the sample, were related to between one and five other households, while 29, 25 per cent of the sample, were related to over five households. Wives tended to have more relations on the estate than husbands. In 46 households, kinship relations existed between females, compared to 23 households, where the kinship relationship existed between males. In a further 17 households, both husbands and wives were related to other households in the estate. While in the remaining 31 cases, relationships existed between parents and married children.

Mutual aid among extended families was largely socially motivated. Members of extended family networks were often literally 'carried through' difficult periods. When examining motivations for participation in these aid relationships, it was clear that interest stemmed from a concern for the welfare of extended family members rather than a concern for reciprocity. Extended kinship networks provided a major source of social and economic support for family network members in need.

The most significant aid relationships existed between parents and children. Whether one was primarily a 'giver' or primarily a 'receiver' of aid was related to age. Middle aged parents tended to initiate most aid obligations and these were directed particularly at married daughters or daughters who were unmarried mothers. Unmarried mothers often remained at home and received help and support from family members. Although in some instances, getting pregnant was a ploy to 'escape' from the family home and get independent accommodation from the Housing Executive. Some unmarried mothers though continued to receive social and economic support from extended kin once they had left the family home. The case of Julie, an unmarried mother with two children can serve as an example.

Julie had her first baby when she was seventeen. The father was aged nineteen at the time, was unemployed and had a severe drink problem. Moreover, he tended to become violent when drunk. Julie continued to live at home when the baby was born and despite her family's disapproval, continued to see her boyfriend. Things came to a head when she discovered she was pregnant a second time. Her family refused her permission to see her boyfriend and as a result, Julie left home. She managed to get a house in the next street to her mother and has been living there ever since. At first, relations between Julie and the rest of her family were very strained and initially Julie had no contact with her mother. After the second baby was born though, Julie's mother called to see her and now supports her on an almost daily basis. Julie has no permanent relationship with her boyfriend and receives no financial assistance from him. Indeed, Julie often gives him money to feed his drinking habit. She is thus very dependent on her mother and wider family network. When her second child was born, the family collected money to buy clothes and a pram for the baby. Julie can't afford a washing machine, so her mother brings Julie's washing around to her house and does it in her machine. Other family members continue to support Julie both financially and emotionally.

In other cases, married daughters tend to remain in the family home with their new husbands. This was often at extreme inconvenience to other family members as space was usually scant. Sometimes these were temporary arrangements until the newly wed couple had saved up the deposit for a house. At other times, particularly if the new husband was unemployed, the arrangements could last several years with the young couples commencing families of their own.

Married daughters who moved out of the parental home, often continued to live in the estate, sometimes in the same street or a few streets away from their mothers. Again, almost daily interaction occurred between married daughters and mothers. Mothers and daughters shopped for each other and mothers often minded grandchildren. Emotional and financial support was also freely exchanged, and the flow tended to be from mothers to daughters. Financial assistance was particularly prevalent when the son-in-law was unemployed. In one household, while the interview was taking place, the respondent's daughter called in to borrow money. When she left, the mother stated:

> Look at that wee girl. She has four kids and she just can't feed them. He (the husband) just can't get a job, no matter how hard he tries. I've to help her out nearly every day. Sometimes she has nothing at all for the dinner and she doesn't like to say to me. But you've only to look at her. She's like an old woman with all the worry. You know, she's only twenty eight. I bet you thought she was older. Everybody does. You want to see the weight she's lost.

Sometimes when a marriage breaks up, the married daughter will move back into the parental home. This was usually the case for married daughters with young families. While occasionally the reason was for emotional support, most often it was sheer financial necessity that forced separated mothers to move back into their parents' home. Often marriage break ups did not go through the courts and hence the women received no financial support from their husbands. Even those who did go through the courts, often received minimal financial assistance as their husbands were unemployed. As a result, many separated women could no longer afford to run a separate household and cope with household bills and thus moved back into the parental home.

Once parents become older, they usually become the 'receivers' of aid and support rather than 'givers'. When parents become pensioners, assistance mainly flows from married daughters to parents. Several old aged pensioners told me that their daughters had paid for the installation and running expense of a telephone, even when the parents lived in the same estate. Married daughters often shopped for elderly parents and undertook weekly cleaning duties in their parents' homes. Often married children grouped together to buy modern consumer durables for their parents. Colour televisions and radios were the most popular items.

So far, I have mainly focused on emotional and financial aid and support between kinship and non kinship networks within the estate. This is important because the maintenance of these links demands considerable work and effort. Often, however, communal activity was an extension of the home provisioning and servicing tasks outlined in the last chapter. Hence, the next section of this chapter will expand on the intra household activities discussed in previous chapters by focusing this time on the exchange of household goods and services within the estate.

Communal food production and consumption

In the last chapter, household baking was carried out by thirty four households, 23 per cent of the sample. This baking was mainly directed towards internal household consumption. Only five households baked for external family members. Of these five, two baked for money while the remaining three baked for a circle of friends, relatives and neighbours. Hence there appears to be little communal value attached to this activity. However, if we widen the area of food production to include the making of meals, then the activity takes on more significance. Households often provided meals for other households. The main recipients of these meals were the elderly and sick inhabitants of the estate and the exchanges took place within streets rather than between streets. If a particular household had relations within the same street, then dietary needs of old and sick members were often met by extended family networks. If the household had no relations within the street, then often these requirements would be fulfilled by concerned neighbours or friends.

The dishes that were distributed most frequently were soup and stew. Both these dishes were made by the pot for an indeterminable amount of people and left overs were often given to elderly members of the street. No strict obligation for providing these services existed between households in any particular street. Rather the arrangements were frequently casual with elderly inhabitants being asked if they wanted some of the soup or stew that the family were having for dinner that night, or with elderly inhabitants being handed over such dishes with no prior notice.

On the other hand, often such dishes were made specifically for sick members of individual streets. If a household member, particularly a female became hospitalized, then the husband would be sent over occasional hot meals to tide him over until his wife got out of hospital. Alternatively, when a female was being released from hospital, particularly after having a baby, neighbours or wider kin would have a hot meal ready to lessen the anxiety attached to the first day home. Again, the obligation to participate in these services was sporadic and casual.

Communal knitting

In the last chapter, I outlined intra familial knitting arrangements. Knitting was mainly a female activity and was often aimed at satisfying the needs of young family members. As these children grew up, their clothing tastes changed and knitting was then mainly directed at satisfying husbands' needs. A further aspect of this typical knitting system involves inter kin knitting processes. In twenty nine households, knitting was regularly undertaken for members of extended kinship networks. In each of these households, knitting was originally carried out by mothers for young children and replicated the pattern mentioned above. However, once children got married and had their own children, the knitting process started all over again. This time with the female grandparent knitting for grandchildren. Again the willingness of grandchildren to wear home knitted items was closely related to age with most inter kin knitting being carried out for young grandchildren. The older the grandchildren, the less likely they were to have clothing needs satisfied in this way.

Knitting was also a way of fulfilling social obligations attached to birthdays and Christmas. The obligation to reciprocate affects most people in society. Most of us are under the obligation to give and receive at key points in our lives; birthdays, christenings, weddings, anniversaries and Christmas. Often when we receive a gift, we feel obligated to acknowledge the present with a counter gift. This extends to such trivial purchases as Christmas cards. The days preceding Christmas are often accompanied by frantic dashes to the post office to mail late Christmas cards to people who sent us cards. Reciprocity can be very problematic for people on meagre incomes. Townsend (1979) outlined how old age pensioners go without food and other basic necessities to honour their perceived social obligations. In Newbury, internal familial talents are often utilised to provide gifts to acknowledge social celebrations within and beyond extended kinship networks. This did not just apply to knitting but to dressmaking, photography and flower arranging. Many of those in community economic enterprises (see Chapter Six) commenced their activities within the immediate household, progressed by utilising their skills to honour social celebrations, before finally turning their talents into income generating activities aimed at the wider community.

Community household and car maintenance

Thus far, most of the activities mentioned have been undertaken by females. Males too, participate in communal reciprocal arrangements. Males tend to predominate in communal household and car maintenance. In forty one households, 27 per cent of the sample, painting and decorating was carried out by a friend, neighbour or relative. In eight of these households money changed hands while the rest built up favours to be reciprocated. Even where money did change hands, often the reason was to help someone out rather than purchase extra familial labour. As one respondent told me:

> A fellow we know hasn't worked in years. God help him. He has a young family. Sometimes we get him in to paint and that. We could do it just as easily ourselves but it gives us an excuse to give him a few bob.

Favours were most frequently built up between relatives. Out of the forty one households mentioned above, in thirty four cases, the work was carried out by relatives. Pahl (1984a) states that unemployed males were the least likely group to engage in communal economic activity. One reason put forward to account for this was that informal work for other households usually requires formal skills and unemployed males are the group least likely to possess such skills. This observation does not apply to painting and decorating which requires minimal, easily acquired skills. Painting and decorating is mainly, a time consuming activity rather than a highly skilled one. Unemployed men can easily cope with the time factor and by utilising their labour in this manner can gain access to other more highly developed skills through the build up of reciprocal obligations. The following quotes illustrate this point:

> I've eight brothers. One's a joiner, one's a plumber and one's an electrican. Me, I can do nothing. But you wanta see me with a paint brush in my hand. I do the painting for all of them and then I'm never stuck for what I can't do.

> My brother owns that hairdressers at the top of the road. We can call in anytime and he cuts all our hair and then when he needs it, I do his painting and papering. He hasn't got much time with working all the time, but me, I've got all the time in the world.

> I've tilers, sparks (electricians), you name it, among me own. They do favours for me and I do favours for them. Usually I do painting and decorating because to tell you the truth, I can't do anything else.

Similar observations can be made when looking at other forms of maintenance. Fourteen of the seventeen households who undertook household improvements relied on friends, neighbours and relatives to carry out the work. Thirty six households requiring electrical repairs, relied on friends, neighbours and relatives. While nineteen of the twenty five car owners relied on friends, neighbours and relatives. In some cases, no money passed hands. Favours were built up to be repaid at some unspecified time in the future. Those who did utilise their skills as money making ventures within the community were often reluctant to charge extended family members money. Kinship ties and bargaining over prices were considered incompatible and services were usually offered from motives of sentiment. The repayment of the service was usually left to the discretion of the beneficiary who would decide whether to pay a minimal monetary payment or keep a note of the service in his/her mind and afterwards attempt to even the score by performing a counter favour.

Those in community economic enterprises also stated that it made sound business sense to occasionally make no charge whatsoever for performing a service for a friend or neighbour. Here motivation stemmed from calculated self interest. Obligations could be built up and future business secured. Quotes from two households illustrate the usefulness of this ploy:

> A local bloke always fixes my car. In fact, a fortnight ago I brought it down to him cause it wouldn't go. It ended up, it was only a wire loose at the battery. Two seconds and it was alright. I said, 'what do I owe you mate' and he said, 'Naw, just let it go mate. I'll see you

another time.' How could you bypass anybody like that. If that had been a garage they'd have dug their arm in.

The man up the street fixes anything that breaks down in the house (electrical). Last week, I couldn't get the washing machine to go. He came up and fixed it. It was only a wee wire loose. All he wanted was a packet of fags. How could you go to anybody else when you've decent fellows like that living in the same street as you.

Even where money did change hands, the exchanges were characterised by the indeterminancy of the rates. Most producers of goods and services did not put a fixed value on their activities.

Redistribution

Polanyi (1957) argues that there are three major modes of exchange in human societies; reciprocity, market exchange and redistribution. Market exchange is the exchange of goods and services at prices based on supply and demand. Reciprocity involves exchanges which lie outside the market calculus. Redistribution involves the gathering of economic goods and services to some central place and then their redistribution throughout the populace. Like reciprocity, redistributive patterns are characterised by the absence of equivalency calculations and price mechanisms (Lowenthal 1981,p.101). Each of these three types of exchange co-exist in Newbury. Redistribution, in particular plays an important role in a community where resources are limited and scarce. The community obligations that come to the fore during the death of a street member can be viewed as one example of redistribution. Money is collected from each member of a particular street and then given to the family affected by a death. Tea and sandwiches and other foodstuffs are made by a number of neighbours and distributed to those who call to pay their respects to the dead.

Clothes, furniture and money circulate in a continuous pattern of redistribution. Unemployment and other related benefits are paid to different households on different days. Often this money is redistributed among a number of different households. This is to ensure that households will always have access to some ready cash. This form of redistribution takes place mainly among females and usually relates to Family Allowance Payments. Often up to four households would engage in this redistribution system. Households who participate argue that it is easier to manage on a small assured (almost) daily sum than on a weekly lump sum.

Furniture and clothes were rarely discarded when not needed. Rather they were continually redistributed among friends, neighbours and relatives in the estate. Thirty four households, 23 per cent of the sample, stated that they had received an item of furniture from a friend, neighbour or relative in the area. Money is rarely charged for any of these items. Instead it is left to the discretion of the recipient whether to acknowledge acceptance of the item or not. Sometimes furniture distribution is co-ordinated through the nuns who work in the community. If the members of a household, for example, are throwing away a bed or a settee, they will contact the nuns and inform them of their intention. The nuns will then circulate this information and usually come up with the address of a household gladly willing to take the item of furniture.

Clothes tend to be redistributed among people with whom the household has a prior relationship. Childrens' clothes are the most frequently redistributed clothing items. As children grow out of their existing clothes, the items are passed down to families with younger children. The nuns also engaged in this form of redistribution. They run a 'thrift' shop in the estate where second hand clothes can be purchased for a nominal sum which is then donated to charity.

Pahl (1984a) states that one reason unemployed men are unable to engage in do-it-yourself work is that they are less likely to have access to the appropriate tools. This lack of ownership is partly overcome by the redistributive networks that exist in Newbury estate. On several occasions while I was carrying out interviews, someone called to the household to borrow a tool. Drills, hammers and saws were all freely circulated among unemployed males. Often this redistribution was not solely to assist others to carry out household or communal repairs but to enable them to take on a few days casual employment, if the opportunity arose. Sometimes this circulation took place from employed to unemployed males. This enabled men with no tools or a limited range of tools to engage in work which they would otherwise have been unable to undertake.

Symmetrical and asymmetrical reciprocity

By examining the practice of gift giving in primitive societies, Mauss (1954) argued that we were likely to misunderstand its essential nature. In primitive societies, the gift expresses and cements a social relationship between giver and receiver. The good or service given is a symbol of that relationship and hence has value over and above its material worth. Moreover, the relationship established by the gift implies reciprocity. The exchange may be symmetrical so that an obligation is created to return in kind or the exchange may be asymmetrical in that the giver may be dominant and in giving the gift asserts his/her superior status so that the receiver is obligated to reciprocate with tribute or subordinate services. Sahlins (1974,p.283), in his study of primitive exchange, argues that the return of a gift is only indefinitely prescribed. The time and amount of reciprocation is left contingent on the future needs of the original donor and the abilities of the recipient, so the flow of goods may be unbalanced or even one way for a very long period. Malinowski (1922) on the other hand, argues that participants in reciprocal exchanges believe that everyone tends to profit from the exchanges in the long run, hence it is not considered important who benefits most at a particular moment. As he says:

> most if not all economic acts are found to belong to some chain of reciprocal gifts and counter gifts, which in the long run balance, benefiting both sides equally (1922,p.39).

When looking at reciprocal exchanges in Newbury, the reciprocal expectations attached to the transactions seem to be linked to the gender of the donor of the good or service. Information on reciprocal exchanges between households was gained through responses to specific questions and through general conversations with respondents. The first set of specific questions related to the extent to which households relied on other households. Hence each household was asked if they could rely on their neighbours and, where appropriate, to give an example of the form of assistance this reliance generated. A further aspect of this first set of specific questions related to the production of goods and services within and between households. The data revealed that a considerable amount of goods and services, such as painting and decorating and household and car maintenance, was carried out by the friends, neighbours and relatives of individual households. While occasionally money did change hands in payment for these services, nonetheless most of these exchanges were characterised by the indeterminancy of the rates. Most households were more concerned with the build up of favours rather than with receiving a monetary payment for their services.

The second set of questions focused on work done within households for other households. Questions here were deliberately general. Households were simply asked if they ever did odd jobs or favours for friends, neighbours or relatives within the estate. If the answer was affirmative, then the respondents were asked to specify the favour(s) and state which family member(s) carried out the task(s). Thirty eight households, 25 per cent of the sample, stated that they regularly did odd jobs for friends, thirty four households, 23 per cent of the sample, stated that they did odd jobs for neighbours and forty eight households, 32 per cent of the sample, stated that they regularly carried out odd jobs for relatives. In the majority of these households, the characteristics of the participants were remarkably similar. The instigator of the favours tended in most cases to be unemployed married males between the ages of 25-45, with dependent children. Out of the thirty eight households who carried out odd jobs for friends, twenty four fell into this category. Out of the thirty four households who carried out odd jobs for neighbours, twenty two fell into this category. While out of the forty eight households who did odd jobs for relatives, twenty eight fell into this category.

Two reasons can be put forward to account for the similarity between the donors of these favours. Firstly, unemployed males tend to have a great deal of excess time on their hands and since most of the odd jobs carried out, such as painting and decorating, are labour intensive, they could utilise their surplus time in this way. Secondly, young to middle aged unemployed married men with families were the group most likely to need and to be in a position to return favours. Hence a great deal of male reciprocal activity took place between males sharing similar age, marital and employment characteristics.

This latter point brings to the fore one of the principal differences between male and female motivations to engage in reciprocal economic favours. The responses to the second set of questions grossly underestimate the extent of female involvement in doing favours for others. Indeed, the bulk of the data relating to female mutual support mechanisms was derived from general conversations with the female respondents rather than as direct answers to specific questions. This in turn is related to how females view this kind of social economic activity.

Male motivation to engage in reciprocal economic exchanges stemmed largely from self interest. This is illustrated to a certain extent by the recipients of male reciprocal transactions. In the majority of cases, as mentioned earlier, favours were performed for those households who were most likely to be able to return such favours at some future imprecise date. Secondly, most of the males who carried out favours for friends, neighbours and relatives could immediately recall what specific favour they had performed and simultaneously what they expected in return. Hence reciprocal equivalence was expected. Thirdly, for some males, the exchange of favours was surrounded by ambiguity and often this imprecision was deliberately orchestrated. Some of the males interviewed stated that they were generally unwilling to accept payment for services performed, prefering the recipient to remain indebted to them. This is illustrated by the following quotes:

> Sometimes money is offered but I wouldn't take it. I'd rather be owed a favour. You never know when you might need it.

> You're missing the whole point. If you take money, that's it. The debt's repaid. But if you get nothing then that person is indebted to you for the rest of his life.

The longer the time span between the initial favour and its return, the more uncertainty arises over whether the favour has been fully repaid or not. This locks males into long standing relationships with each other characterised by the build up of favours and counter favours.

This contrasts starkly with female motivations attached to doing favours for others. When asked whether they ever did favours for others, most females replied 'No'. Yet during the ensuing conversations, many mentioned, casually, such activities as going shopping or cooking meals for old or sick people. Their offhand treatment of these activities indicated that no counter favour was expected or even considered. This is further illustrated by the recipients of female orientated favours. Often favours were directed towards those least able to reciprocate them such as the sick and the elderly. Lynch (1987,p.7) terms such activities 'love labour'. She states love labour is the antithesis of the profit and gain relationship in that it is expressly concerned with the realisation of affective bonds for their own sake. Finally, male favours tend to be geared towards producing something tangible. Hence the receiver is always reminded of the labour of the giver. Female favours often tended to be intangible centering on emotional support. As a result, these favours often remained invisible, perhaps not to the recipient, but to the donor of the activities.

Summary

Cohesive, low income populations are often trapped in space. The residents of Newbury have tried to manipulate their space through communal solidarity and mutually supportive patterns of reciprocity. Survival strategies are collective rather than individual or household endeavours. Mutual interdependence exists between most inhabitants of the estate and the chapter outlined the range of goods and services that were exchanged between kin and non kin. Often these goods and services were an extension of the home provisioning work outlined in the last chapter. These commodities and services tended to lie outside market calculations of the value of the exchanges. Rather they were characterised by the principle of reciprocity which mutually obliged the parties involved. Often these reciprocal arrangements were asymmetrical, although males tended to actively seek 'balanced' reciprocity. On the whole reciprocity promoted social integration by bringing the inhabitants of Newbury into binding relationships with other households. Reliance on these social networks filled in where the conventional economy fell short or failed.

This model of self help communities should not be understood as justifying the New Right's attack on the Welfare State. Such a view ignores the unequitable distribution of resources within specific localities. Obviously not all those unemployed are located in a supportive network of peers. For those living in other parts of Belfast, where unemployment is not so highly concentrated, the experience of unemployment may be a more severely constraining and isolating experience. Social contact within the community may be minimal. Even within Newbury, with its highly developed mutual aid networks, there were some households with limited or no access to these mutual support relationships. Participation in these social networks differed from one street to another. In some streets, residents were highly active in reciprocal exchanges, while in others, participation was low. Many exchanges were characterised by the unspecified expectance of equivalence of return. Hence many individuals were motivated by a desire to build up favours. This led some households to establish reciprocal relationships with those who could reciprocate, thus inducing the neglect of the needs of those unable to do so. This means that the old and the sick, those most likely to be unable to return such favours may be left outside the domain of these reciprocal networks.

6 Community economic enterprises

In Chapter Three, I discussed in detail the emergence of the Newbury Estate as a 'dreadful enclosure'. Newbury exists on the periphery of the declining economy in West Belfast. Access to formal goods and services has always been severely limited and scarcity has always been an integral part of daily existence. Scarcity is considered here, to be the result of political and institutional factors as well as competition from 'deserving' Catholics. These in turn generate informal socio-cultural mechanisms and economic transactions among households and individuals as a means of participating in the distribution of goods and services. A central emphasis of the chapter will be the exposition of how certain socio-cultural mechanisms and transactions are utilised by individuals and households in order to gain access to the scarce goods and services necessary for coping with the vicissitudes of daily living. Community economic enterprise is defined here as the utilisation of one's labour power to provide a commodity or service to others in the community for money. The starting point for much of the activity mentioned in the chapter is the community itself. Community economic enterprise is structured around a series of economic processes that both create a protected niche and maximise the importance of informal resources and relationships. The chapter will begin by presenting a descriptive account of the activities undertaken by individuals and households engaged in community economic enterprises. This will be followed by an exploration of the opportunities and motivations that influence people's choice to engage in this type of informal activity. Attitudes of the wider society to this form of informal enterprise will be assessed as will the link between community economic enterprises and the formal economy. Many of the goods and services mentioned here are mainly concerned with satisfying essential wants like food, clothing, shelter and to a lesser extent with assisting community inhabitants to meet the social obligations that have an economic value attached to them such as Christmas and birthdays.

'House shops' and caravans

The most obvious informal practice that exists on the estate is the 'house shops' which are detectable in almost every street in the estate. These 'house shops' supply inhabitants with food and other basic commodities. The reasons for the emergence of these 'house shops' were twofold. Firstly, the inefficent layout of the estate and secondly, the troubles which erupted in Northern Ireland in 1968-69.

The lack of foresight in the initial planning of the estate is clearly and visibly evident. As mentioned earlier, the few official shops that exist in the estate were erected six years after the estate had been built. These shops are located directly in the centre of the estate with houses forming a circle around the shops. A few other shops are located in the upper part of the outer circle of the estate. Depending on where one's house is located, these shops can be very inaccessible. The further one lives from the centre of the circle, (except for those who live at the very top of the estate where a few shops are located) the more difficult it is to shop for daily needs. Up until the outbreak of the troubles many residents experienced the almost daily inconvenience of having to travel a substantial distance if the household ran out of bread or milk or other basic necessities. Once the troubles broke out, it became a positive danger to have to travel such a distance for essential supplies, particularly at night.

In reviewing this tumultuous period of Northern Ireland's history, two events must be singled out for special mention. The first of these was the introduction of internment in August 1971 and the second was the Ulster Workers' Strike in May 1974. Both of these events had a profound effect upon the development of informal 'house shops' in Newbury and other republican estates. These two episodes led to the collapse of the infrastructure of formal services, leaving the people living in the affected areas as the only ones capable of satisfying essential needs. Internment had a particularly devasting effect on the Newbury estate. On the morning of August 9th 1971, fathers and sons were arrested in every street in the Newbury estate. In the ensuing riots which lasted for four days after internment, nineteen civilians were killed and seven of these came from Newbury. The casualities included one woman out looking for her children who were playing in the estate.

During the month of August 1971, essential services were withdrawn from West Belfast leaving areas like Newbury increasingly isolated. No buses operated in West Belfast during the entire month of August and there were no milk, post or bread deliveries for several days at a time. After internment, Newbury emerged as a 'no-go' area. Essential supplies were continually disrupted and the streets were 'blacked out' at night, making it even more perilous to travel any kind of distance, even within the estate.

The Ulster Workers' Strike of 1974 reinforced the commitment that was emerging among the residents of Newbury to set up and support informal retail ventures. During the Ulster Workers' Strike, the Ulster Workers' Council demonstrated its ability to control directly and indirectly, the supply and distribution of electricity, gas, public transport, petrol and foodstuffs. Shortages developed in many areas. Petrol was rationed and in short supply. The electricity service was being run at a reduced level, determined on a daily basis by the Ulster Workers' Council, so that each area was getting power on an on-off basis. Many shops either closed or opened for only a few hours each day and shortages in many foodstuffs emerged.

It was against this background that the first 'house shops' emerged. These 'shops' were located in the hallways or living rooms of several houses in the estate and stocked mainly essential commodities such as bread and milk. Although the establishment of such enterprises was against Housing Executive policy, these 'shops' went undetected for many years. While most of the present 'house shops' cannot trace their origin back to the outbreak of the troubles, nonetheless it is important to look historically at the political and social climate in which such initial ventures emerged. The informal retail outlets that were set up during this period paved the way for the establishment of later informal retail ventures. Moreover, the period provided a rationale and moral justification for both engaging in and supporting informal trading practices.

Today in Newbury, at least one 'house shop' exists in every street in the estate. The 'house shops' take one of two forms. Firstly, like the initial 'house shops', they are located in either the hallway or living room of individual houses or alternatively they are located in caravans, which are placed in the owners' front garden or driveway. The NIHE remain unaware about the exact location of these 'house shops', although one NIHE employee stated that they are aware that such 'house shops' operate in Newbury. If the 'shop' is located in a caravan this means that although illegal, it is highly visible. In order to curtail detection, if the 'shop' is in the form of a caravan, the owners usually only operate at night when it is hoped representatives from the Housing Executive or other agencies are unlikely to visit the estate. The 'shops' mainly stock essential household items. Milk, sugar, tea, bread, sweets, crisps and cigarettes are the most popular commodities. Often the smaller 'house shops' will stock these items only. The bigger or longer established 'house shops' will also stock a limited range of canned foodstuffs and other household items.

Access to interviewing householders who operated 'house shops' proved very difficult. The survey of the area had a 90 per cent response rate. Of the ten per cent who refused to co-operate with the survey, half had a caravan shop located at the front of their house. In all, I only managed to interview four households who used their premises as informal retail outlets. I was however, able to gain supplementary information by asking the respondents of the survey about their shopping habits.

Of the four 'house shops' the survey focused on, two are located in caravans at the front of the owners' dwellings, one is located in the owner's hallway and the remaining one is located in the household's living room. Three operate as retailers of food and other household provisions while the fourth is involved in renting out videos. Most of the people interviewed in the survey of the area either own or rent a video recorder yet there is no formal retail outlet in the estate that hires out videos. The nearest formal video rental outlet is situated about two miles from the estate and is not really accessible without a car. The 'house shop' in the estate which rents out videos therefore does quite a lot of business. The videos are stored in the living room of the household and customers go into the household's living room to make their choices. Videos are usually rented out on a daily basis and are returnable the next day. However, this ruling is not strictly enforced and there is no penalty if videos are not returned on time. Moreover, often customers rent out perhaps four or five videos at a time and are often allowed to keep these videos for a week or more. The charge is £1 per video which usually works out cheaper than formal establishments which tended to charge between £1.50 - £2.50 for new releases at the time of the survey. Moreover, established customers often get free videos. The general procedure is for the established customer to perhaps select seven or eight videos at a time and only get charged for five.

The male head of this particular household, Mr D, has been unemployed for the past twenty years. Mr D was a builder's labourer and he states he was put out of his job in 1969 because he was the only Catholic on the builder's payroll and the builder's premises were located in a Protestant area of the city. He has been unable to find any formal employment since, although he does undertake occasional informal wage labour particularly in the summer time. Mr D is aged 46 and is married with five children. His wife does not have a paid job outside the household and three of his children are still at school. Of the remaining two children, one is unemployed and the other is on a Youth Training scheme. Four years ago, Mr D's wife put a claim in to the Department of the Environment for falling and breaking her leg on a broken pavement outside her home. She won her case and was given £2000 in compensation. Part of this money was used to set up the family video rental business. Most of the videos on hire by the household are pirate copies. Mr D has a contact who rents out videos from formal establishments, makes a copy (or usually several copies) and returns the original video the next day. The pirate copy is then sold to Mr D at less than a third of the normal retail price and Mr D then hires out these pirate copies. Mr D states that he is not the only pirate retail outlet, his contact supplies. Neither the Housing Executive or the Department of Health and Social Services are aware of Mr D's informal trading activities.

Mrs E is a widow. Her husband died two years ago and she has continued to operate the 'house shop' that was in existence before her husband's death. The 'shop' is located in the hallway of her home and sells a very limited range of goods, mostly sweets and cigarettes. Mrs E has three sons aged 10, 21 and 25 respectively. None of her children are formally employed and all still live at home. Mrs E also works formally as a part time cleaner in a local school. While she is working, one of her sons looks after the 'shop'. When she is not working, serving customers is shared out between Mrs E and her sons.

The two remaining informal retail outlets are located in caravans parked in the front gardens of two houses in the estate. One is owned by Alfie, a twenty five year old chef. Alfie has been in full time formal employment since he was sixteen. Last year he utilised the savings he had amassed from his employment to buy a 'caravan shop' that was for sale in the estate. The owner of the 'caravan shop' was selling his business because his activities had been detected by the Housing Executive and he became frightened to continue trading. Alfie is not unduly concerned with detection. He states that if he is found out trading from his parents premises, he will simply move his operations to the garden of another relative on the estate. Alfie is not married and still lives at home with his parents. His father has not worked in the last fifteen years and claims Invalidity Benefit. He takes primary responsibility for the running of the 'shop' while Alfie is at work. Alfie pays his father a nominal sum for his help. His father is not really interested in the potential financial value of his labour. He is very keen for his son to make a profit from his venture and finds working in the caravan very enjoyable.

The remaining caravan is owned by Mr F, a thirty three year old married man with four children. Mr F was formally employed as a bus driver but was made redundant in cutbacks seven years ago. Part of Mr F's redundancy money was used to set himself up in business. Mr F's wife does not work outside the household and helps run the 'shop'. The two eldest children are aged twelve and ten and they also look after the 'shop' for set periods. Moreover the twelve year old female is responsible for putting her younger brother and sister to bed each night, relieving her mother of her household responsibilities and leaving her free to concentrate on serving in the shop.

'House shops' are largely family affairs. Each individual in the family (with the exception of the very young) generally spend some time each day serving customers. Hours are long and the economic return rarely matches the labour output. The caravans usually open from around 6.00pm until the early hours of the morning. Established customers can go directly to the owner's house if the caravan is locked and generally the owner or a member of the family will unlock the caravan and serve the customer. More generally though, some member of the household will remain in the caravan in the evenings and await customers.

The owners of 'shops' located within households work longer hours. The busiest hours of business tend to be from 8.00am to 9.00am when the children of the estate are going to school, lunch time when most of the school age children come home for lunch and 2.30pm to 3.30pm when the children are coming home from school. The peak trading periods thus tend to be structured around the school day. Children often provide the best customers and occasionally very limited informal retail outlets have been able to expand solely on the profit made from selling sweets, crisps and soft drinks to children. The evenings also tend to be quite busy and the 'house shops' will continue to serve customers until the inhabitants of the household go to bed. Hence the 'house shops' are often open from around 8.00am in the morning until the early hours of the following morning. Access to the 'house shop' is gained by ringing the door bell of the dwelling. This means that rather than waiting for customers to arrive, the householders can get on with their daily chores. Slack periods can be utilised to clean the house, make meals or simply have a rest.

Most of the 'house shops' operate some form of credit system. Most keep a 'book' listing customers' names and addresses and daily purchases are entered into this book rather than being paid for on a daily basis. The account is settled on 'giro day', when customers receive their welfare benefit entitlements. If the account is not settled then, no further purchases on credit can be made. These credit facilities are not extended to everyone. They are generally reserved for those with whom the household has a particularly close relationship or for long established customers. Sometimes households facing particularly harsh financial periods will have credit extended to them. These facilities can be very beneficial for families who find it almost impossible to make benefits last the full week but they set in motion a process whereby often up to as much as half of a family's welfare benefit entitlement is owed even before it is received.

Community bakers

The respondents in two other households bake and sell their produce for an extra source of income. Their orders originate from the community and the only time they bake for outsiders is when they bake for the friends and relations of inhabitants of the estate. Their work mainly concerns the baking of celebratory cakes including wedding, birthday and anniversary cakes. One baker is female and the other is male. The female states that she comes from a long line of family bakers. Her husband is in full time formal employment and she herself was in full time formal employment up until last year when she had to give up her job due to ill health. She does not regard her baking as a chore but rather as a pleasurable activity that occasionally generates extra income. She designs each wedding and birthday cake individually and is very proud of her work. While I was interviewing this respondent, she showed me several pictures of wedding cakes she had designed in the past. Her orders come from her friends, neighbours and relatives and at no time does she actively seek orders. Thus the amount of time she devotes to baking has not increased significantly as a result of her unemployment. She is also very pessimistic as to the possibility of this activity generating enough income to be considered as an alternative to formal employment. Rather, she maintains that she is carrying on a family tradition and the income gained from such work rarely compensates her for the amount of time and effort she puts into her baking.

The other male baker was employed for over twenty years in a bakery firm located in West Belfast. The firm closed down in the early 1980's and Mr G was made redundant. He has not been able to find any formal employment since. Mr G is married with five children, two of whom still live at home. He also engages in baking from his house to supplement the money he gets on welfare benefits. Like the female baker mentioned above, Mr G mainly engages in the baking of celebratory cakes. His orders are also generated from the Newbury community. Mr G also occasionally makes 'special holiday' cakes, for example Halloween cakes and St Patrick's Day cakes. Mr G sells these cakes from door to door within the estate. He also advertises in local shops stating that he bakes wedding and other celebratory cakes. Mr G is continuously on the lookout for contacts he can supply cakes to. He states that he could never make enough out of his skill to become financially self sufficient. He is totally dependent on his benefit entitlements and can occasionally bolster his weekly amount by baking to fulfil orders. He states that wedding cakes are the most profitable and says that if he gets a few orders for wedding cakes, he can do quite well. However, for the most part Mr G engages in baking to occupy his time and provide him with a few extra pounds rather than as a viable money generating activity.

Catalogue sales agents

The activities mentioned so far have been concerned with production for immediate consumption. More durable products such as clothes, toys and household goods can be ordered by catalogue from a number of women who operate sales catalogues within the estate. While most households in the estate have been bombarded with literature over the last few years from catalogue sales companies inviting them to become catalogue customers, most householders cannot be bothered with the weekly trips to the post office to make the payments that such a mode of shopping would entail. Thus while many households in the estate make regular purchases from catalogues, most of them will rely on a neighbour, friend or relative to undertake the administrative work such shopping necessitates. Of the 150 households surveyed in the estate, a member within thirteen of these households was responsible for running a catalogue for friends, neighbours and relatives.

Operating a sales catalogue is predominately a female activity. In all thirteen households in which a member engaged in this activity, the participant was female. Nine of the group were married, two stated that they were separated for welfare purposes, one was a widow and another was a single parent. All had families ranging from between one to ten children. This type of informal employment was blended in with other types of formal and informal economic activity within certain households. The widow, for example, also operates a house shop from her dwelling. Two of the group also worked as informal contract cleaners. Eight also engaged in knitting and dressmaking for others for money. One respondent looked after a neighbour's baby in her home, although her financial return for this was only £10 per week. A further two respondents were formally employed as part time cleaners. Both spouses of these respondents claim Invalidity Benefit and their wives' earnings do not affect their benefit.

Selecting and purchasing items from sales catalogues is also mainly a female activity. This form of shopping is largely negotiated among female neighbours, among female friends and among female kin. Shopping in this way is also a predominately social affair. Potential purchases are discussed between customers and the operator of the catalogue. Advice from other customers and the vendor is sought as to the suitability of a particular item. These negotiations take place in a congenial setting, in the home of either the purchaser or vendor and since this trading takes place among friends, neighbours and relatives, then other customers are often present, especially when initial orders are being placed. This is also particularly prevalent when reduced purchases are on offer. 'Special Offers' are displayed in a special booklet which is sent out to the catalogue operator every few months. Often the catalogue operator will gather customers in her house for tea and the booklet detailing reduced items will be passed around and discussed. The operator has an economic incentive for selling in this way as often in this relaxed atmosphere many orders are generated. Once a purchase is decided upon, a small down payment is required and the customer agrees to repay the balance over a set number of weeks.

Indeed the availability of a whole range of goods on credit is the primary incentive for purchasing in this manner for most of the residents of the estate. Purchasing (often essential items) on credit has become very important due to the abolition of Single Payments Grants in April 1988. Prior to April 1988, households experiencing financial hardship and claiming welfare benefits could apply to the Department of Health and Social Services (DHSS) for a 'single payment' towards the purchase of some essential item. Single Payments were allocated towards the purchase of clothes and shoes, beds and bedding and other essential household and electrical equipment. Since April 1988, families who experience financial hardship and are unable to purchase 'essential' items can apply to the DHSS for a crisis loan. Local DHSS offices are allocated a specific amount of money to be utilised as crisis loans. Hence allocation is often not based on need but on a 'first come, first served' basis. Moreover, as the name implies the amounts are loans not grants and these loans have to be repaid. This in turn leads the DHSS to allocate loans to those most able to repay them. As a result, often the most needy do not qualify for a loan. Repayments are often quite high and are deducted from benefits at source leaving needy families in an even more precarious position.

It is against this background that demand for catalogue purchases within the estate has increased. Several householders have informed me that catalogue repayments are often less than DHSS repayments as catalogue items can be repaid over a longer period. In the survey of the area, all 150 households were asked if they made regular purchases from catalogues operated by residents of the estate. The results indicate the importance of this form of shopping. Eighty households, 53 per cent of the sample, stated that they regularly purchased items from a catalogue. Of these eighty households, 46 per cent bought toys from a catalogue, 58 per cent purchased clothes while a massive 82 per cent bought household goods. The abolition of single payments for household items has had the severest adverse affect on the purchasing patterns of needy families. The most popular catalogue requests are for beds, washing machines and other electrical equipment.

The financial incentive for operating a catalogue is quite low. Agents are given either a 10 per cent commission in cash for every £1 spent by customers or 12½ per cent if they are going to utilise their commission to order something from the catalogue. Most of the women I interviewed alternated between accepting commission in cash or utilising it to make further purchases. Sometimes the commission is saved up and used towards the payment of quarterly bills such as electricity and heating. Four of the women stated that they regularly used their commission in this way. These women stated that this was often the only way they could manage to pay such bills. As one woman put it:

> Listen love, you've just no idea what it's like to have bills lying in your hall and no means to pay them. You spend your whole time wondering how long you can put them off. At least by doing this, I know one bill (electricity) is taken care off.

Others used their commission to buy items from the catalogues. Usually household items were purchased. One woman was saving up for a bedroom combination unit when I interviewed her. Another showed me the washing machine she had 'got for nothing' from her commission. Often when the commission was utilised to purchase items from the catalogue, the adjective 'free' was used, when talking about whatever was purchased. Hence I was told about the 'free' bed, the 'free' vacuum cleaner and so on that had been purchased solely from commission, with little or no mention of the amount of work and effort that had been put into generating such commission. Yet being an agent for a catalogue firm, especially if one has a reasonable amount of customers can be a very time consuming activity. Customers have to be wooed and enticed into making initial purchases. Sometimes goods are found to be unsuitable and these have to be parcelled and returned to the catalogue company by the agent. Once purchases are made, the agent has to collect weekly payments for the goods ordered and send this amount to the catalogue company. Calling for weekly payments often involves having a chat and a cup of tea with one's customers and can involve a considerable amount of time. On the other hand, the prior relationship that often exists between vendor and customer dilutes the vendor's awareness that what she is doing is working.

The relationships of the residents of Newbury are embedded in close knit overlapping social networks of relatives, neighbours and kin. Their social life is centred on the extended family and the wider community. Hence they are subject to considerable local social control. This control is important when encouraging families living in financial hardship to undertake a commitment to repay purchases on credit, often extended over a considerable period of time. There is always the risk that fellow residents will purchase several items and then fail to make repayments. In the Newbury estate however, because social and economic lives are so entwined, not to repay one's catalogue credit can adversely affect one's social standing in the community. If an individual does not repay a credit loan for some item purchased through a catalogue, then the future orders of her agent may be put in jeopardy. Her agent and fellow customers may be unable to make future purchases in this way. Moreover, the debtor will probably meet her agent and fellow customers on a daily basis in the local shops, at Mass, at bingo and so on. These circumstances are not very conducive for defaulting on loans. Hence the debtor, if having a difficult week may not pay the insurance man or coal man who come from other estates rather than threaten her relationship with her catalogue agent and fellow customers. This exploitation of social relationships was the reason one woman gave for not considering operating a catalogue as a way of making extra money. As she describes it:

> They (catalogue agents) buy friendship you see. You see them in and out of people's houses getting cups of tea, going to bingo with them (their customers), going for a drink and all they are doing is softening them up to buy from the catalogue. I couldn't be annoyed with that. They practically live with their customers, so they can shame them into making their weekly payments. I'm not like that so I couldn't be bothered running a catalogue. I'd probably be the mug that would be took on.

The commercialization of women's handicrafts

The making and knitting of clothes and other household furnishings provides a source of extra income for several women in the area. Commercial knitting has a long history in Newbury. One of the first talents the Newbury Enterprises (established in 1970) tried to tap was the hand knitting activities that took place in about twenty women's homes in the district. Some of the reasons for the failure of Newbury Enterprises are discussed in Chapter Three. Today, no such organised commercial knitting enterprise is in operation although home knitting and dressmaking still plays an integral part in several women's attempts to generate extra income. Knitting and dressmaking are activities undertaken by many women in the area, although as the previous chapter illustrated, for most of them, such activities form the backbone for reciprocal exchanges among female friends, neighbours and relatives. Here I intend to focus on women who engage in such activities for money.

The following descriptions are based on semi structured interviews with respondents in fifteen households. Thirteen households were interviewed during the survey of 150 households in the area while the other two were interviewed prior to the survey being carried out. In seven of these households, knitting and dressmaking was carried out for money by more than one family member. In six of these households, these activities were shared between mother and daughter. These six households were all extended families with the mothers continuing to live with their married daughters. In each of these households, the mothers had passed their dressmaking and knitting skills on to their daughters. In the seventh household the female respondent was helped by her husband. Thus in all, twenty two respondents were interviewed. The women's ages range from twenty eight to seventy one while the male was aged forty eight. Old age does not appear to be a handicap in this occupation. Indeed, six of the sample were aged over sixty two and their work was in demand because of their years of knitting and dressmaking experience. Thirteen of the sample were married, although one had informed the authorities that she was separated for welfare purposes. Of the remaining nine, four were widows, three were separated and the remaining two were single parents.

A variety of other informal practices were also located in these households. Eight of the sample were also catalogue agents, one worked as a contract cleaner while two had spouses who were also informal wage labourers. In seven households, respondents knitted for money, in two households respondents engaged in dressmaking for money while in the remaining six households, the respondents engaged in both knitting and dressmaking for money. All the knitting and dressmaking is community based and all but two of the respondents who engage in these activities derive their orders from community members or the friends and relatives of community members.

Community knitting

The respondents who engage in knitting get three main types of orders. The first is for knitted or crocheted baby clothes, the second is for hand or machine knitted school jumpers and the third is for Aran cardigans and jumpers. Particular households tend to specialise in one or other of these areas although some households specialise in all three.

Two respondents concentrate on crocheting baby clothes and blankets. They supply local shops with samples of their work and shops act as advertising agents for their work. Many orders are generated in this way and shop owners get a small commission for every order received. Another two respondents concentrate on machine knitting school jumpers and cardigans. Primary school children in the area have to wear a school uniform and hence the busiest time of the year for these two women is August and September when residents of the estate are buying new school uniforms for their children. Both these respondents start knitting quite early on to prepare for the invasion of orders they usually receive prior to September.

While most women in the area can knit, not many specialize in Aran knitting. Hence Aran knitters are in constant demand. Arans are ordered for special birthday or Christmas presents. Hand knitted Irish Arans are also a very popular present for the children of the area to take to families in America they visit on holiday. Community groups in the area participate in a scheme to send children from deprived areas to America for a holiday. The scheme is operated through the primary schools and most ten to eleven year old children get the opportunity to go to an American family for a holiday of up to six weeks. The scheme is subsidized by charitable organizations both here and in America and the cost for a child is usually about £50-£70. The children are sent once only but often the family will invite the same child over the following year and pay the fare.

I have spoken to teenagers who have been going to America annually for the past seven years. The children rarely go empty handed but usually travel ladened with gifts for their American families. This is where the women from the district who knit Arans come in. Most of these women say that many of their orders are generated as a result of these American holidays. Every year children from the area bring over Aran cardigans and jumpers knitted informally by women in the estate.

The amount of capital or equipment needed to engage in commercial knitting varies. Some of the respondents' activities were very small scale, involving hand knitting only for neighbours and relatives. Aran knitting is entirely done by hand and no equipment other than knitting needles is necessary. The amount of capital needed to engage in Aran knitting depends on how frequently one engages in this activity and the amount of customers one has built up. Often customers supply their own wool and only purchase the knitters' labour. Aran knitting is very time consuming and the amount charged to a customer rarely compensates the knitter for the amount of time she will engage in this activity. The women who engage in this work rarely regard this as a problem or a disincentive against continuing with this activity. Most women I spoke too, mentioned the pleasure they derived from knitting Arans. As one woman told me:

> I don't make that much from knitting the Arans. It takes an awful lot of hours to knit a jumper or something and I don't think I would make that much profit. But I don't work it out on an hourly basis. I don't look at my knitting in that way. I can work at home, decide when I start and when I finish and as long as I bring in a few bob I'm happy.

Other women knit on knitting machines and hence have to find the capital to purchase such machines. If one has plenty of work in the pipe line then this does not pose too much of a problem. Often initial machines are second hand and the women only progress to new machines once they know their business has taken off. The Catholic nuns in the district have been organizing knitting classes in the parish centre for many years. Several knitting machines are located in the parish centre for the use of the community. Residents are trained in the use of these machines and can continue to use the machines to fulfil private orders although if they are successful in learning this skill, the nuns endeavour to set them up with their own machines at home. The nuns keep in contact with a retailer who specializes in selling second hand knitting machines and they ensure that the women get a 'good deal'. Sometimes if the women are experiencing severe financial hardship, the 'sisters' will lend the women some of the money to buy their first machine. This money can be paid back to the nuns once orders start coming in. The nuns also buy wool in bulk and then sell the wool in small amounts to anyone in the district wishing to purchase this commodity. The nuns make no profit from this arrangement, thus the women have access to cheaper wool.

Case study - Mrs Armstrong

While most of the women who engage in this activity are generally small scale supplying community needs, one woman, Mrs Armstrong, has built up quite a successful business enterprise based on home knitting. Mrs Armstrong's activities are worth repeating at length. Mrs Armstrong worked as a stitcher up until twenty years ago. Since that time she has attended several local classes in knitting and dressmaking and has a long history of knitting Arans and other garments for friends and neighbours. Mrs Armstrong's husband has no formal trade and he was formally employed as a labourer on a building site up until ten years ago. He has been unemployed ever since. They have two children, a boy and a girl aged twelve and sixteen respectively. Mrs Armstrong's work is highly regarded in the community and she has always been inundated with orders from local residents. Over the past number of years, demand for Mrs Armstrong's work has spread. Friends of friends and an increasingly wider network of neighbours and relatives of neighbours began to continually put orders in for jumpers and cardigans and other items. Mrs Armstrong's products were reasonably cheap and of a very high quality. Moreover, the more Mrs Armstrong engaged in her work, the more ambitious she became, designing her own patterns of exclusive knitwear. Gradually Mrs Armstrong was contacted by a number of formal business enterprises impressed by the standard of the garments worn by their employees (which they had been informed had been made by Mrs Armstrong). Through these initial contacts, orders from formal enterprises began to flood in.

At this stage, Mrs Armstrong decided to expand her business. Her husband had kept pigeons for many years in a shed at the bottom of her garden. Once he became unemployed, he found the pigeons much too expensive a hobby to keep so he sold them. For several years, the pigeon shed lay derelict. Four years ago, Mrs Armstrong decided to convert the pigeon shed into a work shop. She had only one second hand knitting machine. For a few years prior to her decision to convert the pigeon shed, she had been saving up most of the profit she had made from her knitting. The conversion was carried out by Mr Armstrong and some of his friends and relations from the estate. They replaced the roof and windows, put beauty board up on the walls and made benches for knitting machines. The shed was then carpeted and two storage heaters were placed on the walls to heat the area. There are now three second hand machines in the pigeon shed. Space is limited but the shed is quite comfortable. Mrs Armstrong employs one woman from the estate and pays her £2 per hour. The woman is employed informally and works as the orders come in. If there is a slack period, the woman does not work and Mrs Armstrong and her husband manage the orders between them.

Mr Armstrong plays his part in the knitting business. Once the wool is placed on the machine, a to and fro motion will automatically knit another line. Mrs Armstrong places the wool for particular patterns initially on the machine and Mr Armstrong moves the row counter backwards and forwards repeatedly between the same places, knitting a line each time. Anytime there is a change in the pattern, Mrs Armstrong makes the changes and Mr Armstrong then continues with his to and fro movements. Mrs Armstrong also employs her two sisters on a casual basis to knit Arans and mohair which cannot be done on a knitting machine. She pays her sisters the amount she would get for doing the garments herself. She is not interested in making a profit from this hand knitting but rather is mainly interested in maintaining reliability in fulfilling orders. Thus she is grateful to her sisters for helping her out when orders for hand knit garments come in.

Mrs Armstrong's daughter takes a lot of responsibility for housework. This allows her a flexible work schedule. She finds it easier to work in the evenings and will often work until the early hours of the morning. In these circumstances, her daughter will often prepare the evening meal, wash and tidy up and get her younger brother ready for bed. Hence work is an integral part of family life and each family member has his/her part to play in the smooth running of the business.

Community dressmaking

The women who engage in dressmaking fall into two main categories, those who mainly specialize in making wedding and First Communion dresses and christening robes, and those who make a wider variety of less specialized garments and household items such as curtains and cushion covers. The latter also usually offer a repair and alteration service. The six households who engage in both knitting and dressmaking fall into this latter category. Five of these households gain their orders solely from within Newbury estate. As well as commercial knitting, they offer a wide range of dressmaking services ranging from personal garments to household items. Curtains and matching cushion covers are a particular favourite and generate many orders in the run up to Christmas. These household items can cost as little as one sixth of the price for similar items in formal establishments. Occasionally a resident from the estate might see a particularly attractive display of curtain, pelmet and cushion coverings in one of the exclusive house furnishing shops in Belfast and mention this to the dressmaker. The dressmaker will then, on her next visit into the town call into the shop and make a mental note of the pattern display. She will then attempt (often successfully) to replicate the pattern. In this way, popular marketable commodities in the formal economy end up being replicated informally.

Clothes are generally ordered by females and for children. The males of the estate tend to clothe themselves from formal establishments. One old age pensioner though, was making designer waistcoats at the time of the interview which had proved popular among male and female teenagers in the estate. Usually though, the dressmaking is aimed at a female and children's market.

The sixth respondent in this category, Mrs Whyte supplies a wider market than the estate. She makes good quality tracksuits. Her sister works in a major department store in the city centre of Belfast and brought one of the tracksuits in to show her friends at work who in turn made several orders for tracksuits. The supervisor of Mrs Whyte's sister showed the tracksuits to the manager who expressed interest in buying the tracksuits to sell in the store. Mrs Whyte now supplies this major store with children's tracksuits. She charges £5.50 per tracksuit regardless of size while the shop sells the tracksuits from £9.99 to £13.99 depending on the size.

The two households who deal exclusively in dressmaking engage solely in making wedding and First Communion dresses and christening robes. In both of these households, both mother and daughter engage in dressmaking. The female children from the estate make their First Communion around the age of seven. For the occasion, the children dress up in long white dresses and veils, like mini wedding outfits. This traditional Catholic celebration provides some of the women from the estate with opportunities for engaging in informal work. First Communion attire can prove very expensive and the residents of the estate can offset this high cost by purchasing the necessary items informally.

Christening robes and, less frequently, wedding dresses also generate extra income and again the high cost of these commodities in formal enterprises paves the way for individuals to supply these products informally, so that people with low incomes can afford these items.

Community hairdressing

The members of forty households get their hair cut by either a friend, neighbour or relative from within the estate. In twenty nine cases, hair was cut by a neighbour, in seven cases by a relative and in four cases by a friend. Each of these households stated that the prices they were charged were much lower than those charged by formal establishments. Five hairdressers who work informally within the estate were interviewed. None of these hairdressers have any formal employment although all of them were at some stage formally trained as hairdressers and all of them had spent some time working in formal hairdressing salons. Four of the sample are female and one is male, all are married and all have dependent children. The females are married to spouses who receive some form of welfare benefit while the male has never been formally employed since he completed his apprenticeship ten years ago. All five hairdressers either cut hair from their own homes or in the homes of their customers. This service proves invaluable to women with young children as the family's hair can be cut from the mother's own home. If washing of hair is required then this is done in the customer's sink or in the sink of the hairdresser's home. Thus limited facilities are required.

Moreover, home hairdressing is primarily a social activity. Often some prior relationship exists between the hairdresser and his/her customers. Hairdressers supply tea and biscuits to customers or receive these if the cutting of hair is carried out in the customer's house. The activity provides a venue for catching up on local gossip. The male hairdresser is not as successful as the females and blames this social aspect for his failure. The male is related to twelve other households in the estate and gets his business mainly from his relatives. Attempts to expand his service to other residents have proved unfruitful and he blames this mainly on his sex. As he says:

> It's easier for a woman to get that kind of work. A man can do alright in a hairdresser's shop or a barber's but not going around houses. Female hairdressers make tea and have a chat. It's all part of the expected service. A hairdresser is someone you can tell your problems to, have a heart to heart with. People expect this. But if you're a man they just shut up and let you get on with the job.

Community household maintenance

As the two previous chapters indicated, household maintenance tends to be the primary location for household self sufficiency and community reciprocity rather than being a venue for community self employment. For example only eight households paid someone to paint and decorate their dwelling. Rather such work was carried out by internal family members or through reciprocal community relationships. Electrical items were largely repaired and maintained by formal establishments. This was mainly due to the fact that in eighty four households, 56 per cent of the sample, household electrical items such as televisions and videos were either rented or bought along with a guarantee to safeguard against the expense of paying for the repair of any faults that might develop. Hence the maintenance of these items was the responsibility of the establishment in which these items were purchased or rented. The only significant aspect of household maintenance that generated a mechanism for the establishment of a community economic enterprise was the cleaning of outside windows.

Ninety five households, 63 per cent of the sample, paid someone from the estate to clean the outside of their windows. The estate seems to be divided into five or six specific areas for the cleaning of windows. Each area is the responsibility of particular cleaners either working individually or as part of a team. If one of the existing window cleaners gives up his work, then his patch is passed on to one of his friends, neighbours or relatives. Two informal window cleaners were interviewed. Both work in different patches. Each presented me with strikingly similar accounts of how window cleaning operates in the estate. Neither knew any individual formally self employed as a window cleaner. Rather, those who engage in this activity do so to bolster welfare benefits. A standard charge of 80p per house is made and this price is uniform throughout the estate. While the cleaning of inside windows is predominately a female duty, the outside was largely a male occupation. The two window cleaners (both male) knew of no female who worked or ever worked as a window cleaner. One observed:

> Don't be so stupid. How could you expect a woman to go up to the top of a ladder?

The two respondents who worked as window cleaners are aged twenty seven and forty two respectively. Neither have formal training and both are currently unemployed. Sam, the twenty seven year old, has been unemployed for five years and Joe, the forty two year old, has been unemployed for seven years. The twenty seven year old, is married with one child while the forty two year old is single and lives on his own in Newbury estate. Each works as part of a team and neither has his own equipment. Sam has been working as a window cleaner for the past four years. His mate has all the necessary equipment. The respondent works with his mate every day, Monday to Friday and gets paid £10 per day. Sam states that his mate started off like himself, working along with someone else and gradually saved up the money to buy his own ladders and accessories, so that he could start out on his own if the opportunity arose. Sam hopes eventually to do the same thing.

Joe works approximately eighteen hours per week and is paid £30 per week. Although he has been doing window cleaning for the past two years, he still views this work as temporary and has no desire to ever own his own equipment. Joe's main desire is to find formal employment and he does not consider window cleaning as a viable formal occupation.

Community car maintenance

Only twenty five out of the 150 households interviewed owned a car and of these car owners, 32 per cent paid someone from the estate to maintain and repair their car when necessary. Two respondents fix cars informally within the estate. Both are married with families. Dan is aged forty and is unemployed while Fred is aged fifty one and is on Invalidity Benefit. Dan is a self taught mechanic and deals only with elementary repairs. If he can't fix the cars, he sends the customers down to his brother who operates an informal garage in the lower end of the estate. I tried to interview Dan's brother but he refused. Dan's brother works quite openly from his house and the adjacent houses to his dwelling are surrounded by cars. According to Dan, his brother is also claiming Unemployment Benefit but is not concerned with detection. He states that even if someone did call to investigate his brother's activities, they could never prove that money changed hands. The brother would just state that he is doing the work as a hobby or as a favour for a few friends.

Fred, the other car mechanic interviewed has been caught fixing cars informally but blames his previous employer rather than his neighbours for informing on his activities. He had been formally employed for over twenty years in a garage in West Belfast. He had to give up his job ten years ago because he contacted dermatitis. When he gave up his job, Fred put in a claim for compensation. However, once he was unemployed, Fred began to work occasionally fixing black taxis in Newbury estate. His house is located beside the main road and as there is limited room at the front of his house, Fred fixes the black taxis on the main road.

Any time he did repair work, he bought the spare parts from his old workplace and enjoyed having the opportunity to call in and see his boss and previous workmates. Just prior to Fred's compensation case being heard, he was contacted by his solicitor to inform him that the garage owner's solictor was contesting the claim. The garage owner's solicitor stated that he had pictures of Fred fixing black taxis on the main road and receipts for a considerable number of items purchased by Fred from his local garage over the previous number of months. The solicitor stated that if the compensation case was dropped, the garage owner would consider not passing the information on to the DHSS. Fred became very frightened and withdrew his claim. Because of his dermatitis, he is unable to find formal employment. Sometimes he gets such bad attacks of dermatitis that even informal work is out of the question. He still engages in occasional informal work though, and realises that by doing so, he is often aggravating his condition. On the other hand, the forced inactivity and financial stringency imposed on Fred by his illness leaves him with little alternative.

Community scavenging

A scavenger is a person who searches among or collects things unwanted by others. The purpose in scavenging is to personally use, recycle, trade or resell discarded waste materials. The activity is usually associated with developing countries where it can play an integral role in the survival mechanisms of many impoverished inhabitants. In western industrial societies, the activity is often associated with homeless down and outs or with those concerned with our dwindling natural resources who engage in such activities for the purpose of recycling waste products. Media attention has recently focused on our wasteful discarding of aluminium drinks' cans. Jonathon Porritt, Director of Friends of the Earth (Sunday Times February 19th, 1989) states that among all the drinks' cans discarded in the UK every year, there are 40,000 tonnes of aluminium, worth as much as £13 million. Porritt emphasises that cans mean cash and suggests that if the UK introduced a scheme similar to the one operating in Sweden whereby customers get about one pence for every two cans they return, then we could avert this enormous waste and make money at the same time. In Sweden, about 95% of aluminium drinks' cans are recycled while in the UK, the figure is less than one per cent. Some of the residents in the Newbury estate have long recognised the potential financial value attached to collecting aluminium drinks' cans for recycling. These people are not employable in the formal sector and as a result have devised an informal strategy for survival appropriate for their environment.

There are at least four individuals in the Newbury estate who engage in the regular collecting of aluminium drinks cans. Supplementary information was gathered about this activity by talking to several residents within the estate and from the owner of a scrap metal yard situated about half a mile from Newbury. The owner of the yard pays one pence for every can the residents of the estate bring in. The trash collectors start work very early in the mornings usually around 6.00am before anyone else is up out of bed. Because of these early hours, the trash pickers are often invisible workers. For some trash pickers, the invisibility of this activity reduces the embarassment they may otherwise feel at being reduced to such levels to supplement inadequate benefits. The trash collectors go around Newbury and surrounding estates picking up the aluminium larger cans that have been discarded from the night before. The characteristics of Newbury and the surrounding areas make it optimal for this activity. The high population density together with the drinking habits of younger community members results in a concentration of cans in one area.

The cans are collected by hand or by using some kind of home made stick, often with a metal hook attached to the end. The only other equipment needed are rubbish bags and these are continually re-used. The cans are flattened before being placed in the rubbish bags. This means that one large bag can hold quite a lot of cans. Also because the cans are very lightweight several can be carried without it being a problem. Sometimes several bags are collected at once and placed in a make shift cart (often made from an old pram) and then wheeled to the local scrap merchant. It takes one hundred cans to make £1 profit. Hence most trash pickers' weekly return only amounts to about £10. This extra income is however, regarded by these scavengers as a necessary supplement to their benefit entitlements. The practice illustrates how some people left on the margins of the formal sector create their own strategy for survival. The scavengers of Newbury have devised an informal strategy for survival because they are denied the opportunity to function in the formal sector.

Community photography

The forty year old butcher mentioned in the last chapter who works as an informal wage labourer engages in photography in his spare time. He has always had a keen interest in photography and has built up his equipment over the years. His informal employment as a butcher is often sporadic and he supplements it by working informally as a photographer. He takes First Communion and wedding photographs and also takes individual and family portraits. Demand for these photographs comes from friends, relatives and neighbours in the Newbury estate. While this work is too irregular to depend on, nonetheless it supplements his other casual informal employment.

Jack also works informally as a photographer in another part of the estate. Jack is aged 39 and has been on Invalidity Benefit for the past two years. Like the butcher, Jack takes a variety of family and celebration photographs for friends, relatives and neighbours. He displays the photographs he has taken in an album, which he shows to potential customers. He states that he has perfected his skill in this area by reading books on the subject. While this activity does occasionally generate some additional income, he admits that his photography could never match the income formal employment would provide.

As he says:

> Like I mean to say, I'm doing it for people in the same boat as myself. They haven't much to spare, so how could you ask them for much money. You could hardly dig your arm in there.

Community florist

Jack's wife Mary suffers from arthritis. A few years ago, as a therapy, Mary began to make displays of dried flowers. The activity was also beneficial in that the flower displays could be given to relatives and friends for birthday and Christmas presents, as often the family could not afford alternative gifts. Mary received many complements for her flower displays and a neighbour suggested that she should start to make such displays on a commercial basis. Mary took her advice and for the past two years has been working informally as a community florist. Mary uses both dried and fresh flowers for her displays. She makes wedding bouquets and posies for the girls in the estate making their First Communion. She also receives orders for bouquets for birthday and anniversary gifts. Mary buys baby pink and blue ornaments from a wholesaler and turns them into attractive floral gifts with the aid of dried flowers. These gifts are very popular for new mothers and Mary receives quite a substantial number of orders for these commodities.

The wedding of Peter and Jane

Several of the activities previously mentioned are connected with the economic aspects of the celebrations attached to rites of passage such as birth and birthdays, weddings and anniversaries together with rites of passage more specific to the Catholic church such as christening, First Communion and Confirmation. The informal supply of these items enable people with low incomes to display the ostentation attached to these often obligatory social celebrations. The importance of informal communal mechanisms for realising these obligations can be illustrated by examining the wedding arrangements of Peter and Jane. Peter comes from an estate situated about one mile from Newbury while Jane comes from the Newbury estate. At the time of the survey, Jane's family were preparing for her wedding which was to take place the following week. According to Smith (1986,p.212) people are generally more willing to acknowledge paying for unregistered work than reveal income from such work. Hence the wedding of Jane and Peter provided me with an opportunity to explore the extent to which the economic services connected to the wedding celebration were being met by informal or formal means.

In all, the extent to which the economic aspects of the celebration were being supplied informally was remarkable. Jane's aunt was a dressmaker in the estate and had made the bride and bridesmaids' dresses. Mary and Jack (mentioned above) lived in the next street to Jane and Mary was supplying the flowers for the wedding while Jack intended taking the photographs. The wedding cake was also being made locally. A woman from the estate was going to sing hymms during the mass while a neighbour's son played in a group in the evenings and they were going to supply the music at the wedding reception. Finally, a friend of Jane's mother knew someone who ran a small catering outfit and they were going to provide the catering for the wedding. The wedding reception was being held in a local drinking club. Since Jane's father is a club regular, he was able to hire the main hall in the club at a reduced rate. The only other significant expenses were the hiring of the limousine and the hiring of suits for the groom, bestman and father of the bride. These items were being hired from formal establishments. Jane and Peter estimate that the final expenditure on their wedding and reception will be about half what it would have cost them had all these services been purchased through formal mechanisms.

Community firewood

The final enterprise worth mentioning is the stick business' run by George Black. Collecting sticks, chopping them up and making them into bundles for firewood has a long history in the estate. In Chapter Three, I mentioned how young boys in the district would go around fruit shops obtaining used wooden crates to transform into bundles of sticks. While the income generated from these activities was scant, nonetheless it was often a welcome supplement to families in need. When George was a young boy, he used to be involved in this activity. He is now aged thirty eight, has been married for eighteen years and has ten children, the eldest being fourteen. George has no qualifications and no occupational training and has spent most of his life alternating between bouts of unemployment and bouts of informal employment as a labourer. The scarcity of informal labouring work drove George to continually engage in schemes to enhance the family's income.

Eight years ago, George decided to return to the informal economic activity he had engaged in as a child in order to generate extra income. Along with his sons, he began to collect used wood to chop into bundles of sticks to sell in Newbury. There is a large timber yard on the outskirts of the estate which supplies firms and tradesmen in the building trade from all over Belfast. George decided to contact the manager of the timber yard to find out what happened to their scrap wood and was amazed to find out that most of it was discarded. George made an arrangement with the manager to collect some of the scrap wood on a weekly basis for the purposes of using it to make bundles of sticks. The yard is situated about 400-500 yards from his house. Although initially George's needs were very limited, given the fact that he had no transport to remove the wood and few customers, nonetheless over the years he has expanded this activity so that his current needs are quite considerable. Because George had a constant supply of raw materials, he was able expand on his informal trading activity. He travelled around several shops in surrounding districts asking if he could supply them with bundles of sticks. While many children had engaged in this activity previously, they had done so on a sporadic basis so that shops were never guaranteed constant delivery and many refused to accept bundles of sticks to sell. Being an adult, George was regarded as being much more reliable and many shops agreed to accept weekly deliveries. A few years ago he bought a second hand car and trailer and travels over a much wider geographical area supplying shops with sticks.

George lives in an end house with a large side garden and keeps a caravan there to store wood and sticks. He also has a makeshift shed which houses a large chain saw to help chop the wood into bundles of sticks. Previously, this activity was carried out solely by using an axe. His sons also continue to sell the sticks from door to door when they come home from school in the afternoons. George continues to register as unemployed. Although the chain saw he uses is very noisy and can be heard in the next street, George has no fears about any of his neighbours 'touting' on his activities. He states that while this economic activity generates a reasonable income in the winter, in the summer time he generally reverts back to almost total dependence on benefits.

Motivations to engage in community self employment

Financial considerations are important when looking at community economic enterprises but they are by no means the only motivations. Many interviewees who were involved in community economic enterprises stressed the relative autonomy, the flexibility and the control they had over the labour process. Although several stated that they needed the money, nonetheless there was more a sense of personal choice attached to this type of informal economic activity. Moreover, since most of the activities mentioned here were community based, and since often one's customers were also one's friends, relatives and neighbours, this often lessened individuals' awareness that what they were engaging in was work.

Many of those engaged in community economic enterprises stressed their inability to meet the social obligations attached to mainstream celebrations such as birthdays and Christmas and this inability necessitated their initial involvement in informal trading activity. It was often only after a period of fulfilling social obligations in this way that many decided to capitalize on their individual skills. Some of the evidence also indicates that these informal economic practices are themselves subject to internal inequalities, injustices and abuses. This is particularly noticeable when looking at the trading activities of the 'house shops' in the district. As Newbury has very poor shopping facilities and since many of the residents do not own a car, then the inhabitants of the estate have no option but to utilize these 'shops'. The 'shops' in turn, aware that they are providing a service not otherwise available, charge exhorbitant rates for all the commodities sold. One pensioner showed me some items her housekeeper had purchased on her behalf in the shopping centre on the outskirts of the area. Each item was substantially more expensive in the 'house shop' compared to the shopping centre. For example, the pensioner was charged 62p for a pot of jam from the 'house shop'. The same pot of jam cost 46p in the shopping centre.

Opportunities to engage in community economic enterprises

Robin Ward (Roberts et al 1985) argues that the more culturally alien the minority, the more opportunities for economic enterprises within the community. I have already outlined in Chapter Three, some of the reasons for the alienation of the residents of Newbury from the wider Catholic community. This alienation has encouraged their self reliance. Consumer demand is dependent on the wants and needs of the community and hence to a certain extent constitutes a protected market. While this is in many respects advantageous, it provides limited scope for upward mobility. Production and exchange is locally based and dependent on the manipulation of kin and neighbourhood ties and this acts as a deterrent against even the most successful participants moving out of the community to set up elsewhere. Moreover, the clandestine nature of most of the activities mentioned means that profits are rarely banked as it is feared that this will foster the authorities' suspicion. Hence profits from the most successful ventures are either ploughed back into the business or spent on upgrading dwellings. This results in stark differences between houses in the district from dilapidated dwellings on the one hand to dwellings cloaked in ostentatious consumer trappings on the other.

While the history and isolation of the estate enhance self reliance, not everyone has the opportunity to engage in community economic enterprises. This is partly due to the fact that some of the activities mentioned previously, need a certain amount of capital to get off the ground. This is particularly the case for the 'house shops', where redundancy money, compensation payments and life savings were utilised to fund these trading ventures. Shops need a reasonable amount of stock to make them viable and while purchases can be made on credit once one is an established customer, when one is only starting off, most wholesalers will demand cash for any purchases made. This lack of capital may prevent many residents from the estate considering this activity as a realizable option. This in turn prevents the estate being swamped by house shops and increases the chances of survival for those who have the capital to fund such ventures.

Other activities need limited capital. Pahl (1984) states that the unemployed are the least likely group to engage in informal work/employment because they do not have the money to buy the materials necessary to engage in informal economic activity. While this does represent a problem for the unemployed, nonetheless it ignores the possibility that the purchaser of commodities produced informally may supply the materials in advance and simply purchase the labour power of the informal worker. Hence individuals requiring Arans, wedding dresses, cakes and other commodities may pay for the raw materials in advance or supply their own raw materials. This means that individuals with marketable skills but no capital are not denied access to informal economic activity

Some of the activities mentioned, such as can picking require no capital nor any skills. Here what seems to be important is where the idea to engage in these forms of economic activity originates from. Often the originator of novel forms of informal activity secure a sort of moral monopoly over the activity. Hence the can pickers have their own well defined and recognised patch for their informal economic activity and other individuals are often reluctant to intrude on someone else's territory. Where individuals flout these unwritten rules, the originators of the activities may defend their area by force if necessary.

Polarization between households with multiple formal and informal workers and households with no access to formal or informal work/employment was also evident when looking at those involved in community economic enterprises. The male family head in the household which operated a video shop also works as an informal wage labourer. The widow who runs a 'house shop' is also formally employed as a part time cleaner and is also an agent for a catalogue firm while the owner of one of the 'caravan shops' is also in full time formal employment. The spouse of the female baker is in full time formal employment and she herself was in full time formal employment until one year ago. Of the thirteen catalogue sales agents, one runs a 'house shop', two work as informal contract cleaners and two are formally employed as part time cleaners, one minds a neighbour's baby for money, while the remainder knit and dressmake for money. Two of the spouses of those who knit and dressmake also work as informal wage labourers while a further respondent who knits for money is also employed as a contract cleaner. Finally, one of the photographers also works as an informal wage labourer. Hence the estate is divided between enterprising households who are involved in a whole range of paid formal and informal economic practices and households who do not have the capital, the skills, the ideas nor the contacts to gain access to paid formal or informal economic activity.

Attitudes of the wider society

Community economic enterprise is not as negatively viewed as informal wage labour. Throughout the 1980's the state has been involved in schemes to encourage individuals to set up their own businesses. Current attempts to stimulate economic revival in West Belfast are focused on efforts to tap the supposedly large informal sector and put its energies to even more productive use. The failure of De Lorean and other large scale business ventures in the area has focused the attention of policy makers on the need to provide credit and technical assistance to small scale often informal business enterprises as an alternative economic regeneration strategy.

During the research, I was approached by representatives from Work West Belfast (a state funded organisation aimed at encouraging the setting up of local business units in West Belfast) and an Enterprise Unit situated about one mile from Newbury estate who hope to tap the talents of the female residents of the Newbury estate by encouraging them to formalise their existing informal activity. Both these organisations have a number of self contained individual units that they hope to rent to people ready to set themselves up in business. Rents and other overheads are quite low and both organizations will also supply the newly recruited self employed business person with financial and other business related advice. However, these enterprise officials not only grossly exaggerate the amount of informal activity that supposedly exists within low income estates but they also misunderstand the nature of much community based informal activity.

The applicability of market based notions of exchange to situations in which economic and social relationships cannot easily be disentangled is debatable. Many of the females in particular placed greater value on the intrinsic satisfaction of work rather than on profit maximization. Moreover, much of the economic activity mentioned here gave priority to the social needs of the community, its festivals, religious feasts and other occasions, and work and production were often aimed at fulfilling these. This indicates how social and in a sense non economic factors also profoundly influence people's economic behaviour. Moreover, goods and services are not always sold at their potential price. Rather pricing is often influenced by the relationship between trading partners.

The respondents interviewed in this chapter related an extremely complex process whereby payment is negotiated and renegotiated. All the interviewees who provided a service within the community (except for the owners of 'house-shops') charged fees well below prices charged in formal establishments. Yet, this is not to say that a uniform price structure exists. For the immediate extended family network of those involved in community economic enterprises, payment is usually in kind. Individuals engaged in community economic enterprises are usually reluctant to charge extended family members money. Instead, they will usually receive something in kind, a small gift for themselves or their children or a favour returned. For the other customers of those involved in community economic enterprises, a twofold price system seems to be in operation. Friends and immediate neighbours are charged the lower of the two prices while friends of friends are charged the higher of the two prices. Initial observations thus indicate that payment is related to the relationship of the vendor to the purchaser. The more impersonal the relationship, the more market orientated the pricing procedure becomes.

On further investigation, it became clear that this pricing procedure was not as straightforward as it first appeared. Age and financial circumstances of clients are often taken into consideration. If a friend of a friend turns out to be a pensioner, then a lower charge is made. Furthermore, quite often friends would relate background histories of other friends whom they were requesting a service or commodity for. If it was discovered that the prospective customer was experiencing a bad time, such as a marriage break up, then a lower charge was made. In all these ways, many of the individuals mentioned in this chapter provide a source of economic assistance without being subject to market calculations of the value of their service or commodity.

The services and commodities of most of the small scale enterprises mentioned here are priced to suit local markets. Indeed they are often attractive because of their cheapness. Moreover, individuals who engage in community economic enterprises are able to operate the complex socially based price structure mentioned above because their activities are unregulated, they always have benefits to fall back on and since most activities take place in their own homes, they have low overheads. These advantages would disappear with formalization. Moving to an enterprise retail unit would increase overheads and prices would have to change accordingly. This would have either one of two effects. Those in community economic enterprises would either lose their attractiveness when in direct competition with other formal organisations or if they were successful they would no longer benefit low income areas such as Newbury who depend on the existence of cheap, unregulated informal commodities and services.

Formalization, for the females in particular may also introduce added stresses to marriages. Women who engage in dressmaking and knitting in the community usually have very supportive husbands who are happy enough that their wives can engage in informal economic activity. The husbands rarely feel threatened by their wives income generating activity and do not regard this economic activity as undermining their role as head of household and economic provider. To many, the women are just doing what they are naturally good at. No stigma is attached to men whose wives can make additional money from knitting and sewing. However, if these women were to become self employed business women running their own premises and receiving all kinds of business advice, these activities may be viewed differently. The spouses of these female business women might begin to experience feelings of inadequacy and isolation. Female orientated activities which presently act as a safety valve for discontent and social tensions by enabling families to maintain or improve their living standards may transform to an explosive situation through formalization.

Formal and informal aspects of community economic enterprises

Of course, it may be argued that some of the practices mentioned in this chapter are already formal economic activities. For example, the women who work as catalogue sales agents could be defined as outworkers for a large formal organisation. However, none of the women interviewed classified themselves in terms of this income generating activity. Rather, they defined themselves in terms of their part time formal employment or as housewives. Moreover such activities are usually omitted from government surveys as being far too minor and insignificant to be worth the effort of identifying and counting them as jobs (Hakim 1989,p.481). The Family Expenditure Survey initially identified people earning small amounts from casual work such as mail order selling as self employed, but from 1982, such people have been re-classified as unoccupied. Cragg and Dawson (1981,p.21-22) suggest that women who engage in this type of economic activity ususally fail to report earnings because they are too small to be regarded as a 'proper job' by the women concerned. Hence, the loss of such work does not count as 'unemployment' in the eyes of the women involved (Cragg & Dawson 1984,p.20).

The 'house shops' operate without the knowledge or consent of the NIHE. These outlets can be regarded as informal trading units as their trading practices operate in the absence of official regulation. The shop keepers do not acknowledge their trading activities and as a result do not pay any taxes or follow other official administrative procedures. While occasionally 'house shops' in the estate have to cease trading because of detection by the NIHE, my respondents knew of no instance where owners of 'house shops' had been investigated by the Inland Revenue or any other government department.

Most of the remaining participants were mainly involved in providing community members with goods or services. Here a money relationship existed between the producer of the goods or service and the customer. However, this relationship was qualitatively different from the wage relationship that exists between the employers and employees in formal or informal wage labour (see next chapter). Moreover, this money relationship was not constant but fluctuated in accordance with the perceived social and economic situation of individual customers. These transactions took place in cash and the money was not declared to any official body. Occasionally participants in this economic practice supplied goods to formal establishments outside the estate. Mrs Whyte, for example, supplied a city centre store with tracksuits, while Mrs Armstrong provided a range of formal trading outlets with her designer knitwear. Mrs Whyte was paid by cheque for these items, while Mrs Armstrong received a mixture of cheques and cash. Both respondents had bank accounts and either cashed or deposited these payments. Neither respondent officially declared this surplus income and both seemed unconcerned about detection by any government agency. I did not investigate the way in which the formal establishments treated these transactions but it seems likely that the payments made to both women would be recorded in the accounts of the various formal organisations. Indeed the experience of Fred the car mechanic illustrates how the official recording of these transactions may be used against individuals unofficially engaged in such activities.

Links between formal economy and community economic enterprises

A focus on community economic enterprises indicates that the links between formal and informal economic activities are multifaceted and complex. Most of those involved in community economic enterprises depend on the formal economy for raw materials or goods for re-distribution. The knitters, the dressmakers, the bakers amongst others are directly dependent on the purchase of raw materials from the formal economy before they can apply their skills to transform these raw materials into commodities for informal distribution. The 'house shops' receive direct deliveries from formal suppliers. On many occasions I have been on the estate and witnessed these deliveries. The 'house shops' are on the driver's route together with the other formal establishments in the area, often being supplied from the same source. The only difference is the more complex trading mechanisms utilised by the 'house shops' to distribute these formal products. The easy accessibility of these 'house shops' and the credit system many of them have in operation may ironically increase the estate's consumption of formal products.

Informal economic enterprises may be connected to the formal economy in another way, that is by being structured around the salvage of goods produced in the regular economy. This is particularly evident when looking at the activities of the can pickers in the area and the stick business organised by George Black. Both activities depend on products discarded by the formal economy. The can pickers recycle the aluminium cans purchased in the formal economy and thrown away by the owners when empty. George collects the scrap wood no longer needed by the timber yard in his area and his activity transforms the useless wood into serviceable commodities which then find their way back into the formal economy.

Moreover, in relation to the can pickers, Portes and Sassen-Koob (1987,p.38) commenting on marginal workers who collect trash from garbage dumps in developing countries, suggest that these apparently self employed workers end up supplying large formal industries with significant quantities of substitutes for raw materials at a fraction of their market costs. Hence according to these authors, such workers can be viewed as industrial outworkers who labour under the illusion of self employment but who actually work for the large firms. This further emphasises the subtle links between formal and informal economic activity.

The case histories of Mrs Whyte who makes tracksuits for a city centre store and Mrs Armstrong who supplies formal enterprises with exclusive knitwear further illustrate the intricacies of the relationship between the formal and informal economy. The materials that these women use to make their commodities are purchased in the formal economy. These raw materials are transformed informally into finished goods and these finished goods find their way back into the formal economy by being put up for sale in formal establishments. At first glance, this appears to be evidence of the parasitic relationship between the formal and informal sector whereby the formal sector feeds off the most successful informal enterprises. But the process is two way. The pirating of formal videos and the replication of household interior designs displayed in the formal economy paves the way for people involved in informal economic activity to exploit successful formal sector products and services.

Summary

This chapter sought to demonstrate that there is no lack of entrepreneurial skills available among low income populations. Community economic enterprise is often gender based. For example knitting, dressmaking and running sales catalogues are predominately female activities. On the other hand, some activities were not as clear cut. One of the hairdressers and one of the bakers was male while the 'house shops' were family affairs. The chapter commenced with a descriptive account of these informal economic trading activities. This was followed by a brief discussion on actors' motivations and opportunities to engage in these types of informal economic strategies. The positive perceptions of the wider society to this type of economic activity was outlined and some of the links between the formal and informal economy were explored. The chapter focused on the vitality, based on local cultures, kinship and friendship relationships, and on the goods and services not usually supplied by outside formal institutions. The social as well as the economic aspects of informal trading within the estate were assessed. The existence of the 'house shops' and the manipulation of social relationships by the catalogue sales agents indicated that there was not a complete absence of economic individualism. This indicates that informal trading relationships within communities are far from straightforward and may foster co-operative, competitive or individualistic economic behaviour.

7 Informal wage labourers

This chapter is concerned with exploring actors' accounts and perceptions of their employment as informal wage labourers. Informal wage labourers are people who are employed 'off-the-books' by those who mainly operate in the formal economy. 'Off-the-books' economic activity refers to a wide ranging set of activities that are unregulated, untaxed and unmeasured. Hence these activities often remain invisible in official statistics on the economy. Mattera (1985) provides a host of examples to illustrate the diverse nature of 'off-the-books' economic activity. Those in formal employment, for example, may engage in moonlighting, that is, they may take on additional, unregulated work to provide them with extra, untaxed income. This additional unregulated work stretches from tradesmen who take on undeclared 'homers' to those in the service industries who pocket tips to academics who pocket the undeclared income derived from publications and guest lectures. Employers may also participate in 'off-the-books' activity in an effort to avoid compliance with state regulations and in the process evade taxes. This tactic leads self employed individuals, small businesses and large corporations to under declare their profits and overstate their expenses in order to achieve these ends.

What all these types of 'off-the-books' activity have in common is that they are all mainly dependent on formal employment. Evading income or value added tax (VAT) is usually dependent on legitimate employment. Similarly, those who engage in moonlighting generally depend on their formal employment for basic economic security. Hence, 'off-the-books' economic activity refers to a heterogeneous group of people from a variety of social backgrounds and occupations.

By contrast, the informal wage labourers discussed in this chapter come from specific disadvantaged backgrounds. Most possess no formal skills. They occupy the lowest rungs of the labour market and often sheer financial necessity compels them to seek informal wage labour employment. Many of the respondents interviewed in this chapter are on welfare benefits and find it almost impossible to meet their families' basic needs by relying solely on welfare benefits. Hence, where the opportunity arises, they attempt to find informal employment. This leaves them open to exploitation by unscrupulous employers seeking cheap, easily manipulated workers. The chapter will focus on two specific groups of informal wage labourers; women, whose husbands are unemployed and hence their additional income would affect their families' benefit entitlements and men who 'do the double', that is work while claiming welfare benefits.

The first two sections of the chapter will relate specific histories of individual male and female wage labourers and explore the underlying connections that link these two groups of wage labourers together. Particular emphasis will be placed on how access to informal wage labour is both enhanced and constrained by gender status. The next three sections will explore specific topics in more detail. Attention will focus on actors' motivations to work and attitudes to this type of employment. Wider public perceptions of this type of economic activity and the opportunities that exist to formalise this type of informal economic practice will also be considered. Wage labour is the most common form of formal economic activity. Informal wage labour illustrates the strong links between formal and informal economic activity. Hence the final section of the chapter will explore the connections between the formal and informal economy uncovered by a concentration on this particular type of economic activity.

Male informal wage labourers

The following discussion is based on semi structured interviews with thirty seven men from the Newbury estate, all of whom work as informal wage labourers. Fourteen of the sample were interviewed during the early part of the research. I was put in touch with eight of these men through contacts I had made while working in the community school in the area. The other six worked informally with some of the men in this initial sample and were interviewed in a snowball pattern. All the men in this group were interviewed twice, while just over one third were interviewed three times. The remaining twenty three men were interviewed during a survey of 150 households in the estate. All of these men were interviewed once only. Twenty four of the sample work as wage labourers for small scale subcontractors in the building industry. Supplementary information was gained by interviewing two subcontractors who reside in West Belfast. These two subcontractors live about one mile from Newbury and employ wage labourers from the Newbury estate.

None of the informal wage labourers had any formal educational qualifications. Eleven respondents had served an apprenticeship since leaving school. Nine had served their apprenticeships in the various trades associated with the building industry while the remaining two had trained as butchers. The other twenty six men had never undertaken any form of occupational training since leaving school and most had held a wide variety of unskilled manual jobs.

The following table (7.1) provides a breakdown of the age range of the males interviewed in the overall sample:

Table 7.1
Age of male respondents (a)

Occ. Status	20-29	30-39	40-49	50-59	60+
Formally employed	19%	31%	15%	54%	10%
Informally employed (b)	33%	31%	49%	23%	10%
Unemployed (c)	48%	38%	36%	23%	0%
Retired	0%	0%	0%	0%	80%
	100%	100%	100%	100%	100%
	N.21	N.29	N.33	N.13	N.21

Total: 117
(a) Includes 14 males interviewed in snowball sample.
(b) The males in this group are officially registered as unemployed.
(c) The unemployed includes fourteen people registered as sick/disabled

Unemployment was the most likely destination for males aged between 20-39. 81 per cent of the males aged between 20-29 were unemployed while 69 per cent of the males aged between 30-39 were unemployed, although a substantial number of this group were able to find occasional or regular informal employment. More than half of the males in the age range 40-49 were able to engage in informal employment. Thereafter, access to informal employment decreased. Only 23 per cent of the males aged between 50-59 and only 10 per cent of the males aged 60+ participated in this type of informal economic activity.

Table 7.2 provides a breakdown of the number of children of the male respondents:

Table 7.2
Male Respondents: number of children (a)

	0	1-3	4-5	6+
Occ. Status				
Formally employed	4	7	10	6
Informally employed (b)	1	10	6	20
Unemployed	5	12	10	9
Retired	1	1	4	11
	11	30	30	46

Total: 117
(a) Includes 14 males interviewed in snowball sample.
(b) This group are officially registered as unemployed

The table indicates that the more children there are in the household, the more likely the male will seek informal employment.

The following table (7.3) gives a breakdown of the range of occupations held by male informal wage labourers from Newbury:

Table 7.3
Male informal wage labourers: occupations

Construction Industry		Other Occupations	
Joiner	3	Butcher	2
Plasterer	1	Barman	3
Bricklayer	2	Doorman	2
Plumber	1	Dry cleaning agent	2
Painter	2	Van driver	1
Unskilled labourer	15	Betting clerk	1
		Shop asst.	1
		Taxi depot clerk	1
Totals	24		13

In the following paragraphs, the jobs, working conditions and wage levels of male informal wage labourers will be outlined and discussed. The male wage labourers in the construction industry will be discussed separately from the male wage labourers in other occupations. The first group I am going to focus on are the thirteen men employed in the range of occupations under the heading 'other occupations' outlined in Table 7.3. The two butchers are the only skilled workers in this group. They are aged 29 and 40 respectively. Both are married and both have children. One has three children and the other has six. The spouses of the two butchers are housewives. Both butchers have served apprenticeships to the butchery trade and have each spent periods of formal employment as butchers. The twenty nine year old butcher has been unemployed for the past three years, while the forty year old butcher has been unemployed for the past five years. Both blame the entry of women into the butchery trade as shop assistants for the slump in occupational opportunities for trained butchers. They state that most butchery concerns now only employ one or two trained butchers and a number of female counter staff. The butchers carve up the carcasses and display the meat while the women serve the customers. This leads to an overall reduction in wage costs to the employer. The women are usually employed part time at wage levels well below the standard rate for trained butchers.

The two respondents state that they regularly travel around various butchery retail outlets in West Belfast and the City Centre inquiring if there are any vacancies. This practice has resulted in each butcher acquiring seasonal and casual employment. Both state that they can generally find informal employment during the summer holidays as holiday relief butchers and at busy festive periods in the year, particularly during the weeks preceding Christmas. The two butchers state that they have a number of contacts among butchery retailers and they are contacted whenever these retailers require additional help. During July and August and the month of December, they can find almost constant full time informal employment. For the rest of the year, their employment tends to be more sporadic, perhaps one or two days per week, while it is not uncommon for several weeks to go by with no informal employment at all. When employed informally, each butcher is paid £2.50 per hour.

The two doormen are related to each other. They are brothers-in-law. They are aged fifty three and fifty four respectively. Both are married and both have six children, although some of these children have married and left the parental home. The wives of the two doormen are also employed informally as contract cleaners. Neither of the two doormen have any formal educational qualifications or occupational training. One of the doormen has spent most of his working life employed as a labourer in a variety of building sites. He has been unemployed for the past ten years. The other doorman was a factory worker in one of the multinational companies attracted to Northern Ireland during the 1960's. The company pulled out of Northern Ireland in 1972 and the respondent has been unemployed ever since. Both men are employed informally as doormen in a republican drinking club located in West Belfast. The club has been in operation since the early 1970's and both men are long standing members. One respondent has been a doorman for the past seven years, the other has been a doorman for the past five years. Their job entails standing in the hallway of the club and vetting potential customers. Each customer must sign a visitors book, giving their name and address. On certain occasions, only club members and their friends are permitted access to the premises. If the security forces pay the club a visit, the doormen press a button in the hallway to warn others in the club about the impending visit. Each respondent works every day from 2.00pm to 6.00pm and each is paid £2.00 per hour.

The three barmen are aged twenty six, forty five and sixty one respectively. All are married and all have children. The twenty six year old has two children, the forty five year old has four children while the sixty one year old barman has ten children, although most of these are married and have left the parental home. Two of the spouses of the barmen are housewives while the other is employed informally as a caterer. None of the barmen have any formal educational qualifications and none have served any kind of apprenticeship to the bar trade although the sixty one year old respondent has spent most of his life working in the same bar. The sixty one year old barman was the eldest respondent interviewed. He started working in a bar in the city centre thirty years ago. Initially he was employed as an occasional helper. His employer was impressed with his standard of work and he was taken on full time, although he had never served a proper apprenticeship. He remained in the job until two years ago, when he retired. At the time of his retirement, he was the manager of the bar. He is now employed informally by the owner of the bar and is responsible for the lunch time catering. He works each day from 12.00 to 3.00pm and is paid £4 per hour.

The other two barmen work in republican clubs located in West Belfast. Each is employed part time, one works three evenings per week and the other works five evenings per week. Their hours of work are not consistent. Each start work between 6.30 and 7.30pm and work up until the bar is cleared and all the glasses are washed. Some nights they are finished their work around midnight while other nights they may have to work until 2.00am. They are both paid a standard rate of £15 per night regardless of whether this entails working until 12.00pm or 2.00am. The twenty six year old respondent has been working constantly in a republican club for the past two years while the forty five year old respondent has been working informally in a republican club for the past eight years. The twenty six year old barman has never had any kind of formal employment. He has been unemployed since he left school at the age of sixteen. The forty five year old barman has worked formally in a wide variety of unskilled jobs. He has been unemployed for the past twelve years.

Two respondents are informally employed by a dry cleaning firm. One is aged twenty nine and is married with one child. The other is aged twenty three and is engaged to be married. Both have no formal qualifications, although the twenty three year old was studying for two GCSE's at night classes when the research was carried out. Neither respondent has served an apprenticeship nor undertaken any type of occupational training. The twenty three year old was away for fourteen months in a religious order and had intended becoming a monk. He has been unemployed since he returned to Newbury three years ago.

The firm that both respondents work for is owned by a Pakistani family. They also own several dry cleaning retail outlets throughout the city of Belfast. The firm specialise in a door to door dry cleaning service. The two respondents are involved in this aspect of the business. They call from house to house in Newbury and surrounding estates and ask the occupants if they have any garments that they want dry cleaned. The garments are taken away, dry cleaned and brought back three or four days later. At this stage money changes hands. The two respondents are best friends and have a company van for carrying out this work. The twenty nine year old has been informally employed for just over one year while the twenty three year old has been engaged in this job for the past eight months. Both are very badly paid, usually averaging around £1.50 per hour. However, they supplement these earnings by putting through extra garments to be dry cleaned and pocketing the money. This activity will be discussed in greater detail in the next chapter.

The van driver is aged forty six, is married and has six children. His wife is a housewife. The van driver has no formal educational qualifications and has never served an apprenticeship nor undertaken any form of occupational training. The respondent's brother was a skilled cabinet maker and used to bolster the income he derived from his employment by making cabinets at home for friends and neighbours. The respondent used to help him and gradually became quite skilled at making cabinets. Thirteen years ago the respondent and his brother decided to go into self employment. They were quite successful and were able to expand by selling their cabinets to a number of retail units. Their self employment continued for just over two years, during which time the respondent states, they were making quite a lot of money. However, they were not paying the proper taxes and after two years, they were investigated by the Inland Revenue and fined £2,000 for the non payment of taxes. The respondent and his brother were both frightened of keeping meticulous accounts yet felt that if they didn't they would be investigated once again by the Inland Revenue. They decided to terminate their self employment. The respondent has been officially unemployed ever since. Ten years ago, the respondent became a van driver for a large wholesale delivery firm located in West Belfast. The respondent delivers wholesale orders to various outlets throughout Belfast. He is employed full time (off-the-books) by the firm and his wages at the time of the interview were £90 per week. He does not work when the firm closes at Christmas, Easter and the twelfth of July week. During these periods, the respondent is paid half his usual wage.

The taxi depot clerk is aged thirty four, is married and has two children. His wife operates a dressmaking and knitting business from her home. The taxi depot clerk has no formal educational qualifications and has never been engaged in any form of occupational training. He has been unemployed for the past twelve years. Two years ago, he started work in a taxi firm located in West Belfast. He works at the desk, taking in-coming calls and passing the customers' requirements on to the taxi drivers employed by the firm. The firm employs a mixture of formal and informal taxi drivers. The respondent works between three and four nights per week from 8.00pm to 2.00am. He is paid £12 per night if he works during the week and £18 per night if he works on a Friday or Saturday night.

The betting clerk was the youngest respondent interviewed. He is aged twenty and is engaged to be married. He left school at sixteen and went on a Youth Training scheme for one year. He has been officially unemployed ever since. Three years ago, he started working in a bookmaker's office in the city centre of Belfast. For the first two years he worked Monday to Friday from 1.00pm to 5.30pm and all day Saturday. He was paid £44 per week. One year ago, he transferred to working full time (still informally) for the bookmaker, five days per week, from 9.00am to 5.30pm. He gets one day off per week, although it is usually a different day from one week to the next. His wages were increased to £65 per week. His ultimate ambition is to be taken on legally by the bookmaker.

The final respondent in this category works in a shop located in Newbury. He is aged forty two, is married and has six children. His wife is also employed informally as a contract cleaner. The respondent has no educational qualifications and has never had any form of occupational training. He has been unemployed for the past twenty years. The respondent is unsure how long he has been helping out in the local shop but states that it is 'many years'. The shop is located at the corner of his street and the respondent calls in on a daily basis to help out. He called initially to chat with the owner who is a 'good friend' and gradually began to serve customers while the owner had a cup of tea or went to the toilet. His employment remains very minimal. He basically hangs around the shop in the afternoons and serves customers if the owner is busy. He works no set hours and some days he doesn't bother to call to the shop at all. The owner gives the respondent £5 any afternoon he does call in and all the cigarettes he can smoke while in the shop. The respondent enjoys the company and the 'crack' as the customers are also friends and neighbours. He keeps any money the shopkeeper gives him and uses it to go out for a drink with his mates. Being able to get 'free smokes' while in the shop also prevents vital family income being spent on this 'luxury'.

Construction workers

The next group of male wage labourers are the construction workers. Since all these individuals work in the same line of business, then I intend to discuss their informal activities en masse rather than present individual case histories. This group is comprised of twenty four individuals and as Table 7.3 illustrates includes nine skilled and fifteen unskilled workers. The skilled workers all served an apprenticeship when they left school while the unskilled workers have never engaged in any form of occupational training. Like the group of male wage labourers discussed earlier, none of this group have any formal educational qualifications.

The skilled workers (See Table 7.3) include three joiners, two bricklayers, two painters, one plasterer and one painter. Their ages range from twenty seven to forty six. Eight of this group are married with dependent children. One of the wives of this group is also employed informally. All of this group have been officially unemployed for a number of years. Five of the group have been unemployed for between four to nine years, while the other four have been unemployed for over ten years. All of this group are employed informally by small scale self employed subcontractors who operate mainly in West Belfast. Six of the group state that their informal employment is fairly constant. They state they are usually fully occupied during the seasons of spring and summer while their employment becomes more sporadic during the winter months. Demand for the two painters is not as consistent as their trades are not required as often as the other trades. However, the two painters get painting jobs from friends, neighbours and relatives and this helps them overcome lean periods in employment from subcontractors.

Only one of the group (the only member not married), a thirty year old bricklayer was unhappy about his access to informal employment. The firm this respondent worked for went out of business, one year after he served his apprenticeship and he has been unemployed ever since. He does manage to get periodic informal employment but states that it is too sporadic and undependable. He states that bricklayers usually work in squads, whether they are formally or informally employed and if one doesn't belong to a squad then it is very difficult to gain employment. The respondent does not belong to any squad and is only taken on when any of the squads he has contact with need a pair of extra hands. This only happens when they are nearing the end of a set deadline and then he is only taken on for a few days at a time.

The fifteen unskilled labourers are also employed by small scale subcontractors who operate in West Belfast. Their ages range from twenty seven to sixty. Fourteen of this group are married with children, although two have informed the authorities that they have separated for the financial incentives mentioned earlier. Four of this group have been officially unemployed for between seven and nine years while eleven have been officially unemployed for over ten years. Three of the wives of this group are also informal wage labourers while a further three are engaged in some form of community economic enterprise. Eight of the group state that they can gain fairly constant informal employment, fluctuations again being related to the seasons of the year. The other seven state that their employment is much more undependable, each stating that they can be inactive for months at a time.

It is worth at this point, discussing in greater detail, the type of work that these subcontractors engage in. The Northern Ireland Housing Executive is responsible for public housing in Northern Ireland. The body came into existence in 1972 and was formed from an amalgamation of the Belfast Corporation and the Housing Trust. The Northern Ireland Housing Executive inherited from these two bodies years of housing neglect and sectarian housing allocation policies. Indeed, Northern Ireland contains some of the worst housing in Europe. In an effort to redress these years of bad planning and policy application, the Housing Executive adopts three strategies. Firstly, from 1972, it has embarked on an extensive policy of demolishing and clearing slum areas to make way for new housing estates. Secondly, it renovates property that fails to meet certain minimum standards. Thirdly, it supplies financial assistance to private householders in houses of a certain age and rateable value, to upgrade their property and bring it in line with basic standards prevalent throughout most of Europe. The small scale subcontractors that these twenty four wage labourers from Newbury work for, derive most of their work loads from this third strategy.

The Housing Executive's annual budget includes a sum set aside specifically for grants to private householders to upgrade their property. At the time of the research, to qualify for financial assistance the applicant's house must have been built in the pre-war period and have a rateable value not exceeding £225. The extent of financial assistance depends on the financial circumstances of the applicant. If the applicant is receiving Supplementary Benefit (now Income Support) then he/she is entitled to a 90 per cent grant, if not then the applicant can qualify for a 75 per cent grant. The way the procedure works is important because it paves the way for 'cowboy builders' to engage in grant work or for legitimate contractors to take on a range of informal wage labourers.

The first step for the applicant is to send in a letter requesting a Building Inspector to call and inspect proposed improvements and renovations. Because of the extent of applications and a continuous backlog of work, the time lapse between this letter being sent in and a Building Inspector calling out can be several months. The Inspector's purpose in calling out is to satisfy himself that the improvements and renovations are really necessary. The most common improvements are bathroom and kitchen extensions. To qualify for a kitchen extension, the applicant's existing working kitchen must measure under a certain square footage. Houses qualifying for a bathroom extension usually have no existing bathroom and only an outside toilet. The most common renovations are the replumbing and rewiring of a dwelling and the replacement of windows and doors.

Once the Inspector has agreed with the applicant about what needs to be done, he will send out a typed list of recommended repairs for which financial assistance will be made available. When the applicant receives this form, he/she has to contact a builder to furnish the Housing Executive with an estimate of the total costs of the building and/or repair work. The Housing Executive's only stipulation here, is that the estimate is typed on business headed note paper. The intention here is to ensure that the applicant employs a recognised legitimate builder. Once the estimate is sent in, it is checked against the rates furnished by the Housing Executive's own quantity surveyors in order to ensure that the builder or applicant are not furnishing the Housing Executive with an inflated estimate. Once the Housing Executive approves the estimate they will notify the applicant that they are willing to fund either 75 per cent or 90 per cent of a fixed amount. The applicant can then contact the builder and proceed with the work.

At no point in this procedure has the Housing Executive any contact with the builder named on the estimate. Thus, having an estimate from a specific builder is no guarantee that he will actually carry out the work. The householder and the Housing Executive deal directly with each other and it is the responsibility of the householder to ensure that a proper builder carries out the work. The only safeguard in the system is that the Housing Executive will not pay out any money until its representatives inspect the completed work. What happens is that the applicant notifies the Housing Executive when the work is completed and a Building Inspector is then sent out to inspect the improvements and renovations. If he is satisfied, a cheque for the agreed amount will be posted out to the applicant in due course. If unsatisfied, the Building Inspector will draw up a 'snag list' of points. The applicant then hands the 'snag list' to the builder who can then carry out the recommendations. Once this is done, the applicant then re-notifies the Housing Executive and the Building Inspector is sent out again to repeat the process. This will continue until the Building Inspector is satisfied with the standard of workmanship. While this can act as a deterrent against shoddy building work it does little to ensure that the work is carried out by a registered builder as again throughout this process the dealings are between the Housing Executive and the applicant.

The applicant may be sorely tempted to employ the services of a 'cowboy builder' because of the cheaper costs involved. The term 'cowboy builder' is usually applied to individuals working off-the-record, often with no formal training as builders. Since 'cowboy builders' have no overheads, they can usually carry out the work much cheaper than a formally registered builder. For example even a small scale extension costing £10,000 will involve an added payment of £1500 for VAT alone. The two subcontractors I interviewed told me that they frequently furnish householders with an estimate for repairs or renovations and later discover that the work has been carried out by non registered builders. It is often difficult for legitimate builders to keep tabs on dwellings for which they have given the householder an estimate as the time period between putting an estimate into the Housing Executive and getting notification to commence the work can be as much as a year or more. As one subcontractor put it:

> sometimes you're on to them right away. You know rightly that they have no intentions of getting you to do the work. All they want is your bill head. Other times you think you're on to a sure bet, you go out and see the job, you put your price in, you get the bloodly thing typed up and all and then you past the job a lot of months later to find that some fucker has gone and done the work and all.

This same contractor now charges a fee of £25 for estimates which is refundable once he starts the contract.

The main drawback in using 'cowboy builders' is that often they will demand money 'up front' while the applicant has to wait until the Housing Executive has approved the completed works before being able to claim any grant money. If the 'cowboy builder's' work is not up to standard then the applicant runs the risk of not getting any financial assistance for this work. None of the twenty four male wage labourers interviewed worked as, or for, 'cowboy builders'. All twenty four were employed as wage labourers for small scale legitimate builders in West Belfast. The mere presence of 'cowboy builders' however, mean that legitimate builders have to do some work off-the-books to keep their prices competitive and this in turn facilitates the employment of informal wage labourers.

The two subcontractors I spoke to, stated that most of their building work comes from grant-aided Housing Executive improvement and repair work. The subcontractors put some of these jobs through their books and keep others private. They state they are compelled to do this because of the competitve nature of their business. Both are extremely small scale organisations, being little more than self employed individuals. They distance themselves from 'cowboy builders' and state that they have to stand by all their work as any kind of shoddy workmanship would ultimately affect their legitimate opportunities. They state that, while they get most of their work through word of mouth recommendation, nonetheless their clients often approach two or three builders and tend to accept the cheapest estimate.

Sometimes the clients want the building work done for the value of the grant. With legitimate overheads it is very difficult to reduce costs to these levels. The two subcontractors state that the only way they can reduce their costs is to take on some work off-the-books. Often they will undertake cash jobs and not charge the customer VAT. This saving can be considerable at times amounting to between £1,000 to £3,000. When the two subcontractors are engaged in work off-the-books, they will only accept cash payments from the customer instead of cheques. Each subcontractor employs a number of informal wage labourers either as casual workers or for prolonged periods. Both have a small number of core informal workers who they can give almost constant employment and a number of more expendable workers who they can call in and lay off when required. The two subcontractors employ on an informal basis five of the twenty four male wage labourers I interviewed. The remaining nineteen work for subcontractors in similar situations and their accounts support those given to me by the two subcontractors interviewed. When in constant employment, the unskilled labourers receive an average wage of £80 per week while the skilled tradesmen receive from between £100 to £120 per forty hour week.

Female informal wage labourers

This section is based on semi structured interviews with twenty four women from the Newbury estate, all of whom work as informal wage labourers. I was put in contact with thirteen of this group through relationships formed while working in the community school in the area. The remaining eleven women were interviewed during the survey of 150 households in the estate. These eleven women were interviewed once only while the other thirteen were all interviewed more than once. Sixteen of the sample are employed informally as cleaners for subcontractors in the contract cleaning industry. Supplementary information on this group, was gained by interviewing a representative from the Irish Trade Union Congress (who were engaged in a dispute over the introduction of subcontract cleaning in the Health Service during the time of the research) and the manager of one of the top five cleaning firms operating in Northern Ireland. The firm in question employs women informally from Newbury estate.

The following table (7.4) provides a detailed breakdown of the age range of the female respondents in the overall sample:

Table 7.4
Age of female respondents (a)

Occ. Status	20-29	30-39	40-49	50-59	60+
Formally employed	2	6	4	7	6
Informally employed (b)	8	9	5	1	1
Housewife (c)	13	21	12	10	0
Retired	0	0	0	0	22
	23	36	21	18	29

Total: 127

(a) Includes 13 females interviewed in snowball sample.

(b) The females in this group are officially classified as housewives.

(c) Unemployed females were classified as housewives as none of the women who described themselves as unemployed were officially registered as such.

While several of the older women in the sample were in part time formal employment, informal employment was largely restricted to women between the ages of 20-39.

The following table (7.5) gives a breakdown of the number of children of the female respondents:

Table 7.5
Female respondents: number of children (a)

Occ. Status	0	1-3	4-5	6+
Formally employed	1	9	9	6
Informally employed (b)	0	7	5	12
Housewives (c)	3	22	15	16
Retired	0	1	7	14
	4	39	36	48

Total: 127

(a) Includes 13 females interviewed in snowball sample.
(b) This group are offically registered as housewives
(c) Unemployed females were classified as housewives as none of the women were officially registered as unemployed.

Half of the women who were employed informally had six or more children. Twenty three of this latter group were married while the remaining respondent was a single parent with two children. The spouses of the women who were married were all unemployed and all qualified for some form of welfare assistance. The declaration of the women's extra income would have, in some cases, affected benefit entitlements and hence went unreported. Thus, technically speaking some of these women were breaking the law. Like most other claimants, the unemployed are able to earn a small amount without loss of benefit. Earnings above this 'disregarded' amount are deducted pound for pound from benefits and therefore leave the claimants no better off. In some cases it may leave them worse off as extra declared income may affect entitlement to other benefits.

Up until April 1988, all of the women's husbands were on means tested Supplementary Benefit. This was assessed on a family basis and was affected by any income over £4 earned by either spouse. Since April 1988, either spouse is allowed to earn up to £15 per week before it will affect benefits provided that the male head of household has been unemployed for at least two years. Thirteen of the sample were interviewed before these changes were implemented but it is interesting to note that not one of the remaining eleven women were aware of these changes in the regulations. All twenty four women referred me to the £4 threshold. Thus, while some of the sample were earning £15 or under per week, all were under the impression that they were working illegally and that if their income was known, it would drastically affect their benefit entitlements. Eight of the sample also have husbands who work as informal wage labourers. Since sixteen of the women are employed as contract cleaners, then accounts and descriptions of this occupation will be presented en masse. Of the other eight women, five are employed as shop assistants. Again, their accounts will be presented en masse while separate accounts will be presented for the remaining three women.

Three of the five shop assistants are employed informally in shops located in Newbury estate while the remaining two work in shops located in areas adjacent to Newbury estate. None of the five women incur any travelling expenses getting to and from work. The three women who work within Newbury, work in shops specialising in grocery provisions. They are each paid £1.30 per hour and each work part time. One works from 8.00am to 2.00pm, four mornings per week, while the other two work from 2.00pm to 6.00pm, six days per week. One of the respondents works in a video shop close to the Newbury estate. The shop rents videos for £1.50 per night. The respondent hands out videos, takes the money and makes a note of the borrower's name and address. She works in the video shop six nights per week, from 6.00pm to 10.00pm. The remaining shop assistant works in a Chinese takeaway. She takes orders from customers and payments for meals. She works four nights per week, from 8.00pm to 2.00am and is paid £1.75 per hour. Four of this group are married, while the remaining shop assistant is a single parent. Two of those married have husbands who are employed informally as labourers in the construction industry.

One respondent is a thirty seven year old hairdresser. She is married and has three children. Her husband is also employed informally as a labourer in the construction industry. The respondent is employed informally in a hairdresser's salon close to Newbury estate. The establishment is owned by a friend of hers and she has been working there for the past six years. She is employed two days per week, Friday and Saturday. The hairdresser who owns the salon is officially registered as a self employed hairdresser. However, she does not attract enough customers to take anyone on full time, either formally or informally. The only time an extra pair of hands are needed is at the weekends. The respondent is paid between £12 and £15 per day, depending on the number of customers. She also keeps any tips given by individual clients. The respondent is employed for longer periods prior to Christmas and the summer holidays when demand increases.

Another respondent is employed informally in a package warehouse for a large retailing firm that operates in the city centre of Belfast. The warehouse is situated about two miles from Newbury and the respondent has to pay transport costs to get to and from work. The respondent is thirty eight years of age, is married and has three children. Her husband is also employed informally as a joiner in the construction industry. She works from 10.00am to 2.00pm, five days per week and is paid £1.50 per hour.

A further respondent is employed informally by a friend who operates a small family run catering business. The business caters mainly for weddings, anniversary celebrations and Christmas functions. These parties are usually held in local halls and republican clubs that do not normally have a food licence. The respondent does silver service waitressing. Her duties include laying and waiting on tables and serving the food. Her periods of employment and hours of work tend to be sporadic. In the spring and summer, she will work almost every Saturday, while she will be employed most evenings in the weeks preceding Christmas. She will usually work for three or four hours at a stretch, although occasionally she may work for longer periods than this. She is allowed to go home once the full meal has been served, although if she is working far from home, she will usually wait until everyone has cleared up in order to get a lift home. When this happens she will usually wash dishes and help other people with their duties. At the time of the interview, she was paid £8 for an evening and £10 for a Saturday's work.

Female contract cleaners

The remaining sixteen women are employed as contract cleaners. The following table represents a detailed breakdown of the women's hours of work, hourly rate and take home pay:

Table 7.6
Contract cleaners' hours worked, hourly rate and take home pay

No of Cleaners	Weekly Hours	Hourly Rate	Take Home Pay
1	10	£2.00	£20
2	12	£1.50	£18
1	10	£1.50	£15
1	12	£1.40	£16.80 (gets £17)
2	15	£1.40	£21
2	15	£1.30	£19.50
2	15	£1.20	£18
2	15	£1.00	£15
3	15	£1.00	£15
16 (Total)			

From this table we can see that ten of the sample earn over the £15 threshold, although as I stated earlier, all of the women speaking on this issue referred me to the defunct £4 threshold. All the women have to make their own way to and from their place of employment and this involves added expense which they have to deduct from their already low wages. Fifteen of the sample are employed in the city centre of Belfast and the usual mode of transport is the black taxis which operate in West Belfast and charge 30p per journey. This means that most women on average, have to pay around £3 per week on transport costs.

Cleaning is archetypical of low paid, low status work. Most women will spend some part of their daily lives involved in cleaning duties, usually under the guise of housework. Indeed, if cleaning is carried out at home by the housewife, then it is not deemed worthy enough to be called 'real work'. Cleaning only becomes officially categorised as 'real' work when it is removed from the boundaries of home, family and marriage. The sixteen women interviewed were typically involved in cleaning large shops and office blocks in the city centre of Belfast. Some were confined to the one building while others may clean two or more smaller buildings. The women were generally allocated specific areas to clean while more heavy cleaning such as toilet areas were usually shared on a rota basis. Their main duties include cleaning, polishing and dusting. At certain times of the year, they were expected to give their areas a more thorough overhaul.

The women either worked on their own or as part of a team. This was dependent on the size of the premises in which they were employed. The smaller the premises, the less contact the women had with their supervisors. Hence those involved in cleaning small shops or offices only saw their supervisor once per week, usually on pay day. (All the women were directly paid in cash). If the women worked in a larger concern, then their supervisor either worked alongside them or remained in some part of the building. In these circumstances, the standard of the women's cleaning duties was constantly scrutinized.

The supervisors were not a uniform group but came from varying backgrounds. Seven of the sample stated that their supervisor was a male. None of these males engaged in any direct cleaning work but were rather described as company officials who handed out wages and inspected work. The male supervisors were generally responsible for a number of premises and travelled around from one site to another supervising workloads and dealing with administrative problems. The female supervisors had often been previously employed as contract cleaners and had gained promotion. None of the sixteen cleaners interviewed was a supervisor, although one respondent stated that after eight years of working informally she was offered the chance to become a supervisor. She declined saying that supervisors were not well liked and she didn't want to lose all her friends. The increase in wages offered to her was only 50p per hour and as she states; 'it simply wasn't worth it for all the extra hassle'. Several of the female supervisors had their own cleaning duties but mostly they were responsible for overseeing the rest of the work, making sure it met a particular standard and allocating cleaning materials where necessary.

Often the women had to operate with inadequate cleaning materials and this created difficulty between the cleaners and the supervisors. No bags to put rubbish in, insufficient cloths and cleaning agents and no hot water were the most frequent complaints. This meant that some of the women could not do their jobs properly and often had to bear the brunt of office employees' complaints if they happened to be working overtime. This motivated one woman to occasionally bring in cleaning materials from home. Another woman brought in cleaning materials on a regular basis because she had developed a pathetic pride in her work. Her story is worth repeating at length.

She states that the trouble started when a new male supervisor was appointed to the office building in which she was employed. She believes that this supervisor engaged in fiddling by keeping the cleaning materials and products issued to clean the building and reselling them privately. (Whether such fiddling is common practice or not is outside the scope of this study.) Eventually, she states that the cleaning products dried up altogether and the cleaners were expected to dust with dry cloths and clean with 'plain' water. By this stage, the respondent states that she had started to take great pride in her work. She believes that the area designated to her to clean outshines all other areas.

Previous supervisors had complemented her on the standard of her work and often office employees working overtime would commend her on the quality of her work. So great was her pride in her work, that she began to take cleaning materials from her own house to work, in order to maintain the high standards she had set herself. At one stage, she states her husband caught her out doing this and as she puts it, 'hit the roof'. He said, 'they murder you enough there without them having the cheek to let you bring in your own stuff'. At the time of the interview, the woman was continuing to bring in materials to work smuggling them out of her house without her husband's knowledge. The cleaner in question is paid £1.00 per hour.

Other cleaners state that when complaints were made to the supervisor, the onus was placed back on their shoulders, the supervisors usually stating that the cleaners were too extravagant with the cleaning materials allocated to them. Most women received a quota of cleaning materials to last a specific time and if they ran out before the time limit, they had to resort to cleaning with ordinary water. Most women felt that these quotas were inadequate to meet the cleaning workloads allocated to them.

The sixteen women interviewed were employed in some of the best known shops and business concerns operating in Belfast. None of the women were directly employed by the owners of the premises in which they worked. Rather, they were all employed informally by large scale subcontractors who specialise in cleaning retail and business premises. The subcontractor is employed directly by the owners and/or managers of individual office blocks and retail units. Since cleaning contracts rarely make stipulations regarding the volume, deployment, organisation or conditions of contract labour, then the contractor has total freedom in these matters (Daly 1986,p.23). The contract cleaners interviewed rarely had any contact with the staff employed in their building of work although the women working in office blocks occasionally met workers engaged in overtime. They also had no contact with cleaners in other buildings. The women who worked in large shops had to come in and work later on Thursday nights to accommodate late night shopping. Typically they began work on Thursdays between 9.00-9.30pm, and worked until around midnight. They were paid no extra for this disruption in their work routine. The women complained that at peak periods during the year, especially around Christmas, their work load intensified due to additional late night shopping or office parties. Yet again they often received no extra payment to compensate for this, although six of the sample stated that they received a Christmas bonus of either £10 or one week's wages.

Cleaning requires few imputs apart from labour. Wage costs remain the major costs and according to Coyle (1985,p.12), contractors' strategies for reducing their wage bill have developed into an art form. Coyle states, the secret is to employ a lot of people for a short time, rather than to employ a few for longer. Short hours remove the necessity either to pay employer's National Insurance contributions or to provide tea and coffee breaks. None of the women interviewed in this study had any time allocated for a tea or coffee break. At best, the women could slip out to the toilets for a 'quick smoke' if the supervisor wasn't around.

Male and female informal wage labourers

The preceding paragraphs have provided a largely descriptive account of the employment of male and female wage labourers. At this stage, I want to present a brief overview of some of the similarities and differences between male and female wage labourers from Newbury. What I want to argue here, is that the social patterning of informal employment presented above can best be examined with reference to the same range of organising concepts that are conventionally used to comprehend formal employment (Edgell & Hart 1988,p.15). Thus the distribution and social significance of informal employment, as indeed with formal employment, varies according to class, sex, ethnicity, age and so on. For example, gender is a fundamental feature around which the formal labour force of modern society is fragmented. The gender structure of informal employment parallels the gender pattern of formal employment. The two groups of wage labourers discussed above occupy gender specific occupations. The bulk of the men were involved in construction work while the bulk of the women were employed informally as cleaners. While the women were usually in constant informal employment compared to the men, whose employment was more casual, nonetheless when both groups were in informal employment the women tended to work part time while the men tended to work full time. Not one woman in the sample worked full time informally. Domestic circumstances, including the occupational status of their husbands have influenced the decision of the women to work part time rather than full time.

Domestic duties and informal wage labour

The female wage labourers worked between 10-24 hours per week. Only six of the sample were employed during the day time. The other eighteen worked in the evenings usually between the hours of 5.30-9.30pm. These hours were very conducive to combining the traditional housewife role with informal employment. Most of these female wage labourers had their household duties by and large completed before they went out to work. Only where there were young children in the household was the husband's participation noticeable and this involved putting the children to bed. In this respect, the study parallels Oakley's (1974,p.138) observation that there is a greater tendency for men to take part in childcare than in housework. In only one case was there a significant input from other family members in carrying out domestic household duties. This was the case of a contract cleaner who also held two other informal jobs. This particular respondent cited the delegation of her household duties to other members of her family as a major motivation in encouraging her to work outside the household. As she says:

> I usually get stuff in for the dinner the night before and one of the sons or daughters makes it. The kids also do all the housework. There is nothing I like better than coming in to a clean house and a bit of dinner. Now don't get me wrong, it's not that I don't like cleaning, it's just it's so boring in your own house. When you do it outside it's not the same. It's not like work.

This quote also typified a view held by many other contract cleaners.

Cleaning was regarded as a routine, monotonous chore by most of the women. Yet once this activity became embedded in an employment relationship the negative connotations attached to the task became less transparent.

Flexibility and informal wage labour

The range of occupations held by both male and female wage labourers is very limited and class specific. Most are unskilled, marginal activities. For example, most of the females are cleaners. The only skilled participants specialized in occupations commonly held by the skilled manual working class. For males, these usually centred around skilled trades in the construction industry. The work practices of the male and female wage labourers illustrates some of the main aspects of capitalism's new emphasis on flexibility in working practices. The key feature of this flexibility has been the break up of the labour force into increasingly peripheral, flexible groups of workers clustered around a stable core group which conducts the firm's key activities. The shift to flexible working practices has been enhanced by the government's privatisation programme. As the government increasingly contracts out a whole range of public services, shops, offices and firms are being encouraged to contract out the more peripheral aspects of their organisation such as the cleaning of their premises to private contract cleaning firms. 67 per cent of the female wage labourers work for such private contract cleaning firms. Their job descriptions illustrate how the contract cleaning industry can exploit the flexibility of women's labour and as Thompson puts it 'the elasticity of housework' (Thompson 1983,p.196).

This flexibility in working practices does not just exist between formal and informal employment. The job descriptions of the male wage labourers in the construction industry outlined above indicates that such flexibility is apparent within informal employment. The male wage labourers in this study are made up of two distinct groups. One core group of skilled tradesmen and experienced labourers who find almost constant informal employment (allowing for seasonal fluctuations) and form the core workforce of several small subcontractors. The second group is made up of unskilled labourers whose experience is not as extensive as the first group and who are more peripheral to the concerns of the small scale subcontractors who employ them informally. This group endures more sporadic informal employment.

Male and female wage labourers' motivations to work informally

Informal wage labour was rarely a deliberate choice. Renumeration was the wage labourers single, most important concern. Most of the wage labourers interviewed simply could not manage on the benefit entitlements allocated to their families and needed whatever extra money they could get. These dire financial circumstances meant that most of them were not interested in job satisfaction. There were, however, stark differences between male and female wage labourers in their attitudes to their additional income. The wages earned by the female wage labourers was rarely spent on luxuries but was vital to providing basic essentials for the whole family as the following quotes illustrate:

> Look love, £12 a week mightn't mean much to you, but for me it means the difference between either have a joint for the Sunday dinner or not have a joint for the Sunday dinner. It's as simple as that.

> Well, I could never buy big things with my wages, it went on wee things like ribbons for the kids' hair, socks, knickers, you know. All those things cost a fortune you know. They all mount up and without my wee job I couldn't even afford these bits and pieces.

> I know it's not much especially after you pay your bus fares up and down but it's £15 I otherwise wouldn't have and I need it. The whole family depends on it.

The male wage labourers, while stressing their inability to stretch welfare benefits to meet family demands, nonetheless exhibited a more cavalier attitude to their additional income. This can be illustrated by the following quotes:

> She gets most of it but I'm not working for nothing you know. You have to hold something back.

> Look, the dole's (unemployment benefit) hers. She can do what she wants with it and when she needs something extra I also pull her out

Some of the women interviewed also expressed a different attitude to the additional income earned by male wage labourers:

> If he'd no work I'd be out of pocket, I couldn't afford to buy cigarettes out of my benefit. Also he keeps money for a wee drink with his chums so I get all the benefit.

> I like to see him with a few pound in his pocket. It makes him feel a man again

Word of mouth recruitment

The previous section suggested that male and female wage labourers were motivated mainly by financial circumstances to engage in informal wage labour. Social considerations were also found to be important. Attitudes to jobs are closely bound up with the way the male and female wage labourers in this study were recruited into informal employment. Pahl's (1984) study on the Isle of Sheppey uncovered significant degrees of polarization between multiple earner households and no earner households. Access to informal employment was closely bound up with formal employment. Thus, those without formal employment were denied access to informal employment. For the male and female wage labourers in this present study, access to informal employment was linked, not to those in formal employment but to those already in informal employment. Most of the male and female wage labourers interviewed were recruited through a network of friends, neighbours and relatives already in informal employment. The result of this is that localities which prove most unattractive for the formal economy can function as recruiting zones for informal workers. Hence formal employers can exploit the social networks of existing informal workers to take on additional labour when needed.

This indicates more complex patterns of polarisation than simply divisions between the employed and unemployed. It indicates that polarization may exist among unemployed households with multiple informal workers and unemployed households with no access to informal employment. Eight of the male wage labourers interviewed also had wives working informally. Moreover in two of these cases, the women held more than one informal job. One of the contract cleaners had also worked as a waitress for the past five years in a bar in Belfast's city centre. She worked seventeen hours per week and was paid £2.30 per hour. Her involvement with contract cleaning tends to be sporadic with her moving in and out of jobs during peak periods in her family's expenditure especially prior to Christmas. Her sister and two neighbours work for contract cleaning firms and since the subcontractor's work load coincides with her family's increased expenditure periods, she has little difficulty in securing casual informal employment. She has been involved with contract cleaning on a sporadic basis for the past three years.

The other respondent holds down three informal jobs. She cleans a small shop in the city centre from 6.30-8.30am, every morning, Monday to Saturday. She is employed directly by the shop owner who pays her £1.60 per hour. She then works in a pork factory close to the city centre of Belfast, from 10.30am-2.30pm. Her hourly rate there is £1.70 per hour. Finally each evening Monday to Friday, she works for a contract cleaning firm cleaning a major office block in the city centre, for which she receives £1.50 per hour.

Five of the sixteen contract cleaners were related, although not all to each other. The sample included two sisters and a sister-in-law and another two sisters. Two of the male wage labourers were brothers-in-law and another three were cousins. Others interviewed stated that they had been recruited by a relative. This indicates that polarization may occur, not solely within individual households but across extended kinship networks located in specific communities.

Employers' motivations to recruit informally

Formal employers wishing to take on labour 'off the record' may have little option other than to rely on informal recruitment as formal procedures could increase the risk of discovery. This manipulation of the recruitment process enhances the loyalty, docility, fear, dependence and self discipline of the workforce. Informal recruiting mechanisms operating through social network patterns are very conducive to creating bonds of mutual trust and obligation. As Jenkins et al point out (1983), labour recruited informally via an intermediary already employed by the organisation can to some extent be controlled by peer group pressure. This is because the employee introducing the recruit will feel responsible for ensuring their continued good behaviour. Recruiting informally can often identify in advance the potential troublemaker or layabout (Jenkins, 1988). Morris (1985,p.349) suggests that the need to bring ties of personal obligation to bear in the recruitment and control of the workforce will be strongest amongst employers employing workers off-the-books.

Consequences of informal recruitment

In order to illustrate the consequences of informal recruitment, I intend to focus specifically on the experiences of the women employed as contract cleaners. Since all sixteen of the women employed as contract cleaners (as with all the other wage labourers in this study) were working unofficially, then they were not entitled to any form of employment protection or benefits. Thus, if one of the women was off sick or had to deal with some family crisis, then she did not receive payment for any time she took off, regardless of her length of service to the organisation.

Furthermore, subcontracting firms are involved in a constant effort to fulfil contracts and make profits and this results in a continuous intensification of the labour process. Thus if employees take time off work, this can put the implementation of the contract into jeopardy. These problems were averted by the women in this sample, through the manipulation of social relationships within the workplace. All the women interviewed stated that when a close colleague had to take time off work, then her chain of social contacts within the organisation joined together and distributed her workload between them. This typically happened among friends, neighbours and relatives but often extended over a team of cleaners working in the same part of a building. The women usually co-operated knowing that they may need the favour returned at some future date. In the process, the women taking time off work were guaranteed their weekly wage, their employment was not placed in jeopardy (unless this was a frequent occurrence) and the smooth running of the contract was ensured.

A further benefit of informal recruitment along social networks, for the contracting company, was the inability of the female cleaners interviewed to do anything constructive to change their situation. This inability was not just due to the informal nature of their employment but also to the fact that each cleaner had a friend, relative or neighbour also working for the organisation. Maguire's (1986) study of a telecommunications firm in Northern Ireland, revealed how the encouragement of worker, family or community dependence on one firm tends to maximize control and reduce industrial conflict.

Similar observations can be made from looking at the experience of one of the cleaners interviewed. Occasionally contract cleaning firms are involved in cleaning out newly built houses. The work is very messy, the cleaners moving in after a variety of tradesmen have completed their individual construction tasks. Since the work is much more sporadic than their usual contracts, the contract cleaning firms involved generally rely on casual workers who can be called in or laid off as necessary. Alternatively or simultaneously, they can rely on existing contract cleaners to take on this work at weekends. Frances, one of the contract cleaners interviewed, was approached by her supervisor and asked if she would be interested in doing some overtime by working on these houses over the weekend. Frances agreed and worked from 9.00am to 8.00pm (including breaks), on the Saturday and Sunday of one weekend. No hourly rate was agreed in advance but Frances was convinced that because she was engaged in overtime, she would be paid double her usual rate. When she received her pay packet the following Thursday, she found that she was paid £1 per hour, her usual rate, for her work the previous weekend. Frances summed up her feelings as follows:

> I was so angry. My clothes were ruined. I was filthy. Muck was stuck to my hair and for what - £1 an hour. Its an insult. I wanted to do something about it. I felt they should be reported or something. It couldn't be right to pay people that little, especially for overtime. I didn't care if I got into trouble for not letting on about my wages to

> the dole. But what could I do. My sister and sister-in-law still worked there. In the end, I just walked out and never went back. But I still get angry every time I think about it.

A further advantage of recruitment on the basis of informal contacts is that it makes this form of exploitative employment less alienating. While all sixteen of the contract cleaners interviewed, stressed that they were working above all else for instrumental purposes (ie they needed the money) nonetheless, eleven of the sample stressed the close companionship of their workmates as an added incentive. Since their workmates were also their friends, neighbours and relatives, and since family obligations prevented the women from meeting as often as they would have liked; informal employment provided a venue for catching up on local gossip and keeping up to date with news regarding the welfare of a wider range of friends and relations than they could otherwise have managed.

The informal recruiting process is reflected in the uneven pay structure illustrated in Table 7.6. No standardised wage structure exists for informal workers in the contract cleaning industry. Rather the new cleaners were paid according to the level paid to the person responsible for informally recruiting them. The persons responsible for recruitment of the sixteen cleaners were informal wage labourers already employed by the cleaning firms. Thus, if the friend, neighbour or relative of a new recruit was paid £1 per hour, then she would be paid £1 per hour. Similarly, if the existing cleaner was paid £1.20 per hour, then the new recruit would be paid £1.20 per hour and so on. Often the wage structure was uniform within specific buildings. Thus a team of cleaners would get £1 per hour for cleaning a certain building, while another team would get £1.30 per hour for cleaning a similar building for the same subcontractor. Given the scattered nature of the contract cleaning industry, cleaners in one building had no opportunity to interact with cleaners in another building, thus these wage disparities often remained hidden. Even if the women became aware through personal relationships outside work that friends, neighbours or relatives were being paid higher than them for similar work, they could never be sure that they were employed by the same subcontracting firm.

This latter point reflects a further aspect of the informal recruitment process. Most of the women interviewed knew very little about their employing company. Knowledge about employers was linked to the size of the organisation in which an informal wage labourer was employed. All the men in the sample knew their employer because all of them worked in very small scale concerns where the employer was also a worker, usually working alongside the informal wage labourers he hired. Similarly, the eight women interviewed along with the contract cleaners, all knew and worked beside their employer. Twelve of the sixteen contract cleaners had no idea who they worked for, a typical response being, 'Well, I think it's a big company from across the water'. Of the remaining four women, three knew the company they worked for by name but this was the extent of their limited knowledge. The remaining cleaner knew a certain amount about her employer and was the only one to have actually met her employer. The other fifteen had no contact with their employer. Usually the supervisor was the only company employee they knew apart from their immediate work group. The supervisor was often responsible for the hiring of new cleaners and for the day to day management of the cleaning team. New recruits were put into contact with the supervisor through existing informal workers employed by the company.

Wider attitudes to informal wage labour

This form of informal economic activity creates a considerable wave of public indignation and moral outrage. In the introductory paragraph of this chapter, I pointed out some of the differences that exist between informal wage labour and other types of off-the-books economic activity. These differences are very apparent when looking at societal attitudes to different forms of off-the-books activity. While individuals who engage in off-the-books economic activity are all engaged in attempts to defraud the public purse, nonetheless, tax evasion tends to be regarded as a shrewd business practice rather than fraud, while DHSS fraud is regarded much more negatively as scrounging from the state.

Tax offenders are not as severely punished as DHSS abusers. The Inland Revenue tends to seek settlement rather than prosecution and relies on negotiations between the taxpayer and his/her advisers, and the revenue to arrive at a mutually agreed figure of tax which has been underpaid. During 1986-1987 (Cook 1989,p.151-153) there were 439 Inland Revenue prosecutions compared to 8090 Supplementary Benefit Prosecutions.

The media continually foster images of individuals engaging in social security abuse 'living it up' with luxurious lifestyles. Fast cars, continental holidays are the prizes that can be gained from engaging in this form of off-the-books activity. Others suggest that the presence of social security fraud indicates that there is plenty of employment opportunities around for those who genuinely seek them. These 'myths' are soon evaporated when we look at the specific types of employment often involved in such frauds. There appears to be a strong link between low paid, part time and casual employment and social security fraud. The amalgamation of welfare benefits and sporadic wages of the informal wage labourers in this study rarely, provided any of them with the scope to lead a luxurious lifestyle. At best, these people could afford the consumer products most of us now regard as 'necessities' to modern living such as washing machines, colour televisons and video recorders. But more usually, particularly for these female wage labourers, the additional, often pitiful extra income, did little more than enable their families to obtain basic, bare necessities.

Opportunities to formalize

Twenty three of the twenty four female wage labourers interviewed were married with husbands claiming welfare benefits. Thus, the opportunity for these women to formalize their off-the-books activities ultimately depends on their husbands' ability to gain formal employment, hence leaving them free to compete in the formal market. The high levels of unemployment in West Belfast generally and in Newbury in particular, make this an unlikely proposition. All the husbands of the twenty three married female respondents had endured long term unemployment, had no educational qualifications and had little or no occupational training. The women shared these characteristics with their husbands. Only one of the female wage labourers interviewed held any form of educational qualifications, having three O levels. She had no formal occupational training, however. The remaining twenty three respondents' previous employment experience included a variety of unskilled occupations such as cleaners, barmaids, waitresses and shop assistants.

The thirty seven male wage labourers had all experienced varying spells of unemployment as the following table indicates:

Table 7.7
Male informal wage labourers' length of time unemployed

No of Years Unemployed	No of Male Wage Labourers
0-4 years	5
5-9 years	14
10-14 years	10
over 15 years	8
Total	37

There appear to be two opportunities available to these men to formalize their informal activities. Firstly, they could become formal wage labourers or secondly they could set themselves up in self employment. Since none of the thirty seven males held any educational qualifications and since only eleven had any form of occupational training, then this latter option only really applies to these eleven men. Self employment in turn needs capital and this may act as a deterrent against the possiblity of any of these eleven men availing themselves of this option. Becoming a formal wage labourer depends on the availability of formal jobs. West Belfast is a notorious unemployment blackspot and as I outlined in a previous chapter, the men from Newbury are doubly disadvantaged by having a Newbury address. The recession in the building trade makes it unlikely that any of the skilled tradesmen would find permanent secure formal employment. The two butchers have already travelled extensively throughout West Belfast and the city centre trying to find formal employment and up to the time of the interview only succeeded in finding casual informal employment. The men with no skills whatsoever could only compete in the formal market for low paid, unskilled jobs and may find that it makes economic sense to remain as informal wage labourers even though this employment is unpredictable.

Expanding on this last point, opportunities to formalize depend on the individual's motivation to formalize. This in turn depends on how consistent the informal wage labour is. Most of the women interviewed expressed no desire to seek formal employment. While some of them expressed some sort of general awareness that their conditions of work were poor, nonetheless most of them were grateful for the opportunity to earn extra income and realised that because of the nature of their husbands' employment status, they had little alternative.

The skilled tradesmen also expressed little desire to seek formal employment. Most of these men were able to find reasonable constant informal employment and were only laid off during the adverse climatic conditions that affect formal and informal workers engaged in construction work. One of the bricklayers had been in self employment for a short period before transferring to informal employment. He stated that while at times he earned quite substantial amounts, when this was spread over the whole year to cover the periods of inactivity that usually plagued him in the winter months, the return was not as significant. He states that he now prefers the peace of mind he gains from knowing that no matter what, he has the security of weekly welfare benefit.

The unskilled labourers were more divided in their attitudes to informal employment. Those who engaged in consistent informal employment stated that when they amalgamated their informal income with welfare benefits they achieved a higher return than they could ever hope to achieve in the formal market, given the fact that they had no marketable skills. Other unskilled labourers who could only secure sporadic informal employment were much more dissatisfied. Their ultimate goal was a secure formal job. The two butchers were also unhappy about the casual employment they were able to secure. Their overall purpose in continually travelling around butchery retail establishments is to find formal employment, not casual informal employment.

For the males, consistency of informal wage labour was not the only factor influencing their appreciation of this type of economic activity. The general observation emerging from the interviews with the men is that the younger the respondent, the more likely he is to feel dissatisfied with his status as an informal wage labourer. Hence the younger unskilled wage labourers expressed more desire to return to formal employment than the older unskilled wage labourers, regardless of the consistency of their informal employment. The older the men in the sample and the longer they had been formally unemployed, the less important they viewed formal employment as a priority in their lives. Casual informal employment backed by the security of welfare benefits was the norm in their lives.

Opportunities to formalize also depend on the state's attitude to this form of informal activity. It is naive to assume that the present government is interested in formalizing all aspects of informal economic activity. For example, in an era of savage welfare cuts, the government has no interest in formalizing voluntary work, preferring to emphasise the duties of individuals and communities to their weaker members. The government is however, very interested in formalizing paid informal employment. Some conservatives believe that the existence of informal wage labourers inflates the rate of unemployment for specific areas. The existence of informal wage labourers is also very costly to the government. Firstly they are paying these households unnecessary welfare benefits. Secondly they are denied the National Insurance Contributions and Income Tax some of these people would be liable to pay if they were in formal employment. Finally, the availability of casual informal wage labour plus benefits deters some people from applying for low paid, unskilled jobs. These attitudes however, ignore the ways in which the state gains through privatisation and the subtle important links that exist between formal and informal employment.

Links between formal and informal employment

I think that it is important to initially stress that it is formal enterprises that employ informal workers. Employers' motivations for employing off-the-books wage labourers depends on the nature of the industry and the size of the organisation involved. For the contract cleaning industry, employing informal wage labourers is an effective way of maximizing profit. The contract cleaning industry provides a visible illustration of Marx's classic theory of surplus value. Surplus value is extracted more easily and more effectively from casual informal workers. On the other hand profit is not the only motive in this decision to employ off-the-books wage labour. Subcontracting firms are involved in competitive tendering whereby the most successful tender is generally also the cheapest. The cleaning industry is a labour intensive one, the bulk of its expenditure relating to the payment of wages. Thus to be successful and secure a contract, the subcontractor is continually involved in attempts to increase workloads, intensify work practices and lower the wages of the cleaners he employs. According to Mitter (1986,p.55), the effective use of a flexible and non unionised labour force is a necessary condition for survival in the cut throat competition among subcontractors today. Employing labour off-the-books is one of the most effective means of keeping costs low. In relation to this particular study, attempts to do this are facilitated by the large number of males unemployed in Newbury estate which generally excludes their wives from the formal labour market.

Other small scale enterprises may need the existence of informal wage labourers to remain economically viable. Corner shops, self employed individuals and small business concerns may be unable to afford legitimate workers. Once an employee earns over a certain amount per week, the employer is responsible for deducting National Insurance Contributions and Income Tax. If an employee works over 24 hours per week, the employer has a responsibility to adhere to various occupational regulations such as the payment of Sickness Benefit, Maternity Leave and so on. These administrative and financial obligations that employers have to their employees may act as a further deterrent to small business concerns.

The problem of maintaining legitimate employees is particularly prevalent for the small scale building contractors mentioned earlier. The presence of informal wage labourers help these small scale employers cope with such crises as the recession in the building industry, fluctuating seasonal demands and unpredictable weather and remain in business. One of the most interesting aspects of this particular occupation has been the observation that a uniform price structure seems to exist in West Belfast for informal building workers. Labourers are paid around £80 per week, tradesmen around £100 per week, while bricklayers working on extensions tend to be paid £120 per week. Five of the twenty four building workers interviewed worked at one time or another for the two subcontractors interviewed. The other nineteen were employed by a wide variety of building contractors operating in West Belfast yet this uniform price structure largely prevailed. Most of the men interviewed when asked about their wages stated that they were 'paid the going rate plus benefits'. This almost subconscious amalgamation of informal wage plus benefits was also reflected in the two employing subcontractors' attitudes to this type of employment. They also referred to 'going rates' and stated that these rates took into consideration the fact that these men would also be claiming benefits. This in turn influenced the degree of exploitation experienced by these men. Since neither workers nor employers regarded the wage rate in isolation but referred to it in the wider context of informal wage plus benefits, then the two subcontractors interviewed did not feel that they were exploiting their informal workforce while the informal wage labourers in turn rarely felt exploited.

All the informal wage labourers in this chapter were paid in cash and none of the sample ever received a pay slip or written record of payment. The ways in which the individuals and organisations who informally employ workers 'off-the-record' deal with their own bookkeeping in order to conceal or account for this activity is outside the scope of this study. The two subcontractors I interviewed state that they deal with this by underdeclaring the amount of work they undertake over any given period. This in turn leads to Income Tax and Vat evasion.

The wages paid to informal workers ultimately finds it way back into the formal economy. The informal wage labourers in this study use their income to purchase the goods and services they could not otherwise afford. This in turn benefits the formal economy. Small shopkeepers in areas of high unemployment may for example, be only able to remain economically viable because at least some of the 'workless' population have alternative sources of income.

Summary

This chapter began with descriptive accounts of male and female wage labourers and outlined some of the similarities and contrasts between them. It was suggested that differential access to informal employment between males and females reflected patterns in operation in the formal economy. At this stage, some contrasts with Pahl's work on the Isle of Sheppey were outlined. In particular, Pahl's observation that informal employment was linked to formal employment was found to be only partly applicable to this study. Informal employment is ultimately linked to formal employment but rather than informal workers being recruited by those already in employment (as Pahl's study indicated), the informal wage labourers in this study were recruited by friends, neighbours and relatives already in informal employment. These individuals acted as intermediaries between formal employers and informal recruits. This in turn leads to polarization not just between employed and unemployed households but among unemployed households themselves between those able to gain access to paid informal employment and those unable to gain access to either formal or informal employment. The consequences of informal recruitment practices for both employers and informal employees were outlined and the attitudes of the wider society to this form of informal economic activity was explored. This was followed by a discussion of the opportunities informal wage labourers have to formalize their situation. The final section of the chapter outlined some of the links between formal and informal employment.

Notes

Part of this chapter is based on a paper submitted to the British Sociological Association Annual Conference held at the University of Surrey in April 1990. The paper is published in S. Arber and N. Gilbert, (eds), *Women and Working Lives, Divisions and Change*, MacMillan, 1992.

8 Shady economic transactions

In this chapter, I want to focus on the final aspect of informal economic activity to be explored in this book. The chapter concerns the more dubious forms of economic trading practices that take place in the estate. Some of these activities are overlooked by the wider community while others are deplored and subject to paramilitary punishment squads. The chapter will focus on three main areas. Firstly, fiddling and its relationship to informal wage labour. Secondly, the economic benefits attached to joy-riding. Thirdly, a more general discussion on the various shady ways in which residents of the estate gain access to scarce resources. Actors' motivations for engaging in, and supporting these practices will be outlined. This will be followed by a discussion of the tolerance of the community towards these various practices. Finally, the links between the economic transactions discussed in this chapter and the formal economy will be explored.

Background to the data

> We may have trouble locating practitioners of the vices we are interested in, or locating them in such a way as to ...get any information about their deviance, because they will not engage in it in our presence or because they will not admit.... that they engage in it. (Becker 1970,p.30)

Those involved in shady dealings are perhaps best studied using covert methods. However, apart from problems of access and the ethical issues involved, my interest in the various aspects of informal economic strategies discussed so far, and my use of the survey method precluded this choice of method. On the other hand, studying sensitive activities overtly by allowing oneself to be known as a researcher or outsider may severely limit the amount of information one can obtain. The controversial nature of the topics under study here, limited the range of methods available.

The survey of the area for example proved an unsatisfactory mechanism for locating the perpetrators of the activities outlined in this chapter. The survey was useful though, for giving me an insight into community attitudes to the various shady transactions that take place in the estate; for example how the community accept and justify some dealings and reject and condemn others. The survey was also useful for enabling me to witness how extensive the trading of stolen goods is. On many occasions, while interviewing householders during the survey, I was shown leather boots, clothes and other commodities that had been obtained 'cheap'. The survey was less successful at locating those involved, however. A high degree of trustworthiness must exist between researcher and respondent if the latter is to 'come clean' regarding shady transactions. It is difficult to establish this level of trust using the survey method. The survey approach was useful for exploring other 'illegal' activities such as 'doing the double' because this practice was considered widespread and justifiable. Here, blame was placed on the state for not providing adequate welfare benefits and enough secure 'properly' paid formal employment. Joy-riding, fiddling and stealing are more controversial activities and are more difficult to justify. They are also dealt with more severely by formal organisations. For example, some joy-riders have been injured or fatally wounded by the security forces. Hence, perpetrators of these activities are unlikely to recount their experiences to a 'stranger'. As a result, the activities outlined in this chapter are based on very scant evidence.

Only six respondents in all were engaged in shady transactions, although accounts were backed up by information gained during the survey of the area. The six included two males who participate in fiddling, two male joy-riders and two sisters who engage in stealing from city centre stores. One of the males who engaged in fiddling attended a night class I taught in the community school in the estate. He was known to me for approximately one year before I interviewed him about his fiddling activities. During that time, I met the respondent on a weekly basis during the class and was often in his company at socializing events organised by the school. He put me in touch with his mate who also engaged in fiddling. The mate put me in touch with one of the joy-riders who then put me in contact with the other joy-rider. The sisters were introduced to me in a similar way. This snowball approach enabled my introducers to vouch for me and hence enhanced my trustworthiness.

Each respondent was interviewed at least three times. Moreover, each duo were interviewed separately and together. The separate interviews enabled me to check the validity of the account given by each participant in each activity. Hence for example, the account given to me by each individual joy-rider could be checked against the other. The separate interviews were casual and informal and were not meant to give the impression of a cross examination. Thus I feel it was unlikely that respondents would have clarified their accounts with each other before talking to me. On the other hand, the small sample size and the fact that all the respondents were willing volunteers suggests that the accounts will not represent the full range of experiences and social types engaged in each of these activities from the Newbury area.

Fiddling

Various self report studies indicate that pilfering and fiddling at work is a common activity. Between 75 per cent and 92 per cent of employees admit pilfering and stealing from their employers (Henry 1981,p.12). Ditton (1977) argues that certain kinds of industry, particularly the service industries are more amenable to shady economic activity than others. This observation has been backed by a whole range of occupational studies; hotel waiters (Mars 1982), milkmen (Bigus 1972) and breadsalesmen (Ditton 1977). All these examples of fiddling have been linked to formal employment. Employees commonly engage in fiddling to add to the low wages traditionally earned in the service industries. What I want to do here, is to link fiddling to informal employment. The account which follows is based on detailed interviews with two males who work informally for a dry cleaning firm. Like the occupations mentioned above, the job provides optimal opportunities for fiddling. This is not to say that this is the only example of fiddling attached to the informal employment experiences of residents in the estate. For the reasons mentioned above, data on this practice was difficult to collect. On the other hand, the main informal employment opportunities available to residents in the estate did not give the participants much scope to engage in fiddling. Most of the men worked in a labouring capacity in the construction industry. They were generally employed on very small scale projects involving the renovation of individual properties. They often worked alongside their employer who himself was attempting to complete the work at a fixed price. Hence opportunities for lucrative extras seemed slight. For females, the most common form of informal employment was contract cleaning. Again contractors were involved in attempts to undercut each others' tenders and the whole process was characterised by low wages, scant cleaning materials and continuous intensification of the work process. Indeed, instead of pilfering materials to bring home, some of the women increased their cleaning materials allocation by bringing products into work from home.

Fiddling and informal employment

Brief details about the two respondents who work as dry cleaning agents were outlined in the previous chapter. Both are best friends and work together covering the same route. One is aged twenty nine and is married with one child. He has been employed informally in this occupation for just over one year. The other respondent is twenty three and is engaged to be married. He has been employed informally for eight months and was initially recruited by his friend. Both work for a Pakistani family which has several dry cleaning retail outlets throughout the city of Belfast. The firm also specialises in a door to door dry cleaning service. Because of the overt political image of Newbury and surrounding estates, the Pakistani family are reluctant to become directly involved in the collection of garments to be dry cleaned. Furthermore, because rioting breaks out from time to time in Newbury and surrounding areas, it is difficult to employ 'outsiders' to the area to work as dry cleaning agents. Hence the Pakistani family, where possible, recruit indigenous workers from specific areas to be responsible for collection of items to be dry cleaned in their own 'patches'.

According to the two respondents interviewed, the Pakistani family tend to employ most of their work force on an informal basis. Working conditions are poor, wages are low and fringe benefits are non existent. The two respondents interviewed earn around £1.50 per hour. They have a company van which they use to collect and return items for dry cleaning. They work in Newbury and surrounding estates and go from door to door, asking householders if they have any garments they want dry cleaned. Orders are collected and the owner is given a ticket numbering the garment. The same number is attached to the garment and the owner's name and address is written on the back of the ticket. The identification tabs used are 'cloakroom tickets' which can be purchased at any stationery store. The garments are brought to the main premises to be dry cleaned and returned to the customer two or three days later. It is only at this stage that money changes hands.

According to Mars and Nicod (1981,p.68), the simplest forms of pilferage are overcharging and short changing. Both these options were regarded by the respondents as unsuitable and a undesirable mechanism for fiddling. Leaflets advertising the dry cleaning service and price lists were usually distributed in the area prior to the dry cleaning agents commencing their rounds. The price lists were comprehensive giving standard prices for the cleaning of particular items of clothing. Most households only gave in one item at a time to be dry cleaned, hence spreading out the costs. Payment was collected when the garment was returned. Given these circumstances, opportunities to fiddle the customer were limited. Moreover, both respondents felt it morally unjustifiable to 'take from one of your own'. Hence fiddling was practiced at the expense of the employer leaving customers unaffected and unaware.

The procedure followed was to purchase a duplicate set of 'cloakroom tickets', the same colour and with the same numbers as the authentic ones. Although serial numbers were stamped in small print on each ticket and these differed, the owners were unaware that two almost identical sets of tickets were in operation. The bogus tickets were given out to customers and garments taken, cleaned and paid for without the knowledge of the owners. Hence for example, two customers wanting coats cleaned would be given yellow ticket number seven. One coat would be put through the books, the other would be cleaned without the knowlege of the owner and the payment pocketed by the respondents. The procedure was supported by a woman who worked in the main premises and was responsible for dry cleaning the garments. The woman was also employed informally by the Pakistani family and was paid £1 per hour. She conspired with the two respondents to clean surplus garments without the owners knowledge and the proceeds were divided between the three participants. The two males received on average £25 per week on top of their wages while the woman made around £15 extra per week.

Joy-riding

Joy-riding has become a very common form of deviant behaviour for young males in working class urban areas in Northern Ireland. The procedure generally involves stealing a car, driving it around for a few hours and then abandoning it. To enhance the thrill value attached to the practice, joy-riders often engage in attempts to involve the police or army in a high speed car chase. Often by the time cars are eventually abandoned, they are practically 'write offs'. The exploit can be a very dangerous one. Often joy-riders crash through security road blocks or barriers and as a result come under fire from the security forces mistaking them for IRA 'terrorists'. The practice is often frowned upon by local communities as many residents have become road victims of the joy-riders careless, reckless and inexperienced driving. One man I interviewed was left a cripple after an accident caused by joy-riders within the Newbury estate.

Joy-riding is commonly seen as an example of Cohen's non utilitarian crime (1955). Satisfaction is gained solely from stealing and wrecking someone else's car. The joy-riders I spoke to stated that while initial satisfaction is limited to simply stealing and joy-riding in the car nonetheless through time some joy-riders come to see the economic potential that can be derived from the exploit. Articles left in the car can be utilised. Car radios and cassette players can be removed and sold. The car itself can be stripped and batteries, tyres and other parts can be traded. Hence through joy-riding a pattern of buying, selling, trading and swapping emerges.

According to the two respondents I spoke to, there are about thirty young males from Newbury engaged in 'commercial' joy-riding. The average age of joy-riders is between thirteen and twenty five. The two respondents I interviewed were aged sixteen and seventeen respectively. Both state that joy-riders tend to work in groups of at least three. Each group have their own identifiable patch in the estate where their trading activities take place. Often a number of groups will operate from the same patch. These trading grounds are where most of the joy-riders' transactions take place. They deal with two main types of people, casual customers and fences. Casual customers are people the joy-riders deal with on a one-off basis. They are people who hear through the grapevine that certain items they desire are for sale. These may be car parts or other commodities. The casual customers turn up at the joy-riders' trading ground, ask for him by name, state who sent them or told them what was on offer and negotiate the price for the desired item. The joy-riders' state that if the customer is unknown to them then they must give specific details about the source of their information before trading can commence.

Both joy-riders I interviewed supply fences on a regular basis. Usually these people require specific orders and commercial' joy-riding will be aimed at satisfying the fences' particular requirements. The joy-riders work with two fences who each specialise in different commodities. One deals with car parts including radios and cassette players. The other deals with household electrical goods and clothing. Occasionally, houses are robbed to satisfy the requirements of the latter fence, the stolen car being used to cruise potential areas to rob and to provide a getaway vehicle. Video recorders are the most popular item. The joy-riders state that there are two reasons which encourage them to deal with fences. Firstly, they state that they do not have enough contacts to dispose of stolen goods themselves. Casual customers can never be relied on. Secondly, working through a fence minimises the risk. While fences themselves may be a security risk in that if they are caught there is always the possibility that they may 'tout', nonetheless their specialisation at distributing stolen goods makes them a crucial link in the relationship between sellers and buyers, that is, thieves and receivers of stolen goods (Klockars 1974). As one of the joy-riders says:

> Look we can hardly advertise our goods. You have to be careful in this business. I can get rid of a whole load of gear through P., no problem. I don't have to haggle with customers. He just takes the stuff and

gives me the money. It couldn't be easier.

Prices charged to casual customers and fences also differ. The joy-riders state that if the item is relatively new, they usually charge casual customers about half the price they would have to pay elsewhere while the fences can get the same goods for as little as a quarter of this price.

Stealing from formal retail establishments

A variety of studies (Henry 1976, Ditton 1977, Mars and Nicod 1981) link the source of stolen goods to formal employment. Employees pilfer goods from work to sell through their social networks. As a result, in particular communities, a range of goods can be obtained 'cheap'. Pahl's study (1984a) of the Isle of Sheppey revealed how everyone on the island seemed, at one time, to be related to someone who worked in the docks and as a result, a whole range of products ended up in the homes or fridges of the residents of the island. In Newbury, opportunities for formal employment are scant. Hence 'cheap' goods pilfered from formal employment establishments are rare. This is not to say that 'cheap' goods are not then available. The area is a very low income one. Formally produced goods and services are often priced beyond the capabilities of most of the residents of the estate, thus the residents have to turn to more shady means for satisfying their needs and wants. They do this by purchasing items directly stolen by members of the estate from formal retail outlets.

Again information on the extent of this practice is very limited due to the difficulties in locating respondents as mentioned earlier. Only two females who directly participate in this activity were interviewed, although the data is to some extent enhanced by the responses of residents during the survey of the area. The two females are sisters and state that other members of their immediate and extended family network also engage in stealing. They typically steal items of clothing and other small household goods from city centre retail units. They state that the bigger the shop premises, the easier it is to steal. The girls believe that the secret to being a successful thief is to be as blatant as possible. As the girls told me:

> Look, if you slink about looking all around you, you're only drawing attention to yourself. What I do is go in, lift whatever it is and walk calmly out the door with it.

> I go in with no coat and take a coat off the hanger and put it over my arm and then go and ask the doorman the time or something. I get a

> real kick out of standing there with something I've stole and nobody being any the wiser. People expect you to look guilty or something. I don't and that's why I get away with it.

The girls steal items at random and also to fulfil specific orders. Sometimes customers will see something in the town and go and ask the girls to specifically steal the item. If it is an item of clothing, the customer will state his/her size and the colour required. The girls will steal the item and pass it on to the customer within a few days of the request being made. To prove the accuracy of their accounts, the girls, on several occasions asked me to go around the town and pick out something that I would like and they would then steal it for me. Whether a researcher should allow himself/herself to become directly involved with illegal behaviour to enhance validity is a matter of judgement. In this case, I preferred to remain an observer of the trading in stolen goods rather than a receiver of stolen property. On a separate occasion I did witness a customer receiving a stolen item that had been requested previously from the girls.

The opportunity to steal is not enough. There must also be a demand for the commodities stolen and a willingness for customers to receive stolen goods. Shady economic transactions become legitimised in an economy of scarcity. During the survey, I was shown several items that had been obtained 'cheap' on the estate. The illegal aspect of receving stolen goods was in no case referred to. This was simply viewed as another means of obtaining otherwise unaffordable resources.

Customers have three main resources for obtaining stolen goods. Firstly, they can go to certain houses in the estate where families are known to engage in stealing and make specific orders for goods. The two sisters mentioned in the previous paragraph operate in this way. Secondly, they can go to a public bar on the outskirts of the estate where stolen goods are regularly traded. As one respondent told me:

> You can buy anything from a television set to a pair of socks. You don't need to approach anyone. Just go in and sit down and through time someone will approach you and ask if you are looking for anything 'cheap'. If you're not they'll just go away again. Some people won't buy anything in case there's a kick back. But they'll still turn a blind eye to what's going on. The rest will buy away because that's what they're there for.

Thirdly, stolen goods are occasionally sold from door to door. One respondent who is formally employed as a van driver recounted the following incident:

> I was in the bar having a few bevies when these two guys came in. I knew them to see like. They asked me if that was my van outside and when I said it was, they asked me to run them up to the estate. We had to call round to this house first like, and there they had about a hundred pair of ladies boots. The whole living room was full of them. They had knocked off some lorry or something. I run them up to the estate and they gave me two pair of boots for the lift. The boots cost twenty eight quid and they were selling them for a tenner. They had got rid of them within two days. Everybody knows what goes on around here unless they're stupid or they live in another planet or something. The boys went to key houses to get rid of the stuff but key houses can only take so much. These guys sold the rest around the doors. Here nobody asks no questions and then they're told no lies.

The fact that such a method is used for selling stolen goods illustrates the tacit assent of the residents of the estate regarding these activities.

A variety of other shady practices were prevalent on the estate. Some residents spoke with relish about how tools and other materials utilised by the Housing Executive to upgrade the estate continually disappeared overnight. On three occasions while admiring the gardens of residents of the estate I was told that the plants were 'borrowed' from a local cemetery. In the aftermath of the Gibraltar killings, Newbury was plunged into one week of severe rioting in which many buses, lorries and cars were stolen and burnt on the estate. Some of the more enterprising rioters stripped vehicles prior to burning and sold the parts. Buses were regarded as the most profitable vehicle with several residents stating that around £600 could be made from the carcase of a bus. Hence, no possible income generating opportunity is allowed to slip away.

Changes in Government legislation may also transform the boundaries between legal and illegal activity. Because of the 'troubles' in Northern Ireland, the sale and purchase of fireworks is banned. Hallowe'en can therefore no longer be celebrated in the traditional way. In response to this state of affairs, a number of households in the Newbury estate import fireworks under rather dubious circumstances, from Britain. Aware that they are providing a product not otherwise available, these households charge exorbitant rates for these fireworks and are able to make a handsome profit during the lead up to Hallowe'en. Such a practice illustrates that legal constraints do not eliminate the demand for a product but rather ensure that such a demand will be met illegally.

Motivations to engage in shady economic dealings

Motivations to engage in shady economic practices were varied. For the two respondents who engaged in fiddling, the desire to bolster up low wages was the primary motivation. Both respondents believed that they were being exploited by the Pakistani family whom they worked for and thus felt they were quite justified in earning extra cash 'on the side' using whatever means were open to them. The joy-riders and the two sisters stated that they were also mainly motivated by the desire to make money. Henry (1976) states that while most respondents when questioned about illegal transactions will state they are 'doing it for the money' nonetheless often non economic factors are just as important. Henry bases this judgement on the fact that most of the amateur traders he interviewed did not make very much money from their transactions. To Henry the cementing of friendships were more important to the amateur traders than the potential financial gain from their activities. Ditton (1977), on the other hand argues that the economic motive is the primary one but illegal traders will emphasise other social motives to underplay the monetary benefits they derive from their activities. However, the respondents in both studies depended on their formal employment for their mainstream income. Hence their trading activities were a boost to their income rather than a necessary supplement. The joy-riders and the two sisters who steal make no excuses regarding their primary motivation for dealing in shady trading. Simply, they need the money and they will use whatever means are available to supplement inadequate benefit entitlements. This is not to say that all transactions are tinged by the same economic rationality. The thief may give things freely to his immediate family and friends and charge others. Even where charges were made, like the other traders discussed previously, no standard pricing structure existed. Prices varied depending on how close one was related to the trader and the frequency with which the trading took place.

Community tolerance of shady economic transactions

The community also, by and large, supported the shady economic transactions discussed so far. This was mainly because given the residents' lack of access to mainstream resources, receiving stolen goods was the only mechanism open to them to satisfy their wants and needs. Even those who were unwilling to receive stolen goods were willing to turn a blind eye to the transactions provided no one in the community was robbed. Tolerance by the community could be guaranteed provided no resident was ever robbed. Where this happened, the community reacted adversely to these economic practices. When city centre stores were robbed, most residents tended to believe that no one was really harmed. Stores could well afford to lose some of their goods and anyway the insurance would always pay up. Likewise when people were robbed in more affluent areas (outside West Belfast), a similar rational was used to justify the actions. People in affluent areas didn't really suffer if their houses were robbed as again they could easily afford it and their insurance would always ultimately 'collect the tab'. But where 'one's own people' were the victims, the community reacted in a hostile way calling on the paramilitaries to exact justice on prolonged offenders.

Different terms were often used to distinguish between those who committed crimes outside the community and those who made the community suffer because of their activities. The term 'hood' was utilised by some members of the estate to describe the first category of offender while the term 'thug' was used to describe the latter type of offender. As one respondent told me:

> There's a hell of a difference between the ones that steal in the town and the ones that rob neighbours. Like, the ones that steal in the town are stealing from businesses right. I mean nobody really owns the money or the things you nick from a big store. But the ones that steal in people's houses. They're just thugs. Nobody wants anything to do with them. Breaking into somebody's house and stealing a video or a TV is beneath a lot of hoods.

Throughout the survey of the area however, I was told of many instances where residents of the estate had been victims of robberies. Often these robberies were not pre-meditated. Rather locals would take the opportunity to steal anything that was left unguarded on a doorstep or in the front garden of any property. Hence bikes, prams and other items continually disappeared if left unattended. One respondent told me that her baby was crying in her pram and she lifted her out of the pram and brought her into her house. Less than five minutes later when she went out to bring in the pram, it had disappeared. Others stated that when they went on holiday, by the time they returned, the coal in their outside bunkers had disappeared. Car owners were often particularly badly affected. Three respondents told me that they had to give up their car because the petrol was regularly siphoned from their tank. Another two respondents had the wheels of their car removed during the night. Others were the victims of pre-meditated house robberies. Videos and televisions were the most popularly stolen items. In some instances however, the perpetrators of these activities were subject to harsh community punishments.

Paramilitary justice

The extent to which paramilitary racketeering was prevalent on the estate is outside the scope of this study. I justify this exclusion for three reasons. Firstly, to question survey respondents and other informants too closely about paramilitary activites may have jeopardized the whole research project. Secondly, from their literature review of the informal economy in Northern Ireland, Harding and Jenkins (1988,p.121-122) note four areas of economic activity in which paramilitary organisations seem implicated. These were, fraud in the building trade with respect to the use of 714 Tax Exemption Certificates, protection rackets involving retailing shops and chains paying out 'insurance' money, paramilitary involvement in the black taxis and finally gambling machines and the licensed trade. With respect to the first point, there has been no new building work in Newbury over the past number of years, hence while the construction industry as a whole may provide paramilitaries with opportunities for illegal earnings, this potential only exists outside the estate. With regard to the second point made by Harding and Jenkins regarding protection money being paid by retailers, I have no knowledge of any retail units within Newbury paying out such 'insurance' money. Even if this was the case, the shops within Newbury are small scale ventures servicing a community where money is scarce, hence their profit margins are very low and they are unlikely to be in a position to pay out large sums in 'insurance' payments. With regard to the third and fourth potential source of illegal revenue, both the black taxis and the licensing trade have been subject to considerable scrutiny over recent years. For example, new licensing laws introduced in 1988 curtailed the opening hours of drinking clubs in an effort to reduce their profits. Moreover, the clubs have to fulfil a whole range of legal technicalities before they can operate as licensed traders. Again the drinking clubs in Newbury are servicing an unemployed community and again profits are bound to be affected. The black taxis have been subject to similar scrutiny making it difficult for them to employ workers 'off the record'. The only link between the black taxis and the paramilitaries is that positive discrimination seems to be practiced in that former political prisoners are more likely to be hired as formal black taxi men.

Within Newbury (and other republican strongholds), paramilitary groups operate as a community police force responsible for dealing with 'anti-social elements'. Community justice is by no means a new phenomenon. According to Whelan (Henry 1981,p.171) the system of justice has always been supplemented by informal institutions. Key social structures such as the family, the church and trade unions played in the past, and continue to play an important role at the base of the judicial pyramid. Ferdinand (Henry 1981,p.187) from his studies of early colonial America argues that the church, family and community maintained a firm hold on its members and the community in particular was a more powerful determinant against crime than written law.

Henry (1981,p.179-191) focusing on modern day justice systems argues that the formal judiciary system only handles the tip of the iceberg of criminal offences. This is because the majority of offences are handled within the contexts in which they occur by informal disciplinary procedure groups. For example, theft at work is often handled by the employer/manager of the premises issuing verbal warnings, formal written warnings or perhaps dismissal notices. Universities, prisons, trade unions, lawyers, doctors, dentists, pharmacists and social workers all decide disciplinary procedures within their own communities. Each group has the power to impose their own sanctions and ultimately withdraw the membership rights of the individual. However, while there is evidence of a significant degree of decentralised criminal processing, there is little evidence of decentralised justice. These disciplinary courts often provide rough justice since they are often victims, prosecutors, judges and juries. This rough justice is very apparent when looking at justice procedures exercised by the paramilitaries in working class communities.

There has been no 'normal' policing of the Newbury area for over twenty years. The police seem preoccupied with political crimes. Males in the estate are frequently stopped and interrogated by the police. The army often accompany the police as they patrol the estate or call to question or arrest a resident. Hence the police are seen as one of the primary upholders of the British State in Northern Ireland and as a force not to be trusted. 'Ordinary' crimes are rarely reported to the police. Because money is so tight for many households in the area, many people do not even report house break-ins as often they have no insurance policies, preferring to save the money and take the risk. Moreover, to inform on 'one's own' to an enemy force could place the family's future position in the community in jeopardy. The stigma attached to 'touting' runs deep in Irish society (Burton 1978). In these circumstances, residents turn to the paramilitaries for protection against anti-social elements in their communities. This means that judges and those who are judged are part of the same society.

The paramilitaries deal with undesirable elements in their areas in a number of ways. Social pressure always precedes punishment. The perpetrator will be publicly labelled as an 'anti-social element' and privately warned to cease his activities or risk physical punishment. Potential traders with the labelled person will also be encouraged not to continue dealings or have any future connections with whoever has been labelled. If this fails, the perpetrator risks being knee-capped. This is a procedure whereby the 'victim' is shot in one or both knees. The technique has become so refined and the paramilitaries so expert at carrying out the punishment that they know exactly where to aim to cause the most damage. This often results in 'victims' having to have their lower leg amputated. If this fails to deter the 'victim' (and it often does) then the perpetrator may be brought before a kangaroo court and told to leave Northern Ireland or risk being executed. During the time of the research, two brothers from Newbury were given this ultimatum. They left Northern Ireland the following morning and have been in England ever since.

Obviously this is a very rough form of justice, much more severe than that practiced by formal institutions. Some community members believe that these punishment squads go too far. Yet, amazingly, these tactics have not deterred 'anti-social elements' from continuing their dubious activities. The failure to protect Newbury from its more undesirable elements has proved a constant source of embarrassment for the paramilitaries and calls into question their effectiveness as a community police force.

Link between formal economy and shady economic transactions

This chapter focused on the trading activities of people who fiddle or steal and sell stolen goods. The activities outlined in this chapter fall between the sphere of work and employment. Fiddling, for example, is dependent on regular employment, either formal or informal. The two respondents who engage in fiddling in this chapter are informally employed by the owner of the dry cleaning business in which they work. The owner informally utilises the labour power of the two repsondents to increase his trading outlets and profit. The two respondents bolster the low wages they receive from their informal employment by fiddling to gain extra money. The joy-riders and the two female respondents do not depend on any employment relationship for the opportunity to trade in stolen goods and no employment relationship exists between them and their eventual customers. Their activities further illustrate the interpenetation of both the formal and informal economy. The respondents trade goods produced in the formal economy through a network of shady informal transactions. Their activities increases the residents' consumption of formal products. The illegal nature of these activities directly feed into insurance claims drawn from the formal economy. This is particularly the case for car thefts. Similarly the punishment squads draw on the resources of the National Health Service as 'victims' need intensive medical attention after knee-cappings.

9 Summary and conclusions

> People talk about work and worklessness. Of all the people I know, I don't know anyone who doesn't work and I resent this whole notion of workless people. The so called unemployed in my district, my neighbours, are among the most hard working people I know. They're not workless and must not be called workless. They may not be getting paid for their work but we have got to make sure that the day is finished when any two bit factory owner is able to tell us that his work in the factory is worth paying for but your work in your home, community or anywhere else is not worth paying for. (Statement by a resident of Newbury estate at a Public Inquiry into Unemployment 1983,p.42).

In Chapter One, I outlined the applicability of sociological accounts of the informal economy to the Newbury estate in West Belfast. The discussion focused, in particular, on Pahl's research into the informal economy in the Isle of Sheppey. Pahl's study was considered to have been the most important research project on this theme in the British Isles and more than any other study raised considerable doubts about earlier views on the extent and significance of informal work. Pahl's choice of location was no accident. He states that it was common gossip among those he talked to in the mainland towns that Sheppey was a 'seething heap of informal work' (1984,p.145). Hence Pahl felt that Sheppey could be regarded as a test case for investigating the extent and significance of informal work. If informal work was not flourishing in Sheppey, then it was unlikely to be flourishing anywhere else.

Pahl's work was taken as the theoretical starting point of the book. I suggested following Edgell and Hart (1988) that we need a case by case approach to informal work in order to dispel the notion that there is any such thing as a typical informal economy. Rather informal economies will differ depending on the locales in which they are set. Hence in order to illustrate the diversity of informal economies, local studies such as this are necessary.

Moreover, I utilised the term informal economic activities/strategies to refer to the practices outlined throughout the book. Hence I tried to move away from accounts which portray the formal and informal economy as separate economic spheres. Rather I focused on the distinctions outlined by Harding and Jenkins (1989,p.10-14) that exist between work and employment and formality and informality. Harding and Jenkins suggest that accounts of informal economic activity rarely differentiate between informal work and informal employment. The latter refers to 'economic activity carried out within a capitalist employment relationship, be it formally or informally organised' (1989,p.14). The former thus refers to forms of economic activity where this employment relationship is absent.

Chapter Four focused on the extent to which households in Newbury engaged in self provisioning by providing goods and services by relying on the labour power of internal family members while Chapter Five concentrated on the reciprocal build up of favours. Both these sets of activities were considered as unpaid informal work. No employment/wage relationship existed between the producers and consumers of the goods and services outlined in these two chapters.

The relationships surrounding the range of activities described in Chapter Six were qualitatively different from the employment relationships attached to the activities outlined in Chapter Seven. In Chapter Six, a market relationship existed between participants in community economic enterprises and their customers. These activities also displayed varying degrees of formality and informality as customers ranged from friends, neighbours and relatives to formal organisations. The chapter also included a discussion about a group of women who work as catalogue sales agents for a large formal organisation. The degree to which the state acknowledges this activity and the women's perceptions of this economic practice were discussed.

Chapter Seven concentrated on people from Newbury who were informally employed by others who operate in the formal sector. All of those interviewed were paid directly in cash and none of the respondents had ever received a written record of payment. The economic activities of this group remained hidden from official recognition as none of the respondents had ever informed any official body about their informal employment. The mechanisms utilised by formally registered individuals and organisations to disguise or account for this economic strategy was outside the scope of the book.

Chapter Eight focused on the trading of stolen goods and illustrated that fiddling can be related to informal as well as formal employment. The

Chapter also looked at individuals who trade in stolen goods not connected to formal or informal employment.

The main theoretical thrust of the book was to emphasize the importance of locality and duration of unemployment as key factors influencing participation in informal economic activity. The book attempted to illustrate the ways in which particular social structures and localities shape, foster and constrain informal economic strategies. The inhabitants of Newbury estate display a high degree of class homogeneity and there is a marked absence of either social or geographical mobility. The majority of residents have lived in Newbury all their lives and also have kin residing in the locality. Informal social ties involving kinship, friendship and locality are considered crucial factors in understanding the opportunities and constraints affecting individuals' participation in informal economic activity. Cultural isolation, long term stability of residence, social homogeneity, extensive kinship and friendship networks and low levels of access to external resources are all considered as conducive to the development of informal economic practices among the unemployed. These factors differentiate the unemployed in Newbury from the unemployed studied by Pahl and enhanced informal economic opportunities for Newbury residents.

In Newbury, survival strategies are collective rather than individual or household endeavours. Hence the analysis moves beyond research which focuses on the individual or the household as the unit of analysis. The study of informal economic activity in Newbury reveals the necessity to examine individual, household and collective responses to unemployment and their interpenetration. To concentrate on one or the other misses the variety of informal economic interconnections between the individual, the household and the community. As Morris argues:

> it is the social network that provides the mechanism by which the household is articulated with its social and economic environment (1988,p.398).

Following Morris, this study suggests that social networks are crucial in facilitating the development, expansion and acceptance of informal economic activity.

Importance of locality and social networks

The importance of locality as an access route to informal or casual employment is very much in evidence when looking at the recruitment of the informal wage labourers described in Chapter Seven. It seems unlikely that informal wage labourers could engage in this economic practice without the acquiescence of the co-residents of the estate. Participation in informal wage labour, over a long period, sets in motion established daily routines. For example, informal wage labourers leave and return to their homes at specific times during the day and this by itself, does much to publicise their activities. Moreover, for the males in particular, informal wage labour was extremely localized. 87 per cent of the males who engaged in informal wage labour worked in Newbury or the surrounding area. This concentration in a small geographical area further publicizes these 'illegal' economic practices. While detection is clearly more difficult for DHSS investigators concerned with administering politically sensitive areas, nonetheless this does not mean that Catholic 'republican' areas are immune from official investigations. Rather it means that more subtle forms of investigation have to be implemented. Hence being reported by one's neighbours remains a potential threat. However, in Newbury, with its consistently high levels of long term unemployment, even the majority of those currently in formal employment have experienced varying periods of formal economic inactivity. Hence most members of the estate have had to resort, at some stage in their lives, to informal economic activity in order to make ends meet. This, in turn, lessens the stigma attached to 'scrounging from the state', as most households in the area have had some experience of engaging in this activity.

Extensive kinship and friendship networks were also prevalent among those who engaged in informal wage labour. Five of the female informal wage labourers and five of the male informal wage labourers were related, although not all to each other. The sample of female wage labourers included two sisters and a sister-in-law and another two sisters. The latter two sisters were also married to two of the male informal wage labourers, while three of the remainder of male wage labourers were cousins. Most of the contract cleaners stated that they had been recruited by a friend, neighbour or relative. Most of the male construction workers also stated that they had been recruited in this way. These social relationships permeated the workplace and for the contract cleaners in particular, the exploitation of these relationships enhanced the security and regularity of wages, during periods of absence from employment, and simultaneously enabled subcontractors to keep to rigorous deadlines.

The community is also the focal point for the remainder of economic activities outlined throughout the book, while kinship and friendship networks provide the backbone for the trading activities that take place. The hardship and poverty experienced by most households within the area encourages the widespread development of reciprocal exchanges. The lack of purchasing power to buy formal goods and services provides a justification for buying stolen goods. This, in turn, provides the impetus for some members of the community to engage in these shady economic activities as the opportunity to steal must be matched by an ability to 'get rid of' the stolen goods. The community's lack of purchasing power also fosters the growth of entrepreneurial activities among some members of the estate. Most of those in community economic enterprises developed their skills in response to their inability to satisfy their internal household needs and fulfil their social obligations by relying on formally purchased goods and services. The skills gained from supplying these needs informally paved the way for those in community economic enterprises to transfer these skills into income generating activities. All these exchanges are emeshed in extensive friendship and kinship ties and the chapters illustrate the salience of the community as the fundamental means of coping with the pressures of economic hardship.

Household composition and informal economic activity

The following Table (9.1) gives a breakdown of the composition of the 150 households in the survey of the estate and illustrates which types of household are most likely to engage in the various informal economic strategies outlined throughout the book. The respondents interviewed in the snowball sample have been excluded from this table.

Table 9.1
Household composition and informal economic activity

Married Couples (Total number = 93)

	H + W formally employed	H or W formally employed	H. unemp.(a) Housewife	H + W Retired
	(10)	(26)	(45)	(12)
Informal Employment	0%	0%	49%	8%
Community Enterprise	0%	27%	58%	17%
Self Servicing	100%	96%	93%	33%
Reciprocity	20%	19%	71%	0%

Single, Divorced and Widowed Respondents (Total number = 57)

	Formally Employed	Housewife (b)	Unemployed (c)	Retired
	(6)	(22)	(13)	(16)
Informal Employment	0%	4%	15%	0%
Community Enterprise	33%	18%	8%	0%
Self-Servicing	83%	50%	92%	37%
Reciprocity	33%	18%	54%	19%

(a) The unemployed married couples included nine males registered as sick/disabled

(b) The Unemployed single, divorced and widowed respondents included five people registered as sick/disabled

(c) Unemployed females were classified as housewives as none of the women who described themselves as unemployed were offically registered as such.

The Table illustrates that none of the formally employed sample engaged in any informal paid employment. Retired households were also unlikely to engaged in this economic practice. Only 2 of the 13 unemployed respondents who were single, divorced or widowed had recourse to this type of informal economic activity whereas just under half of the unemployed married couples engaged in this activity. Marriage increases one's financial responsibilities, especially if the marriage contains dependent children. These responsibilites can be seen as providing a strong impetus to seek informal wage labour as a means of bolstering inadequate welfare benefits and stretching one's income to meet family needs. Moreover in eight of these households, both husband and wife had access to informal paid employment. This suggests that polarization may exist between some unemployed households with more than one member in informal paid employment and other unemployed households with no access to informal paid employment.

Unemployed couples were also more likely than employed couples to engage in some form of income producing activity within the estate. Over half of the unemployed couples in the sample engaged in some type of community economic enterprise. Often this activity complemented the earnings made from informal paid employment. Again, unemployed respondents who were single, divorced or widowed were largely excluded from this economic strategy. Just 2 of the 13 households in this category had recourse to this economic practice. Married couples in households where one member was formally employed also had access to this economic activity. In these cases the husband was in formal employment while the wife engaged in either knitting, dressmaking or catalogue selling for money.

As I pointed out in Chapter Four, most households regardless of employment status tended to participate in some form of self provisioning. Indeed as the Table indicates, married couples in households with one or both partners in formal employment were the group most likely to engage in this economic activity. This was partly due to home ownership. Formally employed households were the group most likely to own their homes and hence be responsible for the upkeep and improvement of their dwellings. On the other hand, as Chapter Seven illustrated, households in paid informal work or employment were also major participants in the household economy. These households engaged in a variety of tasks aimed at improving their dwellings. Hence within Newbury, houses cloaked with the trappings of modern consumerism were situated alongside houses in dilapidated conditions. This was mainly because participants in informal paid work or employment were too frightened to deposit their earnings in any formal establishments and hence had little option but to utilise their money to upgrade their homes, often in the absence of home ownership.

Employment status, marriage and motherhood were influencial in determining the extent to which households participated in reciprocal exchanges with other households. Most reciprocal relationships took place between households with married couples and dependent children, or between mothers and married daughters and vice-versa. As I pointed out in Chapter Five, the males in the survey, who stated that they did favours for others, were mainly unemployed, between the ages of 25-45 and married with dependent children. This group tended to do favours for households containing members sharing these characteristics. The main reason given for concentrating on households with these specific characteristics was that these groups were perceived as the ones most likely to be in a position to return favours. Hence, male participation in reciprocal exchanges was heavily tinged with economic rationality and self interest.

Marriage and motherhood linked older members of the estate into these reciprocal exchanges. Many emotional, social and economic exchanges took place between married daughters and their mothers. Age largely determined who gave and who received within these relationships. Table 9.1 illustrates that no retired married couples engaged in reciprocal favours while less than a quarter of retired single, divorced or widowed respondents engaged in reciprocal favours. This was because as inhabitants of the estate became older they were mainly on the receiving end of favours rather than instigators of them.

Gender and informal economic activity

Many of the economic activities mentioned in previous chapters were gender specific. The division of labour along gender lines apparent in the formal economy was also visible in the various economic practices outlined throughout the study. Distinct gender divisions were apparent among the informal wage labourers. Here the majority of females were employed as cleaners while construction work was the principal form of employment for males. Moreover, males in informal wage labour tended to work full time while females engaged in informal wage labour tended to work part time. This meant that females often had to combine part time informal employment with overall responsibility for family and home.

Work within the household was also sharply divided along gender lines. Women mainly engaged in baking, knitting and dressmaking, while men were responsible for the more strenuous tasks such as painting and decorating and home improvements. The cleaning of outside windows was partly considered to be a gender neutral activity. Here, what determined whether a male or female carried out the task, was whether a price was attached to the service. Females often cleaned windows as part of their duties as unpaid domestic housewives. Some females also cleaned the outside windows of elderly parents' dwellings. However, once a price was placed on the service, the work invariably became the territory of males.

The extent to which males and females could be viewed as rational, self interested economic individuals is also debatable. While males tended to display these characteristics, exchange values among females were determined by social as much as economic values. Hence, throughout the research, there were various examples of males pursuing their own self interest while females were more concerned with the needs of others. The self centred nature of the males was very apparent when looking at how the wages derived from informal wage labour was utilised by both males and females. Females tended to regard their income as the family's wage and used their earnings to provide for the family's everyday needs. Males, on the other hand, used either part or all of the income derived from working informally to satisfy their personal needs. For many the main concession here was that the family could keep the 'dole cheque' intact. Some of the males felt that to hand over the whole income derived from informal wage labour to satisfy family needs would mean that they were working for nothing. Morris (1990,p.181) also found that for some males working informally in South Wales and Hartlepool, informal earnings were used to finance male social activity.

Males and females who engaged in income producing activities within the estate and who had control over pricing levels also tended to adopt different strategies to determine price structures. Males tended to charge uniform prices for the goods or services they were supplying while females operated a variable pricing policy dependent on the perceived purchasing ability of customers. Thus pensioners or people going through a crisis period were often charged lower prices than others viewed as more capable of paying standard charges.

Males and females also displayed different orientations in their attitudes to unpaid informal work. The caring attributes of the community that came to the fore during sickness, deaths or crisis periods were monopolised by women. Males doing favours for others in the community were motivated by the extrinsic economic rewards that could be derived from their involvement, whereas females tended to gain more intrinsic satisfaction from helping others. Hence males were extremely selective in their involvement in helping others, whereas females often assisted those least able to repay favours. This meant that people on the margins of the extensive kinship networks on the estate could have some of their needs met through their acquaintances with these caring females.

Informal economic activity: liberation or drudgery

Some writers have suggested that informal work carries with it the liberating potential of escape from capitalist relations of production and the alienation of work (Redclift and Mingione 1985,p.6). To Shankland:

> The two economies offer different life styles, a new balance between collective and personal work and this choice .... could be a new dimension in human freedom...... unless the formal economy makes its working conditions more attractive it deserves to lose its workers to the informal economy and will do so (1984,p.188).

Informal economic strategies in Newbury illustrate the complexity of human behaviour in the face of certain institutional constraints and illustrate how some inhabitants within the estate did not react passively to these constraints but instead, utilised them to their economic advantage. Some members of the estate experienced a sense of personal power in their ability to satisfy some of their daily needs without being totally dependent on the formal economic structure and this led some inhabitants to believe that they were 'beating the system'.

Participants in certain forms of informal economic activity, particularly those engaged in income producing activities within the community achieved a certain level of autonomy, flexibility and control over the hours and circumstances of their work. Here buying and selling were integrated into an occasion of social interaction. These exchanges were rarely straightforward economic endeavours but were rather governed by norms derived from shared social intercourse. Thus within these systems of exchange, social values played a key role. For example, females in particular, lowered prices for people they felt needed the items and who appeared to be in dire financial straits. These exchanges also provided the impetus for the emergence of a female culture. Female exchanges took place within an atmosphere of intimacy and closeness and hence reduced the social isolation of many housewives. For example, catalogue buying and selling gave females an opportunity to forge networks and cement personal and social ties. Transactions were highly socialised, giving females the opportunity to meet, have tea with, and gossip among, other housewives in the estate.

On the other hand, authors such as Pym (1980), Handy (1984) and Shankland (1984) who focus on the positive aspects of informal economic practices such as those outlined above ignore the manipulative relationships that can often exist between participants in informal economic activities. In many instances the personal social relationships between females in Newbury were manipulated, by the catalogue sales agents in particular, for entrepreneurial advantage. Building up friendships and relationships with others in the estate was often a cultural device, strategically used to make money. Kinship ties were often exploited to obtain special terms on the goods and services offered by those involved in community economic enterprises.

In relation to the informal wage labourers described in Chapter Seven, the liberating potential of this type of informal economic strategy is highly questionable. As Bryan Roberts states:

> A note of caution is needed at this point. Local networks are important in obtaining work, whether in the informal or the formal sector, but I suspect that they serve as much to facilitate economic exploitation as economic independence (1988,p.17).

Informal recruitment operates to the advantage of employers by facilitating the creation of low cost, exploitative employment. Women in particular make ideal informal employees as they represent a relatively unorganised and hence cheaper source of labour. According to Portes (1981), firms that hire in the informal sector, bypass minimum wage levels and fringe benefits and thus reduce their labour costs. These observations are echoed by Mattera who states:

> By toiling off the books, workers give up minimum wage and overtime regulations, health insurance, pensions, occupational safety standards - in other words, social security in the broadest sense. This reversal from established rights back to precariousness is the single most important aspect of the growth of informal economic activity (1985,p.122).

This reversal from established rights is most visible among the contract cleaners described in Chapter Seven. To Mattera (1985,p.38) subcontracting permits larger companies to keep their hands clean and let smaller firms do the dirty work. The current trend towards the privatisation of public services is enhancing this process by altering the terms under which certain groups are available for employment. The study of contract cleaning indicates that processes of polarisation along different axes from those outlined by Pahl are developing. Not only are divisions apparent between the employed and the unemployed, divisions are becoming visible among the lowest paid sector of society between those on minimum wage levels but nonetheless security of employment and access to other employment protection rights and those employed on an informal basis denied even the most basic employment rights.

In Newbury, married women with dependent children are unable to stretch benefit entitlements to meet family needs and hence are willing to work for extremely low wages, where they can get the opportunity to work informally. These circumstances prove very conducive to a labour intensive industry compelled by the competitive tendering process to continually reduce wage costs in an attempt to secure future tenders. Because of the employment status of the spouses of the contract cleaners in this study, they are deterred from entering formal employment. As a result, these women form a 'trapped' section of the workforce and fall easy prey to companies seeking low paid, casual employees.

Informal economic activity, the state and political consciousness

The research also highlights the need to focus on the relationship between particular localities and the wider, social, economic and political system.

Hence, the book attempts to move away from analyses such as Handy (1984) and Shankland (1984) which tend to focus on individuals' autonomous decisions to participate in informal economic strategies. A more adequate analysis of informal economic opportunities, it was argued, should take account of the influence of external factors on individuals, households and localities. It was suggested that only through an examination of the influences outside the household and community could a more complete account of informal economic opportunities be attempted. The research illustrates how the wider social, economic and political system encouraged and at times hindered informal economic opportunities in Newbury. Hence, informal economic strategies were not just individual or household reactions to particular economic situations but were linked to the ways in which households in Newbury as a whole related to the wider social, economic and political environment.

This brings me to a further point, can involvement in informal economic activity influence an individual's political consciousness? In a paper presented to the 6th Urban Change and Conflict Conference (1987), Pahl argues that the more work people do to meet their own needs, the more likely they are to vote conservative. This is because involvement in formal and informal economic activity is matched by employment status. Multiple earner households with two or more members in formal employment are most likely to engage in self provisioning and informal paid work as well. These households are able to maintain high household incomes and substantial affluence. Pahl stresses that this combination of formal and informal work does not just enhance the material possessions of households but also may influence the ideological consciousness of its members. This ideological dimension may help create a new division amongst working people. Households will become polarized, even within the same street, between those who embrace conservative home ownership policies and self help doctrines, and those who end up on the scrapheap unable to plug into formal or informal work strategies. This contrasts with Pahl's earlier work which focused on the ways in which government fiscal policies enlarges the scope for the operation of informal economies and on how such economies are mainly accessible to those strata that have resisted most effectively incorporation into the dominant values of industrial capitalism. Rather, in relation to the working class, Pahl's later research illustrates divisions between affluent privatized conservative working class members and marginalized working class members for whom poverty and unemployment also become privatised. However, certain groups have always had to cope with the deficiencies of the capitalist system. Even in the affluent post-war years, for some groups, poverty was increasing (Able-Smith and Townsend 1965, Field 1975). Many members of the unskilled working class, ethnic minorities and women were denied access to the post-war affluence and never incorporated the dominant values of the privatized worker. Among such groups, existing on the margins of society, traditional ways of 'making out' and forms of mutual aid have persisted.

While the employed households in Newbury did participate in self provisioning within their households, nonetheless they were the group least likely to engage in paid informal economic activities. Rather households where the male head was unemployed were the group most likely to engage in informal paid economic strategies. Following Weiss (1987) and Ferman and Berndt (1981), the research suggests that the origins of informal economic strategies lies in the structural conditions and processes in the larger society and cannot be divorced from them. Many people continue to have relatively low or non existent incomes and hence have to resort to additional ways of 'getting by'. By maintaining ethnic and cultural segregation, the wider society has encouraged the growth of informal economic strategies. Moreover, informal economic strategies contribute to economic growth by providing low cost informal employees for formal enterprises. It seems unlikely that the type of paid informal employment, these workers engage in would affect their ideological consciousness in the way in which Pahl envisaged.

On the other hand, Henry (1982) suggests that involvement in informal economic activity could lead to the development of a radical class consciousness. This study only partly supported this suggestion. The raising of one's consciousness through involvement in informal economic activity was linked to motivations for working informally and whether or not payment was received. For many people, involvement in informal economic activity was motivated by economic necessity. The existence of informal paid employment acted as a safety valve rather than as a threat to the system. Many respondents who engaged in demeaning, low paid informal employment felt that they were 'beating the system'. It is doubtful that they were simultaneously developing a critical awareness of the inadequacies of the system. Even within the politically sensitive locality studied, where the opportunities for radical action were so pronounced, many of the respondents linked to the formal economy by an informal cash nexus remained unpoliticised. For many of these people, the Northern Ireland conflict only conditioned the practicalities of engaging in informal paid employment and work in that some informal economic opportunities were related to the 'troubles' and detection was more difficult in republican estates. Those individuals who displayed a highly developed political awareness were those who were unable to, or decided not to, engage in informal paid work or employment.

Informal economic activity: a panacea for unemployment?

In Newbury, where the realities of daily life are dominated by informal economic activity, pronounced inequalities still remain. The whole area continues to be disfigured by poverty and unemployment. Throughout this study, I have attempted to underline that the economic rewards from informal economic activity can never lead to economic independence. For example, paid informal employment rarely compensates for secure formal employment. The people who engage in the various types of informal economic strategies described throughout the book, do so to supplement not replace social security benefits. Put simply, they cannot manage to stretch their weekly allowances to meet their families' needs and thus have to resort to a whole range of informal economic practices to cope with the shortfall. This may involve working on the side and adding the income to welfare payments to create a manageable livelihood. It may mean commercializing one's talents and exploiting one's friendships in an effort to create occasional extra cash. It may mean doing favours for others that can be reciprocated, hence leaving scarce income for vital necessities where no such option exists and only money forms the medium of exchange. Or it may mean purchasing items illegally when such goods become available.

These activities either singly or together can never compensate for secure formal employment or lead to independence from formal sources of cash, should it be only in the passive sense of receiving a weekly welfare cheque. This incapacity has been utilized by some sociologists to put forward the view that informal economic activity among marginal groups is hence trivial and unimportant. But if individuals, households and even in some cases, whole communities, are actively engaged in a whole range of everyday activities that escape regulation, then surely to dismiss such activities as inconsequential is mistaken. The persistence and resiliency of the various forms of informal economic practices in Newbury deserve sociological attention. The fact that these people still need to rely on formal sources of income only further reiterates the links between the formal and informal economy.

Finally, this book has attempted to move beyond the confines of much of the theorising on the informal economy which separates the formal from the informal or at best focuses on the various sub-economies of a society. The book illustrates the various ways in which the formal and informal sectors of the economy are drawn together in one highly localized site. The various informal economic practices outlined here fit into the interstices of formal structures. Often these links are so obvious that they fail to be recognised. Yet what we should be studying is not separate economies or sub-economies but how individuals, households and communities are shaped by, and in turn shape, the one flexible, adaptive economy.

Bibliography

Abrams, P. (1984), 'Realities of Neighbourhood Care: the Interactions between Statutory, Voluntary and Informal Social Care', *Policy and Politics,* Vol 12, pp413-429.

Aitken, R. (1979), 'Schools, Unemployment and the Work Ethic', *Universities Quarterly,* Vol. 34.

Ashton, D.N. (1986), *Unemployment Under Capitalism,* Wheatsheaf Books Ltd.

Banerjee, N. (1981), 'The Weakest Link', *Institute of Development Studies Bulletin,* Vol 12, pp36-40.

Barnes, J.A. (1979), *Who Should Know What? Social Science, Privacy and Ethics,* Penguin, Harmondsworth.

Beals, A. (1967), *Culture in Process,* Holt Rinehart and Spindler, New York.

Becker, H. (1970), 'Practitioners of Vice and Crime', in R. Habenstein (ed.), *Pathways to Data,* Aldine, Chicago.

Bell, C. and Newby, H. (1971), *Community Studies,* Allen and Unwin, London.

Berg, M. (1988), 'Women's Work, Mechanisation and the Early Phases of Industrialisation in England' in R. Pahl (ed.), *On Work: Historical, Comparative and Theoretical Approaches,* Blackwell, Oxford.

Bew, P., Gibbon, P., Patterson, H. (1979), *The State In Northern Ireland 1921-1972,* Manchester University Press, Manchester.

Bigus, O.E. (1972), 'The Milkman and His Customer', *Urban Life and Culture,* Vol 1, pp131-165.

Birrell, W.D. (1971), *Housing in Northern Ireland,* Centre for Environment Studies, Belfast.

Blair, J.P. (1982), 'Irregular Economies', in G Gappert and R.V. Knight (eds), *Cities in the 21st Century,* Vol 23, Urban Affairs Annual Reviews, Sage

Publications.
Boal, F.W. (1971), 'Territoriality and Class: a Study of Two Residential Districts in Belfast', *Irish Geography.*
Boal, F.W. (1972), 'Close Together and Far Apart', *Community Forum.*
Boal, F.W., Doherty, P., Pringle, D.G. (1974), *The Spatial Distribution of Some Social Problems in the Belfast Urban Area,* Research Paper N.I.C.R.C, Belfast.
Boal, F.W., Doherty, P., Pringle, D.G. (1978), *Social Problems in the Belfast Urban Area,* Occasional Paper No.12, Dept of Geography, Queen Mary College, London.
Bogdan, R. and Taylor, S.J. (1975), *Introduction to Qualitative Research Methods,* Wiley Publishers, New York.
Bradshaw, J., Cooke, K., Godfrey, C. (1983), 'The Impact of Unemployment on the Living Standards of Families', *Journal of Social Policy,* 12:4, pp433-452.
Brannen, J. (1988), 'Research Notes: The Study of Sensitive Subjects', *Sociological Review,* Vol36, pp 552-563.
Brewer, J. (1990), 'Sensitivity as a Problem in Field Research: A Study of Routine Policing in Northern Ireland', *American Behavioural Scientist,* Vol33, No5.
Bromley, R. and Gerry, C. (eds), (1979), *Casual Work and Poverty in Third World Cities,* John Wiley, Chichester.
Bronfenbrenner, U. (1952), 'Principles of Professional Ethics: Cornell Studies in Social Growth', *American Psychologist,* Vol7, No.8, pp 452-455.
Bryman, A. (1988), *Quantity and Qualitative in Social Research,* Unwin Hyman, London.
Bulmer, M. (1986), Neighbours: *The Work of Philip Abrams,* Cambridge University Press, Cambridge.
Burgess, R.G. (ed), (1982), *Field Research: A Sourcebook and Field Manual,* Allen and Unwin, London.
Burton, F. (1978), *The Politics of Legitimacy,* Routledge & Kegan Paul, London.
Cohen, A.K. (1955), *Delinquent Boys,* The Free Press, Glencoe.
Cook, D. (1989), *Rich Law, Poor Law: Different Responses to Tax & Supplementary Benefit Fraud,* Open University Press, Milton Keynes.
Cragg, A. & Dawson, T. (1981), *Qualitative Research Among Homeworkers,* Research Paper No21, London, Dept. of Employment.
Coyle, A. (1985), 'Going Private: The Implications of Privatisation for Women's Work', *Feminist Review,* Vol21, pp5-25.
Dahrendorf, R. (1975), The New Liberty, Routledge & Kegan Paul, London.
Daly, M. (1986), *The Hidden Workers,* Employment Equality Agency, Dublin.

Daniel, W.W. & Stilgoe, E. (1977), *Where Are They Now?*, Political and Economic Planning, London.

Darby, J. & Morris G. (1974), *Intimidation in Housing*, Research Paper, NICRA, Belfast.

Darby, J. (1986), *Intimidation and the Control of Conflict in Northern Ireland*, Gill & MacMillan.

Davis, J. (1985), 'Rules Not Laws: Outline of an Ethnographic Approach to Economics', in B. Roberts, R. Finnegan, D. Gallie, (eds), *New Approaches to Economic Life: Economic Restructuring, Unemployment and the Social Division of Labour*, Manchester University Press, Manchester.

Davis, J. (1972), 'Gifts and the UK Economy', *Man*, Vol7, No3.

Denzin, N. (1970), *Sociological Methods: A Sourcebook*, Butterworths, London.

Ditton, J. (1977), *Part-Time Crime: An Ethnography of Fiddling And Pilferage*, MacMillan, London.

Doherty, P. (1977), *A Geography of Unemployment in the Belfast Urban Area*, Unpublished PhD Thesis, Queen's University, Belfast.

Doolan, L. (1982), *Elements of the Sacred and Dramatic in Some Belfast Urban Enclaves*, Unpublished PhD Thesis, Queen's University, Belfast.

Douglas, J. (1976), *Investigative Social Research*, Sage Publications, Beverly Hills, California.

Dow, L.M. (1977), 'High Weeds in Detroit: The Irregular Economy Among a Network of Appalachian Migrants', *Urban Anthropology*, Vol6, pp111-128.

Edgell, S. & Hart, G. (1988), *Informal Work: A Case Study of Moonlighting Firemen*, Salford Papers in Sociology and Anthropology.

Eisenberg, P. & Lazarfield, P.F. (1938), 'The Psychological Effects of Unemployment', *Psychological Bulletin*, No 35, pp 358-390.

Evans-Prichard, E.E. (1940), *The Nuer*, Clarendon Press, Oxford.

Feige, E. (1977), 'The Anatomy of the Underground Economy', in S. Alessandrini & B. Dallago, (eds), *The Unofficial Economy*, Gower, Aldershot, England.

Feige, E. (1981), 'The UK's Unobserved Economy: A Preliminary Assessment', *Journal of Economic Affairs*, Vol 1, pp205-212.

Ferman, L.A., Henry, S., Hoyman, M. (eds), (1987), *The Informal Economy: The Annals of the American Academy of Political and Social Science*, Sage Publications, Beverly Hills.

Ferman, L. & Brendt, L. (1981), 'The Irregular Economy', in S. Henry, (ed), *Can I have It In Cash*, Astragal Books, London.

Field, D. (1958), *A Report on Unsatisfactory Tenants*, Belfast Council of Social Welfare, Belfast.

Field, F. (ed), (1977), *The Conscript Army: A Study Britain's Unemployed,*

Routledge & Kegan Paul, London.
Frankenberg, R. (1966), *Communities in Britain,* Penguin.
Gallie, D. (1985), 'Directions for the Future', in B. Roberts, R. Finnegan & D. Gallie, (eds), *New Approaches to Economic Life: Economic Restructuring, Unemployment and The Social Division of Labour,* Oxford University Press, Oxford.
Gappert, G. and Knight, R.V. (eds), (1982), *Cities in the 21st Century,* Urban Annual Reviews, Vol 23, Sage Publications.
Gaughan, J.P. & Ferman, L.A. (1987), 'Towards an Understanding of the Informal Economy', in Ferman, L.A., Henry, S., Hoyman, M. (eds), *The Informal Economy: The Annals of the American Academy of Political and Social Science,* Sage Publications, Beverly Hills.
Geer, B. (1970), 'Studying a College', in R. Habenstein, (ed), *Pathways to Data,* Aldine Press, Chicago.
Gershuny, J. (1978), *After Industrial Society. The Emerging Self-Service Economy,* MacMillan Press, London.
Gershuny, J. (1983), *Social Innovation and the Division of Labour,* Oxford University Press, Oxford.
Gershuny, J. (1987), 'Technology, Social Innovation and the Informal Economy', in L. Ferman, S. Henry & M. Hoyman, (eds), *The Informal Economy: The Annals of the American Academy of Political and Social Science,* Sage Publications, Beverly Hills.
Gershuny, J. and Pahl, R. (1980), Britain in the Decade of the Three Economies, *New Society.*
Gershuny, J. and Pahl, R. (1981), 'Work Outside Employment: Some Preliminary Speculations', in S Henry, (ed), *Can I Have It In Cash,* Astragal Books, London.
Grieco, M. (1987), 'Family Networks and the Closure of Employment', in G. Lee & R. Loveridge, (eds), *The Manufacture of Disadvantage,* Open University Press, Milton Keynes.
Gutmann, P. (1985), 'The Subterranean Economy', in W. Gaertner and A. Wenig, (eds), *The Economics of the Shadow Economy,* Proceedings, Bielefeld: W Germany, Oct 1983, Springer-Verlag.
Hall, M. (1986), *Ulster: The Hidden History,* Pretani Press, Belfast.
Handy, C. (1982), *The Informal Economy: An Essay on Contemporary Opportunities & Challenges,* ARVAC Pamphlet, No3, ARVAC, Wivenhoe.
Handy, C. (1984), *The Future of Work: A Guide To a Changing Society,* Blackwell, Oxford.
Harding, P. and Jenkins, R. (1989), *The Myth of the Hidden Economy,* Open University Press, Milton Keynes.
Harris C.C. (1987), *Redundancy and Recession in South Wales,* Blackwell, Oxford.

Harris, P.B. (1977), *Foundations of Political Science,* Hutchinson, London.

Hart, K. (1973), 'Informal Income Opportunities and Urban Employment in Ghana', *Journal of Modern African Studies,* Vol 11, pp61-89.

Henry, S. (1976), 'It Fell Off the Back of a Lorry', *New Society.*

Henry, S. (1978), 'The Dangers of Self-Help Groups', *New Society.*

Henry, S. and Mars, G. (1978), 'Crime at Work: The Social Construction of Amateur Property Theft', *Sociology,* Vol 12, pp245-263.

Henry, S. (ed), (1981), *Can I Have It in Cash,* Astragal Books, London.

Henry, S. (1982), 'The Working Unemployed', *Sociological Review,* No 30, University of Keele.

Henry, S. (1987), 'The Political Economy of Informal Economies', in L. Ferman, S. Henry, M. Hoyman (eds), *The Informal Economy: The Annals of the American Academy of Political and Social Science,* Sage Pub, Beverly Hills.

Hill, M., Harrison, R., Sargeant, A., Talbot, V. (1973), *Men Out of Work,* Cambridge University Press, Cambridge.

Howe, L. (1990), *Being Unemployed in Northern Ireland,* Cambridge University Press, Cambridge.

Howe, L. (1986), *Unemployment: Doing the Double and Local Labour Markets in Belfast,* UK Economic and Social Research Council, Belfast.

Howe, L. (1987), *Doing the Double: Wages, Jobs and Benefits in Belfast,* Paper presented to conference on Economic and Social Research, Belfast.

Humble, S. (1982), *Voluntary Action in the 1980's: Summary of the Findings of the National Survey,* The Volunteer Centre, Berkhamstead.

Hutson, S. (1990), *Saturday Jobs: Sixth Formers Earnings and Spending,* Paper Presented at the BSA Annual Conference on Social Divisions and Change, Guildford, Surrey.

Hutson, S. and Jenkins R. (1988), *Taking the Strain,* Open University Press, Milton Keynes.

Interim Report, (1944), *Housing In Northern Ireland,* Interim Report of the Planning Advisory Board, Cmd. 224, HMSO, Belfast.

Jackson, H. (1971), *The Two Irelands - A Dual Study in Intergroup Relations,* Minority Rights Group, London.

Jackson, I. (1977), *Inequality in American Communities,* Academic Press, London.

Jahoda, M. (1979), The Psychological Meanings of Unemployment, *New Society.*

Jenkins, R. (1983), 'Goals, Constraints and Occupational Choice: The First Twelve Months in the Belfast Labour Market', *British Journal of Guidance and Counselling,* Vol 11, No2.

Jenkins, R. (1988), 'Discrimination and Equal Employment in Britain', in D. Gallie (ed), *Employment in Britain,* Blackwell, Oxford.

Jenkins, R., Bryman, J.F., Ford J, Keil, T., Beardsworth, A. (1983), 'Information in the Labour Market: The Impact of the Recession', *Sociology,* Vol 17.

Jenkins, C. and Sherman, B. (1979), *The Collapse of Work,* Eyre Methuen.

Klockers, C.B. (1974), *The Professional Fence,* Tavistock, London.

Kumar, K. (1984), 'The Social Culture of Work', in K. Thompson (ed), *Work, Employment and Unemployment,* Open University Press, Milton Keynes.

Kumar, K. (1988), 'From Work to Employment and Unemployment: the English Experience', in R. Pahl (ed), *On Work: Historical, Comparative and Theoretical Approaches,* Blackwell, Oxford.

Larrain, G. (1979), *The Concept of Ideology,* Hutchinson, London.

Layard, R., Piachaud, D., Stewart, M. (1978), *The Causes of Poverty,* HMSO, London.

Liebow, E. (1967), *Tally's Corner: A Study of Negro Street Corner Men,* Little Brown, Boston, Mass.

Lowenthal, M. (1981), 'Non-Market Transactions in an Urban Community', in S. Henry (ed), *Can I Have It In Cash,* Astragal Books, London.

Lynch, K. (1987), *Love Labour: Its Nature and Marginalisation,* Paper Presented at the Sociological Association of Ireland Annual Conference, St Patrick's College, Drumcondra, Dublin.

McNeill, P. (1985), *Research Methods,* Tavistock Publications, London.

MacLennan, E., Fitz, J., Sullivan, J. (1985), *Working Children,* Low Pay Pamphlet, No 34, Low Pay Unit, London.

Maguire, M. (1986), 'Recruitment as a Means of Control', in K. Purcell, S. Wood, A. Watson and S. Allen (eds), *The Changing Experience of Employment: Restructuring and Recession,* Explorations in Sociology 22, British Sociological Association, MacMillan Press.

Malcolmson, R.W. (1988), 'Ways of Getting a Living in Eighteenth-Century England', in R. Pahl (ed), *On Work: Historical, Comparative and Theoretical Approaches,* Blackwell, Oxford.

Malinowski, B. (1922), *Argonauts of the Western Pacific,* Routledge & Kegan Paul, London.

Mars, G. (1973), 'Hotel Pilferage: A Case Study in Occupational Theft', in M. Warner (ed), *The Sociology of the Workplace,* George Allen & Unwin, London.

Mars, G. and Nicod, M. (1981), 'Hidden Rewards at Work: The Implications from a Study of British Hotels', in S. Henry (ed), *Can I Have It In Cash,* Astragal Books, London.

Marsden, D. and Duff, E. (1982), *Workless,* Harmondsworth, Penguin/Croom Helm, London.

Marx, K. and Engels, F. (1969), *The Manifesto of the Communist Party,*

Harmondsworth, Penguin.
Mattera, P. (1985), *Off the Books: The Rise of the Underground Economy,* Pluto Press, London.
Mauss, M. (1954), *The Gift: Forms and Functions of Exchange in Archaic Society,* The Free Press, New York.
Mill, J.S. (1924), *Autobiography,* London.
Mitter, S. (1986), 'Industrial Restructuring and Manufacturing Homework: Immigrant Women in the UK Clothing Industry', *Capital and Class,* Vol27.
Morris, L.D. (1984), 'Patterns of Social Activity and Post-Redundancy Labour-Market Experience', *Sociology,* Vol 18, pp339-352.
Morris, L.D. (1985), 'Local Social Networks and Domestic Organisation', *Sociological Review,* Vol33, pp 327-342.
Morris, L.D. (1988), 'Employment, the Household and Social Networks' in D. Gallie (ed), *Employment in Britain,* Blackwell, Oxford.
Morris, L.D. (1990), *The Workings of the Household,* Polity Press.
Moser, C. and Kalton, G. (1971), *Survey Methods in Social Investigation,* Heinemann, London.
Moylan, S., Millar, J., Davies, R. (1984), *For Richer, For Poorer? DHSS Cohort Study of Unemployed Men,* HMSO.
Nichols, T. and Beynon, H. (1977), *Living with Capitalism,* Routledge & Kegan Paul, London.
Nicholson, J.H. (1961), *New Communities in Britain,* National Council for Social Science, London.
Northern Ireland Housing Executive, (1978), *Belfast Household Survey,* Northern Ireland Housing Executive, Belfast
Nukunya, G.K. (1969), *Kinship and Marriage among the Anlo Ewe,* Athlone Press, London.
Oakley, A. (1974), *The Sociology of Housework,* Martin Robertson, London.
Pahl, R.E. (1984), *Divisions of Labour,* Blackwell, Oxford.
Pahl, R.E. and Wallace, C. (1985), 'Household Work Strategies in Economic Recession', in N. Redclift & E. Mingione (eds), *Beyond Employment,* Blackwell, Oxford.
Pahl, R.E. (1985), 'Restructuring of Capital, the Local Political Economy and Household Work Strategies', in D. Gregory & J. Urry, *Social Relations and Spatial Structures,* Critical Human Geography, MacMillan.
Pahl, R.E. and Wallace, C. (1986), 'Polarisation, Unemployment and all Forms of Work', in S. Allen (ed), *The Experience of Unemployment,* MacMillan Press.
Pahl, R. (1987), *The Distributional Consequences of Informal Work,* Sixth Urban Change and Conflict Conference, University of Kent at Canterbury.
Pahl, R.E. (1987), 'Does Jobless Mean Workless? Unemployment and Informal Work', in L. Ferman, S. Henry, M. Hoyman (eds), *The Informal*

Economy: The Annals of the American Academy of Political and Social Science, Sage Publications, Beverly Hills.
Pahl, R.E. (ed), (1988), *On Work: Historical, Comparative and Theoretical Approaches,* Blackwell, Oxford.
Patrick, J. (1973), *A Glasgow Gang Observed,* Eyre-Methuen, London.
Plummer, K. (1983), *Documents of Life,* Allen and Unwin, London.
Polanyi, K. (1957), *The Great Transformation,* Beacon Press, Boston.
Portes, A. (1981), 'Unequal Exchange and the Urban Informal Sector' in A. Portes and J. Walton (eds), *Labour, Class and the International System,* Academic Press, New York.
Portes, A. and Sassen-Koob, S. (1987) 'Making it Underground: Comparative Material on the Informal Sector in Western Market Economies', *American Journal of Sociology,* Vol 93, pp30-61.
Pym, D. (1980), 'Towards the Dual Economy and Emancipation from Employment', *Futures,* Vol12, No.3.
Rainwater, L. and Pittman, D. (1966), 'Ethical Problems in Studying a Politically Sensitive and Deviant Community', *Social Problems,* No.14, pp357-366.
Redclift, N. and Mingione E. (eds), (1985), *Beyond Employment: Household Gender and Subsistence,* Blackwell, Oxford.
Rolston, B. (1978-1979), 'Escaping from Belfast', *Race and Class,* Vol20, Institute of Race Relations, London.
Rolston, B. and Tomlinson, M. (1988), *The Obair Report,* Preliminary Report, Belfast.
Rose, R. (1985), 'Getting by in the Three Economies: the resources of offical, unofficial and domestic economies', in J. Lane (ed), *State and Market: The Politics of the Public and The Private,* Sage Publications, London.
Sahlins, M. (1974), *Stone Age Economics,* Tavistock Publications, London.
Samuel, R. (1977), 'Workshop of the World. Steam Power and Hand Technology in Mid-Victorian England', *History Workshop,* Vol3.
Shankland, G. (1984), *A Guide to the Informal Economy: A Work and Society Report,* Institute of Manpower Studies, Brighton.
Sieber, S.O. (1982), 'The Integration of Fieldwork and Survey Methods', in R. Burgess, (ed), *Field Research: A Sourcebook and Field Manual,* London, Allen & Unwin, pp176-188.
Smith, D.J. (1980), 'How Unemployment Makes the Poor Poorer', *Policy Studies,* Vol 1:1, pp20-26.
Smith, S. (1986), *Britain's Shadow Economy,* Clarendon Press, Oxford.
Spencer, A.C.E.W. (1973), *A Tale of Two Surveys,* Social Studies Dept, Queen's University, Belfast.
Stacey, M. (1969), *Methods of Social Research,* Pergamon, Oxford.

Stack, C. (1974), *All Our Kin: Strategies for Survival in a Black Community,* Harper & Row, New York.

Tanzi, V. (ed), (1982), *The Undergound Economy in the United States and Abroad,* Lexington Books, Lexington Mass.

Taylor, R. (1988), 'Social Scientific Research on the troubles in Northern Ireland', *Economic and Social Review,* Vol 19, pp123-145.

Thomas, K. (1964), 'Work and Leisure in Pre-Industrial Society', *Past and Present,* The Past and Present Society, Kendal, England.

Thomas, J.J. (1990), 'Measuring the Underground Economy: A Suitable Case for Interdisciplinary Treatment', *American Behavioural Scientist,* Vol 33, No5, pp621-637.

Thompson, K. (1984), *Work, Employment and Unemployment,* Open University Press, Milton Keynes.

Thompson, P. (1983), *The Nature of Work,* MacMillan, London.

Townsend, P. (1979), *Poverty in the UK,* Penguin, Harmondsworth.

Trew, K. and Kilpatrick, R. (1984), *The Daily Life of the Unemployed: Social and Psychological Dimensions,* Dept. of Psychology, Queen's University, Belfast.

Van Maanen, J. (1981), 'The Informant Game: Selected Aspects of Ethnographic Research in Police Organisations', *Urban Life,* Vol9, pp 469-494.

Vickerman, R.W. (1980), 'The New Leisure Society', *Futures,* Vol 12, No3.

Walter, E.V. (1976-1977), 'Dreadful Enclosures: Detoxifying an Urban Myth', *Archives Europeenes De Sociologie,* Vol 17-18.

Ward, R. (1985), 'Minority Settlement and the Local Economy', in B. Roberts, R. Finnegan, D. Gallie (eds), *New Approaches to Economic Life: Economic Restructuring, Unemployment and the Social Division of Labour,* Manchester University Press, Manchester.

Warr, P. (1983), 'Job-Loss, Unemployment and Psychological Well-Being', in Van de Vhurt & Allen V. (eds), *Role Transitions,* Plenum Press, New York.

Wax, R.H. (1971), *Doing Fieldwork: Warnings and Advice,* University of Chigcago Press, Chicago.

Weiss, L. (1987), 'Explaining the Underground Economy: State and Social Structure', *British Journal of Sociology,* Vol38, pp 216-234.

Whipp, R. (1985), 'Labour Markets and Communities: A Historical View', *Sociological Review,* Vol 33, pp768-792.

Whyte, W.F. (1955), *Street Corner Society,* University of Chicago Press, Chicago.

Whyte, J. (1983), 'How Much Discrimination Was There Under the Stormont Regime, 1921-1968?', in T. Gallagher & J. O'Neill (eds), *Contemporary Irish Studies,* Manchester University Press, Manchester.

Wiener, R. (1975), *The Rape and Plunder of the Shankill,* Belfast.
Willis, P. (1977), *Learning to Labour,* Westmead, Saxon House.
Wilson, R. (1964), *Difficult Housing Estates,* Tavistock Pamphlet No.5, Tavistock Publications, London.

Index